BRITISH FILM MAKERS

Humphrey Jennings

BRITISH FILM MAKERS

MANCHESTER
1824

Manchester University Press

Humphrey Jennings

KEITH BEATTIE

Manchester University Press

MANCHESTER AND NEW YORK

distributed exclusively in the USA by Palgrave Macmillan

TThe right of Keith Beattie to be identified as the author of this work has been asserted by him in accordance with the Copyright, Designs and Patents Act 1988.

Published by Manchester University Press
Oxford Road, Manchester M13 9NR, UK
and Room 400, 175 Fifth Avenue, New York, NY 10010, USA
www.manchesteruniversitypress.co.uk

Distributed exclusively in the USA by
Palgrave, 175 Fifth Avenue, New York, NY 10010, USA

Distributed exclusively in Canada by
UBC Press, University of British Columbia, 2029 West Mall,
Vancouver, BC, Canada V6T 1Z2

British Library Cataloguing-in-Publication Data
A catalogue record for this book is available from the British Library

Library of Congress Cataloging-in-Publication Data applied for

ISBN 978 0 7190 7855 2 *hardback*

First published 2010

19 18 17 16 15 14 13 12 11 10   10 9 8 7 6 5 4 3 2 1

The publisher has no responsibility for the persistence or accuracy of URLs for any external or third-party internet websites referred to in this book, and does not guarantee that any content on such websites is, or will remain, accurate or appropriate.

Typeset in Scala with Meta display
by Koinonia, Manchester
Printed in Great Britain
by CPI Antony Rowe, Chippenham, Wiltshire

To the memory of my father
and for Julie Ann Smith

Contents

Series editors' foreword

The aim of this series is to present in lively, authoritative volumes a guide to those film-makers who have made British cinema a rewarding but still under-researched branch of world cinema. The intention is to provide books which are up-to-date in terms of information and critical approach, but not bound to any one theoretical methodology. Though all books in the series will have certain elements in common – comprehensive filmographies, annotated bibliographies, appropriate illustration – the actual critical tools employed will be the responsibility of the individual authors.

Nevertheless, an important recurring element will be a concern for how the oeuvre of each film-maker does or does not fit certain critical and industrial contexts, as well as for the wider social contexts which helped to shape not just that particular film-maker but the course of British cinema at large.

Although the series is director-orientated, the editors believe that reference to a variety of stances and contexts is more likely to reconceptualise and reappraise the phenomenon of British cinema as a complex, shifting field of production. All the texts in the series will engage in detailed discussion of major works of the film-makers involved, but they all consider as well the importance of other key collaborators, of studio organisation, of audience reception, of recurring themes and structures: all those other aspects which go towards the construction of a national cinema.

The series explores and charts a field which is more than ripe for serious excavation. The acknowledged leaders of the field will be reappraised; just as important, though, will be the bringing to light of those who have not so far received any serious attention. They are all part of the very rich texture of British cinema, and it will be the work of this series to give them all their due.

Acknowledgements

Staff of the following institutions provided me with assistance as I accessed the collections: The Australian Centre for the Moving Image, Melbourne; Special Collections and the Research Viewing Service of the British Film Institute, London; the Imperial War Museum, London; The National Archives, Kew, Surrey; and the National Film and Sound Archive, Canberra. I would especially like to thank David Edgar of Special Collections at the British Film Institute, Dr Toby Haggith of the Film and Video Archive of the Imperial War Museum, and Jane Rosen, Librarian, Department of Printed Books, Imperial War Museum. Dr Gwenno Ffrancon of Swansea University, Wales, kindly gave me access to her perceptive essay on *The Silent Village*.

Certain scholars have provided me with critical insights into the aesthetics and functions of documentary film. In this relation, I am especially indebted to the work of John Corner, Brian Winston and William Guynn. In another way, details provided in Kevin Jackson's biography of Jennings were helpful.

Brian McFarlane and Neil Sinyard, editors of the British Filmmakers series, and Matthew Frost, Editor, Manchester University Press, were supportive in the best possible ways. I'd also like to thank Associate Professor Ann McCulloch and Dr Joost Coté for making Deakin University a workable environment. While writing this book during 2008 I was Visiting Research Fellow in Film and Visual Culture within the School of Humanities, Faculty of Arts, College of Arts and Social Sciences, at the Australian National University, Canberra. I would like to thank the School and the Faculty for this position.

Email correspondence with friends and colleagues is one way to stave off the feeling of alienation from the world which attends protracted periods of writing. For their email correspondence, and other matters, I am especially thankful to Associate Professor Roy Shuker, Media Studies Programme, Victoria University, Wellington, New Zealand, and Professor Harry Haines, Chairperson, Department of Communication Studies, Montclair State University, New Jersey.

My mother, Beryl Beattie, my sister, Louise Thake, and my brother-in-law, Michael Thake, provided invaluable support during the time spent writing this book. The memory of my father, Reg Beattie, remains a constant source of inspiration and guidance in my life. As ever, Dr Julie Ann Smith offered a sound critical ear as I researched and wrote this book – and provided inestimable varieties of encouragement. 'She is foremost of those that I would hear praised.'

Any errors of fact or infelicities of interpretation in this work remain, of course, my own.

Introduction

'It might reasonably be contended that Humphrey Jennings is the only real poet the British cinema has yet produced', wrote Lindsay Anderson in the early 1950s.[1] Jennings' friend and colleague, the poet and sociologist Charles Madge, said that Jennings' work had a 'meteoric quality'.[2] The cultural and media theorist Stuart Hall, who became professor of sociology at the University of Birmingham, a position earlier filled by Madge, called Jennings a 'film-maker of extraordinary talent – one of the very few authentic exponents of cinematic language in the British cinema'.[3] Ian Dalrymple, the producer of a number of Jennings' films, said that Jennings 'had the artist's gift for setting up his camera at what might be called the *angle juste*'.[4] The documentary filmmaker Basil Wright, who was sometimes critical of elements in Jennings' films, summarised his overall impression of Jennings' filmmaking skills when he called him a 'genius'.[5] Jennings' friend, the poet Kathleen Raine, described him as 'one of the most remarkable imaginative intelligences of his generation'.[6]

The generation in question was roughly coterminous with the beginning of the twentieth century. Humphrey Jennings was born on 19 August 1907 in the village of Walberswick, on the Suffolk coast. In 1916 he was admitted to the Perse School in Cambridge where he contributed to the school's theatrical productions and wrote for the school magazine. Jennings left Perse in 1926 and later that year entered Pembroke College, Cambridge to read English. Many of the friends and acquaintances he made at Cambridge would go on to prominent and distinguished careers in the arts and academia, among them William Empson, later the author of *Seven Types of Ambiguity* (1930) and *Some Versions of Pastoral* (1935), among other leading works of literary criticism. Other members of Jennings' wide social circle at university included the novelist Malcolm Lowry, the painter Julian Trevallyn, the scientist and writer Jacob Bronowski, the actor Michael Redgrave,

Charles Madge and Kathleen Raine.

After graduating in 1929 with a starred first degree Jennings pursued his ongoing interests in set design, poetry and painting. His intellectual enthusiasms were further exemplified in his contributions to Mass-Observation, a project he helped establish in late 1936 with Madge and the anthropologist Tom Harrisson. Mass-Observation used the technique of participant observation derived from sociology and anthropology to study and plot the habits of British citizens in their everyday lives. Prior to his brief involvement with Mass-Observation Jennings joined the Film Unit of the General Post Office (GPO) in 1934, doing so, it seems, as a way of supplementing his meagre income from his painting and stage work. Jennings' sense of the visual gained from his painting, his poet's understanding of the power of language, and his background in acting and stage design were perfect complements for the demands of the documentary filmmaker made by John Grierson, his new boss at the GPO Film Unit. Jennings' outstanding talents as a documentary filmmaker were initially developed within the GPO Film Unit, and subsequently within its successor, the wartime Crown Film Unit. In 1950, the year of his untimely death at the age of forty-three, Jennings was working for the independent film company Wessex Films with his friend from the Crown Film Unit, the producer Ian Dalrymple. Jennings fell to his death from a cliff on the Greek island of Poros while scouting for locations for a film to be included in a series called *The Changing Face of Europe* (1951) dealing with the economic reconstruction of Europe under the Marshall Plan, made by Wessex for the US Economic Cooperative Administration.

Though Grierson recruited Jennings to documentary filmmaking, the two temperaments were ill-matched. In a reflection of his staid character, Grierson perceived Jennings to be a dilettante and aesthete. Jennings, in turn, recognised Grierson as a bully and thought of him as an unenlightened intellect. In broader terms, beyond their personal differences and disagreements, Jennings sits uncomfortably within a British documentary movement founded by Grierson. In this relation it has been pointed out that 'though some reference books have tended to over-simplify matters by referring to Jennings as a leading film-maker of the "Griersonian school", the fact is that his mature films (all of them made a fair time after Grierson had left the [GPO Film] Unit in 1937) have virtually nothing in common with Griersonian orthodoxy – indeed, [they] can be seen as works of outright heresy'.[7] The assessment tends to overstate the case when arguing that Jennings' films have, in effect, nothing in common with Griersonian works. Reconstruction – as the incorporation of the fictional element of acting by non-professional actors within a documentary frame, an approach that Jennings employed to masterful effect in his films *Fires Were Started* and *The Silent Village* (both 1943) – was a foundational aesthetic component of a Griersonianism that interpreted dramatisation as an essential feature of the documentary form.[8]

Nevertheless, many of Jennings' expressive films differ stylistically from the expository mode of voice-over commentary, which dominantly characterised Griersonian forms. Daniel Millar's account of what he calls the 'Jennings style' is useful in this relation. Jennings' filmmaking, notes Millar, has several distinctive features, including: (a) beautifully composed and filmed long shots – 'in these Jennings is as much an English John Ford as an English Flaherty'; (b) a 'sense of literary tradition, especially Shakespeare, in defining the quality of England'; (c) a 'sophisticated patriotism and a desire (Non-Marxist though Leftish) to unify national experience in terms of public symbol and personal definition in relation to it'; and (d) a willingness to experiment with form, especially sound and image relations. 'Editing is a vital synthesising element, in terms of emotional and even geographical collocations'.[9] These stylistic components – which constitute the bases of Jennings' innovations within and deviations from a 'Griersonian orthodoxy' – derive in part from the formative influence of working with Alberto Cavalcanti, who joined the GPO Film Unit the same year as Jennings and who became production supervisor within the unit in 1936. Cavalcanti was responsible for the production of a number of Jennings' early films, including *Speaking from America* (1938), *Spare Time* (1939), *The First Days* (1939) and *Spring Offensive* (1940), and during this period of production the two men shared a close working relationship.[10] As a reflection of their collaboration, Cavalcanti's contribution to *Spare Time* was considerable, and included many ideas and suggestions that were incorporated into the final version of the film.[11] According to Joe Mendoza, who worked as assistant director on Jennings' film *Listen to Britain* (1942), Cavalcanti brought new insights and attitudes to British documentary filmmaking: 'It all goes back to Cavalcanti really ... Cav really trained people to think analytically about what was on the screen and on the succession of images and why it went flat there and nothing happened and why it got better there. That was the way Cav trained people'.[12] Harry Watt, who worked as a director with Jennings and Pat Jackson on *The First Days*, and with whom Jennings co-directed *London Can Take It!* (1940), wrote in his autobiography that 'British documentary films would not have advanced the way they did without Cav's influence'.[13]

Elsewhere Watt reinforced the point when he stated that 'the arrival of Cavalcanti in the G.P.O. Film Unit was the turning point of British documentary ... Cavalcanti was a great professional'.[14] In an important way Jennings gained from Cavalcanti a willingness and the licence to experiment – to exceed Griersonian forms. Though a Brazilian, Cavalcanti's own training in film was largely steeped in a European avant-gardist tradition, from which he derived an aesthetics which informed his remarkable early film, *Rien que les heures* (*Nothing But the Hours*, 1926), an impressionistic evocation of urban life in Paris. Jennings shared this tradition; he spoke French fluently and was schooled in European painting, poetry and theatre. Geoffrey Nowell-Smith argues that Jennings' films are better placed within the context of avant-garde film and European modernist film experimentation than within the British documentary movement.[15]

One of the chief Continental influences absorbed by Jennings was Surrealism. Jennings knew Breton and Aragon personally, translated writings by the French Surrealist Benjamin Péret, and exhibited his Surrealist paintings in the company of works by Dali, Ernst, Tanguy and Man Ray at the International Surrealist Exhibition in London in the summer of 1936, an event he helped organise. As a result of his close association with European Surrealists and his contributions to the nascent British Surrealist movement critics have consistently sought to scrutinise Jennings' films for evidence of Surreal imagery. In this way what are, essentially, certain unusual shots in Jennings' films have been labelled 'Surrealist'. In a more astute assessment one commentator has noted that 'the viewer will search in vain' for Surrealist imagery in his films.[16] However, as is pointed out here in chapter 2, Jennings did incorporate into his films one of the main formal attributes of Surrealism, that of collage. Surrealist collage foregrounds the material heterogeneity of its elements within a juxtaposition of unrelated texts and images. The practice partook of Breton's notion of the *objet trouvé*, the fortuitous found object which, when aligned with other such objects, produces a revised set of meanings for the once separate and distinct parts. In this way the intention of Surrealist collage, a crucial component of the modernist image, is to combine two distant and distinct representations of reality to create a third representational 'reality'. Collage reworks shards and fragments of the real to suggest the marvellous, a Surrealist key-word connoting the realm of mystery, newness and startling apprehension.

As the documentary film theorist Bill Nichols notes in an account of modernist film aesthetics, the practice of rearranging found fragments was common in the early decades of the twentieth century to both avant-gardist and documentary tendencies in filmmaking.

However, under the weight of the institutional forces affecting British documentary, which were endorsed in part by Grierson's directives, the two tendencies gradually diverged.[17] In its deviation from Griersonian forms, Jennings' documentary work constituted a continued negotiation of avant-gardist nonfiction practice within its deployment of a richly expressive associative and collagist montage, in which different and often opposing elements are contrasted and combined within the overall schema of narrative progression. Jennings' montage is not, as certain critics have claimed, a dialectical form such as that developed by Eisenstein.[18] Though Jennings did not consciously emulate Russian film aesthetics, Pudovkin's asynchronous association of sound and image is a closer approximation to Jennings' documentary practice than the shock aesthetics of Eisensteinian montage.

In his study of Mass-Observation, Ben Highmore argues that collage was central to the organisation's aesthetic practice.[19] Using as the basis of his comments the techniques of *May the Twelfth: Mass-Observation Day-Surveys 1937*, a book which Jennings co-edited from the many first-person observational reports written by Mass-Observation volunteers on the day of the coronation of George VI, Highmore notes three features of collage. Firstly, he emphasises that collage produces surprising and unexpected outcomes, arising from the juxtaposition of heterogeneous elements. Secondly, collage permits '*simultaneity* of difference within the everyday to be represented' or, more particularly, collage 'is a synchronous representation of non-synchronous simultaneity'. Thirdly, collage refuses to subsume its multiple and diverse elements into a homogeneous whole: 'Instead of accumulating these elements into a resolved ... unity, collage offers a bombardment of materials that resist narrative resolution'.[20] The last point – the resistance or refusal of narrative resolution or closure – is a product of ambiguity within narrative. In a similar way, references to the 'ambiguous fragment' as the basis of collage and to the 'radical ambiguity of the collage form' highlight the relationship of collage and ambiguity.[21]

Ambiguity in this context is not applied as a pejorative term. In its capacity to encompass the contrasts and juxtapositions basic to modernist collage, ambiguity is a productive condition and a strategic mode of communication, which conveys multiple and opposing positions and images.[22] As a productive and strategic representational form ambiguity encodes ambivalence, 'tension', heterogeneity, polyvalence and polysemy. Thus ambiguity is 'the capacity of a work ... to allow or even provoke different interpretations, all of them pertinent and comprehensive' and, it can be added, comprehensible.[23] In these terms ambiguity is not the deferral or dissipation of meaning into indeterminacy and incoherence; it is the recognition of multiple meanings, an acceptance of alternative interpretations.

Jennings' Surrealist paintings exploited ambiguity of meaning, and he embodied ambiguities, oppositions and inconsistencies within his personality. As Eric Rhode has pointed out, Jennings was a republican who felt the need for monarchy, and a socialist who at times deployed conservative symbols as genuine expressions of the essence of the nation.[24] Extending this point, ambiguity was a central feature of his films. Jennings' films confront and challenge fixed meanings, thereby admitting the opportunity for ambiguity. The construction of multiple simultaneous meanings, in the form of polysemy, as a potential feature of ambiguity, is exemplified in *Listen to Britain* where the intention is not to 'exhaust the meaning of each image and sound, or to dispatch the spectator down a particular avenue of meanings'.[25] Via the construction of multiple meanings Jennings' work displays a '*rich ambiguity*' which constitutes as a 'constant feature of [his] style'.[26] The documentary film theorist Brian Winston stresses the role of ambiguity in his outline of Jennings' filmic practice: 'Of course, film-makers had long since realised that juxtapositions created new levels of meaning ... What is pioneering about [Jennings'] approach is the achievement of syntheses not synthesis'. Winston adds, taking his cue from the methods of *Listen to Britain* in particular, that Jennings' films 'are replete with Baroque moments where two soundtracks, one perhaps continuing from a previous shot, carry over new shots. The whole is connected by subtle notions of contrast and analogy often informed by an abstract framework of implicit reference to British, usually English, social mores, traditions, history and literature. Such moments constitute nothing less than the filmic equivalent of ambiguity run riot ... That is what is new about them'.[27] The filmmaker Pat Jackson captures the effect of Jennings' films as the source of varied and richly ambiguous meanings when he reflected that 'Humphrey would interpret a situation in disconnected visuals ... Then he created a pattern out of them. It was as though he were going out to collect all sorts of pieces, cut already, for a jigsaw puzzle'.[28]

In certain estimations a mosaic of imagery similar to that described by Jackson is the basis of poetry. The frequent references in the critical literature to Jennings as a 'film poet' (Lindsay Anderson's description of Jennings in these terms being perhaps the most notable of such assessments) in part draws on the connection to a dense collection or mosaic of images in Jennings' films. However, among the many references to Jennings in these terms there is no adequate description of Jennings' 'film poetry'. In many cases 'poetry' is used variously in reference to a director's 'personal vision', or a film's 'aesthetic beauty', or the ways in which 'the ordinary' is transformed into the 'strange or beautiful'.[29] A more apt and useful description of poetry is, as Jennings' friend William Empson explains in *Seven Types of Ambiguity*, a form that involves multiplicity, complexity – and ambiguity.[30] Ambiguity is also implicit in Grierson's foundational description of documentary as the 'creative treatment of actuality' – a phrase which can apply equally to fiction and nonfiction.[31] In these ways ambiguity, emphasised here in relation to Jennings' work, is the most cogent definition of the 'poetry' in his documentaries.

Ambiguity is a structural principle within Jennings' films and is central to the forms through which Jennings represented content, as in the mixture of elements derived from both fiction and documentary which characterises the form referred to as story-documentary. Further, the ambiguity in Jennings' work reflects the complexities inherent in everyday experience, what the theorist of film realism, André Bazin, was to refer to as the 'imminent ambiguity of reality'.[32] Jennings held that 'the image' (a term he used to refer to unadorned sights capable of bearing referential significance) should not be invented by a film-maker, but discovered within socio-historical experience.[33] Accordingly, Jennings discovered or 'found' his images within the complex and often contradictory everyday experiences of British society. His concern with the 'everyday' had developed during his brief involvement with Mass-Observation. The focus by Mass-Observation on the habits of the British, including mundane and eccentric activities together with the effect on daily lives of national events such as abdication and coronation, provided Jennings with an orientation towards quotidian experience. Developing his attention in this area to film, Jennings' representation of everyday experience involved a negotiation of national characteristics in their complexity, which in their varying combinations expressed national identity and a collective unity. The process of representing the everyday bases of national identity was, then, a complex one. As Antonia Lant has emphasised, the evocation of national characteristics during the years of Jennings' filmmaking career was a contested process involving a variety of factors. As Lant points out:

> [n]ational identity is not a natural, timeless essence, but an intermittent, combinatory historical product, arising at moments of contestation of different political and geographical boundaries ... War produced the need for images of national identity ... but British national identity was not simply on tap, waiting to be imaged ... 'National characteristics' could not simply be 'infused into a national cinema' however much later writers wished that version of the story to be true.

Instead, the aesthetic and narrative forms used to represent national identity in literature, painting and history had to be rearticulated and transplanted into the cinema.[34]

In explicitly addressing the representation of national characteristics in many of his films Jennings accepted the multiplicity of experiences within British society. Different geographical regions (the North of England and the Home Counties, Wales, city and countryside), differing social classes, differing cultural pursuits and pastimes, varying and often contrasting everyday experiences are acknowledged and addressed within Jennings' films. Extending and informing this practice were the ambiguities implicit in such conditions and activities, which were 'resolved' in the films through allusions and appeals to, and the appearance of, an encompassing social totality. The ideological drive of such representations, then, was the construction of unity from difference – the notion of a national collectivity defined in and through difference.

Listen to Britain is one of many films by Jennings that exemplifies these relationships. As one commentator notes, the 'effect of the film is of unity and harmony, the holding together of difference as variety. National identity is proposed as the sum of this productive variety'.[35] The film presents the nation as a bond between the individual and the group across time and space. While acknowledging variation and distinctions in social life, the narrative constructs an image of the nation which is, ultimately, based on and around the concept of shared, common experience. The representational and ideological outcome of the recognition of variety and difference is an emphasis on 'us', a collectivity which embodies though transcends difference through the ascription of shared cultural assumptions. This effect is central to Jennings' films, and informs their function as propaganda. Brian Winston notes that '[n]o element of wartime propaganda was more important than [the] notion of "one nation"'.[36] He adds that 'settled opinion downplays or even ignores Jennings the propaganda master'.[37] In addressing the critical oversight it can be stressed that Jennings' mastery as a propagandist stemmed from his ability to evoke a unified nation as the outcome of its differences. For Jennings, social consensus, arrived at and actualised through diversity, is expressed in an image of the nation – which is 'imagined as a community, a deep horizontal comradeship', in Benedict Anderson's phrase.[38]

Jennings capably constructed both difference and commonality as valuable components of national identity. In doing so, he subtly inflected the nature of (wartime) propaganda. The so-called 'straight propaganda film' eschews ambiguity within its insistence on a clearly stated 'message'.[39] In this way wartime propaganda has a tendency to simplify issues: stark contrasts replace subtle differences, values are positive or negative, and complexity, contradiction or ambiguity are smoothed over or suppressed within the construction of certain univocal versions of historical experience. In contrast, Jennings' films, by acknowledging multiplicity, diversity and difference within national identity and the processes of representation, admit ambiguity as a productive vehicle for propaganda. It is within the subtlety with which Jennings addressed the complexity of this effect that he emerges as a master of propaganda.

In this relation, the study of British propaganda of World War II has tended to concentrate on the role of the Ministry of Information and its propaganda policy. Such studies frequently ignore the representational forms and the range of texts that encoded policy – from official speeches, to journalism, to documentary films – within a strict focus on the bureaucratic and administrative roots of policy.[40] Central to studies of this type is an empirical method based in archival research. In an associated way a rigorous empiricism is a hallmark of the methodologies of studies of British wartime cinema, and the approach also informs many studies of the broader history of British cinema.[41]

A certain deferral to archival documents is an element of this study. More particularly, though, the approach dominantly adopted here is an analysis of the formal or aesthetic components of significant selected films produced by Humphrey Jennings over his varied though lamentably short career. The central focus of this perspective is the explication of the construction of image and sound within Jennings' films, and their narrativised relationships. In this way the sound and image components and the narrative elements of individual films are, together with depictive aims between and across films, analysed as aspects of Jennings' documentary discourse. The principal archival source for this study is, then, Jennings' films – their images, sounds, narratives and the arrangements for their production. The method pursued here also recognises the historical and ideological contexts which impinged on the production of the films and their formal characteristics. Chief among the historical contexts is the trauma of World War II, though other historical conditions, including Britain's post-war directions and international relations, impacted on the narrative themes of certain of Jennings' films (notably *Family Portrait*, 1950). Ideological contexts include the continued construction and circulation within mid-twentieth-century British society of an agrarian myth and accompanying notions of national identity.

The study of formal components and style of a director's body of work implicates the attention within film studies to auteurism. However, the notion of creative control and individual 'vision' characteristic of a theory of the director as auteur is rendered problematic in relation to the collaborative mode adopted by British sponsored documentary filmmakers of the 1930s and 1940s. Grierson, for one, dismissed any sense of an auteurist documentary filmmaking as 'romantic and old-fashioned':

> I am not interested in single films as such [wrote Grierson] ... Film cannot of its nature be a purely personal art ... The nature of cinema demands collaboration and collusion with others ... and its significance derives from those who can operate and command purposively within these conditions ... [Documentary filmmaking] also demands ... patience and persistence ... not to mention as multifold and various and rich a collection of talents as the project demands and the wit of catalyst/producer dictates.[42]

Despite his desire to banish the auteur concept, it returns in Grierson's pronouncement in the figure of the producer.

The emphasis in Grierson's argument on the role of collaboration in documentary filmmaking has been reinforced in accounts of Jennings' productive practices. As Dai Vaughan among others has usefully pointed out, the editor Stewart McAllister made an important contribution to a number of Jennings' films.[43] Nevertheless, McAllister's role in Jennings' filmmaking should not be overestimated. Jennings *directed* the films on which they collaborated. In this way Anthony Aldgate and Jeffrey Richards perceptively insist that:

> it is hard to accept that the overall conception, the continuing preoccupations, the structure even of the films are not ultimately those of Jennings. Jennings prepared the scripts beforehand, outlining the ideas he sought to express in much greater detail than he has often been given credit for ... Jennings' Surrealist background gave him a full appreciation of the value of juxtaposition of images ... On the other hand, McAllister did not edit *A Diary for Timothy*, a key Jennings work which strongly relates both visually and thematically to the rest of his work. Furthermore, there is no attested evidence of specific interest on McAllister's part in [the thematic concerns in Jennings' films on] England and the English.[44]

Within the limitations on his film practice imposed by institutional and bureaucratic demands, Jennings was able to express his own 'means of vision', a process, he argued, in which 'matter (sense impressions)' are 'transformed and reborn by Imagination: *turned into an image*'.[45] The 'political' component of this vision was infused with the exigencies of producing propaganda. Nevertheless, the stamp of his own point of view is evident in the ways in which his films marry propagandistic and formalist (or 'poetic') aims within and through what is frequently a productive ambiguity expressive of the everyday experiences and identity of British (or English) society during war and peace.

Notes

1 L. Anderson, 'Only Connect: Some Aspects of the Work of Humphrey Jennings', *Film Quarterly*, 15: 2 (winter 1961–62), 5. Originally published in *Sight and Sound* in 1954.

2 C. Madge, 'A Note on Images', in M.-L. Jennings (ed.), *Humphrey Jennings: Film-Maker, Painter, Poet* (London: BFI in association with Riverside Studios, 1982), p. 49.

3 S. Hall, 'The Social Eye of *Picture Post*', Working Papers in Cultural Studies, no. 2 (Birmingham: University of Birmingham, 1972), p. 97.

4 I. Dalrymple, 'The Crown Film Unit, 1940–43', in N. Pronay and D. W. Spring (eds), *Propaganda, Politics and Film, 1918–45* (London: Macmillan Press, 1982), p. 217.

5 Quoted in A. Lovell and J. Hillier, *Studies in Documentary* (London: Secker and Warburg, 1972), p. 62.

6 K. Raine, *Defending Ancient Springs* (West Stockbridge, Massachusetts: The Lindisfarne Press, 1985 [1967]), p. 49.

7 Ibid., p. 134.

8 See B. Winston, *Claiming the Real: The Griersonian Documentary and its Legitimations* (London: BFI Publishing, 1995), p. 54.

9 D. Millar, 'Fires Were Started', *Sight and Sound*, 38: 2 (spring 1969) 101.

10 See I. Aitken, *Alberto Cavalcanti: Realism, Surrealism and National Cinema* (Trowbridge, Wiltshire: Flicks Books, 2000), p. 57.

11 Ibid., p. 59.

12 Quoted in C. Drazin, *The Finest Years: British Cinema of the 1940s* (London: Andre Deutsch, 1998), p. 122.

13 H. Watt, *Don't Look at the Camera* (London: Paul Elek, 1974), p. 65.

14 Quoted in E. Sussex, *The Rise and Fall of British Documentary: The Story of the Film Movement Founded by John Grierson* (Berkeley: University of California Press, 1975), p. 49.

15 G. Nowell-Smith, 'Humphrey Jennings: Surrealist Observer', in C. Barr (ed.), *All Our Yesterdays: 90 Years of British Cinema* (London: BFI Publishing, 1986), pp. 321–33.

16 G. Roberts, 'Soluble Fish: How Surrealism Saved Documentary from John Grierson', in G. Harper and R. Stone (eds), *The Unsilvered Screen: Surrealism on Film* (London: Wallflower Press, 2007), p. 97.

17 See B. Nichols, 'Documentary Film and the Modernist Avant-Garde', *Critical Inquiry*, 27: 4 (summer 2001) 580–610.

18 See Highmore, for example, B. Highmore, *Everyday Life and Cultural Theory: An Introduction* (London: Routledge, 2002), p. 93.

19 Ibid.

20 Highmore, *Everyday Life and Cultural Theory*, p. 94.

21 Roger Shattuck quoted in E. Adamowicz, *Surrealist Collage in Text and Image: Dissecting the Exquisite Corpse* (Cambridge: Cambridge University Press, 1998), p. 187, and C. Russell, *Experimental Ethnography: The Work of the Film in the Age of Video* (Durham, North Carolina: Duke University Press, 1999), p. 251.

22 The productive and strategic communicative capabilities of ambiguity are emphasised in E. Eisenberg, *Strategic Ambiguities: Essays on Communication, Organization, and Identity* (Thousand Oaks, California: Sage, 2007).

23 Christopher Bode, quoted in D. Gamboni, *Potential Images: Ambiguity and Indeterminacy in Modern Art* (London: Reaktion Books, 2003), p. 13.

24 E. Rhode, *A History of the Cinema: From its Origins to 1970* (Harmondsworth, Middlesex: Penguin, 1978), p. 377.

25 A. Higson, *Waving the Flag: Constructing a National Cinema in Britain* (Oxford: Clarendon Press, 1995), p. 201.

26 Lovell and Hillier, *Studies in Documentary*, p. 87. Italics added.

27 B. Winston, '*Fires Were Started* – ' (London: BFI Publishing, 1999), p. 35.

28 Quoted in Sussex, *The Rise and Fall of British Documentary*, p. 143.

29 As in, for example, Higson, *Waving the Flag*, p. 191 and p. 192. Attempts to analyse Jennings' films as poetry include J. Leach, 'The Poetics of Propaganda: Humphrey Jennings and *Listen to Britain*', in B. K. Grant and J. Sloniowski (eds), *Documenting the Documentary: Close Readings of Documentary Film and Video* (Detroit: Wayne State University Press, 1998), pp. 154–70, and B. Sorenssen, 'The Documentary Aesthetics of Humphrey Jennings', in J. Corner (ed.), *Documentary and the Mass Media* (London: Edward Arnold, 1986), pp. 47–64.

30 W. Empson, *Seven Types of Ambiguity* (Harmondsworth, Middlesex: Penguin Books in association with Chatto and Windus, 1961 [1930]).

31 See Winston, *Claiming the Real*, chapter 3.

32 A. Bazin, *What is Cinema?* volume 2 (Berkeley: University of California Press, 1971), p. 68.

33 Raine, *Defending Ancient Springs*, p. 49.

34 A. Lant, *Blackout: Reinventing Woman for Wartime British Cinema* (Princeton, New Jersey: Princeton University Press, 1991), p. 31.

35 Higson, *Waving the Flag*, p. 202.

36 Winston, '*Fires Were Started* –', p. 52.

37 Ibid.

38 B. Anderson, *Imagined Communities: Reflections on the Origin and Spread of Nationalism* (London: Verso, 1991), p. 7.

39 K. Reisz and G. Millar, *The Technique of Film Editing* (London: Focal Press, 1973), p. 170.

40 Studies of this type include M. Balfour, *Propaganda in War, 1939–1945: Organisations, Policies and Publics in Britain and Germany* (London: Routledge and Kegan Paul, 1971), I. McLaine, *Ministry of Morale: Home Front Morale and the Ministry of Information in World War II* (London: George Allen and Unwin, 1979), N. Reeves, *The Power of Film Propaganda: Myth or Reality?* (London: Cassell, 1999), and M. Stenton, 'British Propaganda and Raison d'Etat, 1935–40', *European Studies Review*, 10 (1980), 47–74. Where studies acknowledge the relationship of policy and communicative forms they tend to assume that the Ministry of Information's propaganda policy 'determined' content in an unproblematic way. Empirical studies of documentary, which draw heavily on the bureaucratic manoeuvring behind the British documentary movement, include P. Swann, *The British Documentary Movement, 1926–1946* (Cambridge: Cambridge University Press, 1989). I. Aitken, *Film and Reform: John Grierson and the British Documentary Movement* (London: Routledge, 1990), an analysis of the aesthetic and institutional influences that shaped Grierson's ideas on documentary, is widely informed by archival sources.

41 See, for example, J. Chapman, *Past and Present: National Identity and the British Historical Film* (London: I. B. Tauris, 2005), Higson, *Waving the Flag*, and J. Richards, *The Age of the Dream Palace: Cinema and Society in Britain, 1930–1939* (London: Routledge and Kegan Paul, 1984). A source-based approach is extended in a so-called New Film History. See J. Chapman, M. Glancy and S. Harper (eds), *The New Film History: Sources, Methods, Approaches* (Houndsmills, Basingstoke, Hampshire: Palgrave, 2000).

42 Quoted in P. Rotha, *Documentary Diary: An Informal History of the British Documentary Film, 1928–1939* (New York: Hill and Wang, 1972), pp. 276–7.

43 D. Vaughan, *Portrait of an Invisible Man: The Working Life of Stewart McAllister, Film Editor* (London: BFI Publishing, 1983).

44 A. Aldgate and J. Richards, *Britain Can Take It: The British Cinema in the Second World War* (Oxford: Basil Blackwell, 1986), p. 224.

45 H. Jennings, 'Introduction', H. Jennings, *Pandæmonium: 1660–1886: The Coming of the Machine as Seen by Contemporary Observers*, M.-L. Jennings and C. Madge (eds) (New York: The Free Press, 1985), p. xxxviii.

Modernity, myth, colour and collage: the early films

The early stages in a career are problematic. Biographers and other writers seeking to assess the work of creative individuals either pass over the formative years in a subject's career on their way to discussion of the 'mature' work, or scrutinise the early work for signs of burgeoning creativity. Generally, assessments of Jennings' career fall into the former category, and his early films are either ignored or noted only briefly. According to Kevin Jackson, Jennings' biographer, Jennings' early work 'seems almost hermetically sealed ... from his private intellectual concerns'.[1] Contrary to such an assessment, Jennings' foundational films do connect with and inform his early and ongoing intellectual preoccupations. His lifelong concern with aspects of technological modernity is evident in his earliest films, *Post Haste* and *Locomotives* (both 1934), with their focus on locomotives as symbols of modern experience. In another way his films *The Farm* (1938) and *English Harvest* (1939) apply and exploit features of a myth of rural England, an ideological strain which Jennings analysed in his studies of British poetry and which he also deployed in various forms in a number of later films. Jennings' early work also includes a number of films shot in colour. Working with the British Dufaycolor system, a rival to the US Technicolor process, the films were in many ways experiments in the use of colour stock. While Jennings worked exclusively with black-and-white after the 1930s, the early experimentation with colour presaged his later innovations and experiments with documentary form, particularly his use of reconstruction and a collagist associative montage. In these various ways, then, Jennings' early films point to a number of concerns and themes that characterise his later work. Typically dismissed as negligible, Jennings' films of the 1930s embody themes and practices that he would develop across his filmmaking career.

The engine of modernity

Jennings began to make films in 1934, the year he joined the Film Unit of the General Post Office. In that year he made, in addition to *Post Haste* and *Locomotives*, the short film *The Story of the Wheel*, a simple narrative from prehistory to the advent of the steam engine. Jackson passes over these works as 'modest to the point of invisibility'.[2] Certainly the films are simplified narrative accounts, though to dismiss them outright is to ignore the fact that the films reflect in part Jennings' developing ideas concerning the complex and unsettling place of machines within society and, as a related intellectual strand, his reflections on the emergence of a technologically based modernity. In these ways the films can be seen as ideational antecedents of his monumental (unfinished) study of this theme, *Pandæmonium*.

Jennings was concerned in *Pandæmonium* to examine the effects of the Industrial Revolution, a process he understood to have been experienced across three centuries during which time thought and action were mechanised. He called the book an 'imaginative history' of the Industrial Revolution, and he adopted a method which he summarised in terms of the presentation of 'Images' (selected quotations and passages from writings from various periods), each of which is arranged 'in a particular place in an unrolling film'.[3] The method was enacted in the form of a wide collection of excerpts from sources as diverse as scientific reports, letters, autobiographies, diaries, novels, polemical tracts and philosophical treatises produced within the period 1660 to 1886. The work opens with a description from Milton's *Paradise Lost* of fallen angels constructing 'Pandæmonium', the Palace of Devils. The extract inaugurates the central theme examined within the narrative, the creation of a mechanised and materialistic hell behind which, yet still recoverable, are the lost spiritual values of an older, more satisfying, moral order. Observations from the nineteenth century on the spread of factories embody the theme, as captured in Dickens' description of 'Coketown' as a 'town of machinery and tall chimneys, out of which interminable serpents of smoke trailed themselves ... It had a black canal in it, and a river that ran purple with ill-smelling dye ... and where the piston of the steam-engine worked monotonously ... like the head of an elephant in a state of melancholy madness'.[4] The conflict between industrial machinery and the degradation of nature is posed in many quotations from the era, and the fatalism which infused much Victorian thought concerning the effects of the machine is amply demonstrated in the selected passages. More particularly, Jennings identifies through the use of various excerpts a spreading industrialisation and its relationship with a resistant culture, one that the later social observer Raymond Williams described in terms of a 'whole way of life'.[5] Indeed, Jennings' line of thinking in *Pandæmonium* can be situated within the 'culture and society' tradition of social critique, with its roots in the Romantic movement analysed by Williams.

In another way, the intellectual montage of the work reflects a central aesthetic practice of modernism, that of collage. *Pandæmonium* exploits the potential to create meaning inherent in a Benjaminian juxtaposition of extracts released from their original contexts to reveal a narrative implicit within the combination of fragments. In this way the 'choice of texts refuses any simple, reductionist understanding of the Industrial Revolution and bears testimony to its massive complexity and cultural ambiguity: it is both the "stupendous system of manufacture" and the exploitation and degradation of working people'.[6] Another, more inclusive ambiguity informs the work: industrialism is represented as both a cause of social degradation and a site of societal regeneration. Industrialism may have wrought deleterious effects on physical landscapes, yet such effects can, in an openly utopian inflection of thought, be controlled within a future in which science, technology, poetry and philosophy together function to serve the needs of society.

Occupying a central place within the analysis is the railway and the locomotive engine. *Pandæmonium* includes twenty-five entries related to 'The Railway', more than any other reference to industrialisation. Elsewhere Jennings emphasised the significant cultural implications of the coming of the railway: 'Not only did it create a new architecture and a new type of engineer, new culture of the railway ticket and the railway station – but it altered irrevocably the nature of dreams and of childish fantasy (ambition to be an engine driver) ... It has given us a different conception of space, of speed and of power. It has rendered possible mass activities – the Cup final, the monster rally, the seaside holiday, the hiking excursion – whose ramifying effects on our behaviour and mentality almost extend beyond imagination'.[7] In *Pandæmonium* the experiential impacts of the railway are outlined in equally portentous terms. The railway inaugurates mass transportation; as one extract states: 'At a recent meeting of the Metropolitan Railway Company I exhibited one million of letters, in order to show the number of passengers (thirty-seven millions) that had been conveyed during the previous months'.[8] Other extracts depict the train compartment as a place of social engagement, coincidence and fortuitous meetings. Underwriting each effect of the new technology is the experience of speed: an extract in *Pandæmonium* from 1839 describes the movement of a train as 'the likest thing to Faust's flight on the Devil's mantle; or as if some huge steam night-bird had flung you on its back, and was sweeping through unknown space with you'.[9]

According to Jackson, Jennings' prose-poem 'The Iron Horse' (a description of a steam locomotive in terms of the well-known equestrian metaphor), published in June 1938 in the third edition of the *London Bulletin*, was the earliest prose sketch for the work that would become known as *Pandæmonium*.[10] In the next issue of the journal, Jennings, serving as editor, included extracts from six texts, among them R. M. Ballantyne's *The Iron Horse* (1891). Jackson concludes that 'It is reasonable to assume that, from this time [1938] onwards, he was engaged in the prodigious task of researching *Pandæmonium*'.[11] Given the importance in *Pandæmonium* of the impact of industrialisation and a technological modernity, as centrally represented by the railway and the locomotive, it can be reasonably assumed that Jennings' ideas on this topic are traceable back at least to his earliest films for the GPO, the railway-themed *Post Haste* and *Locomotives* of 1934.

Post Haste constructs a history of the 300 years of the post office through a method reminiscent of *Pandæmonium* – a collagist assemblage of extracts from various historical documents. Stuart Legg argued that *Post Haste* may be one of the earliest examples of a film composed of still images.[12] The soundtrack is also innovative, combining a range of voices reading various descriptions, noises of steam trains, hoof beats, a post horn and sounds of modern modes of transport. The narrative begins in the seventeenth century with the inauguration of a public postal service. The development of the service is illustrated by drawings of mail sorting and delivery on horseback and by stagecoach. The introduction of the railway, and its significance to the postal service, is emphasised in the account, as is the introduction of the Penny Post. The role of the railway in speeding delivery is reinforced through reference to mail sorting in a Post Office railway carriage, and to the track-side hooks which automatically collect mailbags from the moveable sorting room. Beyond such practices, the film outlines the economic expansion of the Post Office, which incorporated the Parcels Post Company in the 1880s and led to the modern Post Office. The function of transportation in the development of the Post Office is extended through reference to varieties of contemporary modes of transport used to expedite mail delivery – vans, trains and aeroplanes.

Like *Post Haste*, *Locomotives* is an account of technological development, without the reference in *Post Haste* to an attendant expansion of business practices. The theory of steam power is sketched through reference to a whistling kettle, which in turn is used to introduce the operation of steam pumps in the mills and mines of the eighteenth century. The same uncomplicated technological determinism motivates the conclusion of the narrative, with its focus on the development of the steam railway engine and an attendant expansion of railways across the countryside. In developing its narrative the film includes numerous shots and close-ups of the workings of models of steam engines. The detailed attention to the mechanical operations of the engines – in effect, a celebration in expressive visual terms (and musical accompaniment: the film is cut to sections of Schubert's *Rosamunde*) of the power and efficiency of technology – is matched by a similar attitude to mechanised power in Arthur Elton's *Aero-Engine*, also produced in 1934. Writing two years earlier in his manifesto 'First Principles of Documentary', Grierson had set out his opposition to what he interpreted as the pure formalism of a modernist work such as Walter Ruttmann's *Berlin: Die Symphonie eines Grosstadt* (*Berlin: The Symphony of a Great City*, 1927), a film which, among images of what Grierson called a 'cross section' of the city, opens with close-ups of a train as it approaches Berlin.[13] According to Grierson, 'What [is] more attractive (for a man of visual taste) than to swing wheels and pistons about in a ding-dong description of a machine, when he has little to say about the man who tends it, and still less to say about the tin-pan product it spills?'[14] The criticism could have been aimed at Jennings, and points to the difference in aesthetic tastes that was to mark the relationship of Jennings and Grierson in coming years.

Jennings edited both *Post Haste* and *Locomotives*, and though the editing is more workmanlike than inspired, it does point to his capacity in this regard, which is commonly overlooked in the critical attention given to the role of editors such as Stewart McAllister in the production of Jennings' later films. The fact that the shots were largely edited from archival footage reflects conditions within the GPO Film Unit in which the recycling of archival and other footage was a common institutional practice. Alberto Cavalcanti described the situation at the Film Unit when he first arrived there in 1934 as one in which 'The working conditions were similar to mediaeval artisanship; the work was collective, the films of [each director] were discussed'.[15] The practices of cooperation and mutual exchange implicit in the collective, collaborative practice noted by Cavalcanti informed attitudes within the Film Unit to accessing film footage whereby appropriation was rewritten in terms of a 'sharing' of resources. In the case of *Post Haste* and *Locomotives* much of this recycled, shared footage concerned trains.

To reduce Jennings' focus on railway engines in both films to a trainspotter's fanaticism is to misread the motivation for the representations. For Jennings, trains symbolised modernity, and it was through the prevalent symbol of the locomotive that he expressed the ambivalent attitude found in *Pandæmonium* towards the ability of industrialism and modernity simultaneously to degrade and improve the quality of life. In another way, the link between locomotives and modernity found in *Post Haste* and *Locomotives* revises the connection evident in certain films of the period between trains and danger and disaster. The image of the dangerous train was widespread during the formative years of the railway; indeed *Pandæmonium* includes an account of a deadly railway accident among its numerous references to locomotives. Drawing on this tradition a number of films of the 1930s expressed the residual fears and anxieties associated with railway travel. Walter Forde's *Rome Express* (1933) and Hitchcock's *The Lady Vanishes* (1938), for example, translate such fears into narratives concerned with murders that occur on trains.[16] Other examples of the dangers and inherently disruptive effect of trains include the opening mesmeric sequence of Renoir's *La Bête humaine* (1938), which registers the dizzy acceleration of a train on its way to the station at Le Havre. A sense of disorder, apprehension and trepidation is associated with the train's return journey from the port to Paris, one marked by murder, suicide and increasing speed. Bernard Vorhaus's low-budget thriller *The Last Journey* (1936) openly exploits feelings of disorientation and danger in a fast-paced narrative dealing with a suicidal plan to smash a speeding train into a terminus station.

The panic associated in these films with trains was allayed in Jennings' films. Just as one aim of *Pandæmonium* was the documentation of the deleterious effects of the Industrial Revolution as a way of transforming 'pandæmonium' (the city of demons) into a civilised place, so Jennings' films 'tame' dangerous locomotives, casting them as efficient (and safe) agents of modernity. In this way, *Locomotives*, especially, explains the workings of a train engine, rendering it a precision machine that can serve, not endanger those who use it. A similar point was made in *Night Mail* (1936), a film that replicates the emphasis in *Post Haste* on the role of mobile mail sorting carriages.

Critical interpretations of *Night Mail* tend to concentrate on the film's formal innovations – night photography, reconstructed scenes, and its expressive, poetic, narration – and downplay matters of content – the routine operations of a GPO mail train. However, it is the latter focus that may be the most relevant to considerations of the aims of the sponsor (the GPO) which, arguably, would require reference in the film to the latest railway postal service. Such an assessment does not suggest that corporate sponsorship necessarily demands or results in specific filmic characteristics or narrative foci. This position is echoed in Annette Kuhn's study of the conditions of sponsorship within the GPO

Film Unit. Kuhn concludes her analysis by noting that 'The question of control on the part of the sponsor over the management of the film units and, relatedly, the nature of the films produced in them, is ... not a simple one'.[7] The conclusion can be recast in the assessment that, though a sponsor may have expected or required particular elements to be included in a finished film, sponsorship nevertheless left room for the use of various aesthetic approaches and narrative elements.

Working within the terms of sponsorship Jennings could criticise modernity – as in his later film *A Diary for Timothy* (1945), in which it is suggested that certain modern conditions have contributed to an impoverishment of social and political life – and elsewhere, as in *Family Portrait*, he would endorse modernity as the engine of British history. The latter position is reinforced in the references throughout his work to locomotives as symbols and instruments of a progressive and benevolent modernity. Images of trains appear repeatedly in Jennings' work in a variety of media, including painting, poetry, photography and film. The powerful appeal of the symbolic potential of trains is evident in his summary of *La Bête humaine*. Writing to his wife Cicely about Renoir's masterful and psychologically complex film he emphasised that it's 'all about railways'.[18]

A dream of England

Among Jennings' preoccupations was a concern with the English countryside. Landscapes – rural and urban – feature prominently in his work, and a pronounced emphasis on rural regions within his films demonstrates an intellectual and emotional investment in the countryside as a reflection of an essential component of British – though more particularly, English – national identity. Jennings' early work includes two films, *English Harvest* and *The Farm*, structured around rural scenes. These two films, together with another film, presumably *Farwell Topsails* (1937), were made during a period when Jennings worked as a freelance film director. A press release dated 5 October 1937 mentions that he was soon to complete films for the producer Adrian Klein: 'Work is practically complete on three short colour films. One of these will be named *English Harvest* ... Another picture has been made of the last few top-sail schooners ... A third film is promised in which an attempt is being made to break entirely new ground in rhythm and colour. The films are being directed by Mr Humphrey Jennings, whose work in recent colour films awakened considerable attention'.[19] As Kevin Jackson points out, the information clarifies some issues of dating certain films. Numerous reference books list the release date of *English Harvest* as 1939, but it was more likely shot in the autumn of 1937. The 'schooner' film, 'lost in the archives until very recently, must be *Farewell Topsails*; and another short now attributed to Jennings, *The Farm*, was either made from *English Harvest* out-takes, or at one time was a much longer piece incorporating all or part of the harvest footage as an extended sequence'.[20] The innovative third film mentioned was either not made or became *Design for Spring*, which was filmed during the winter of 1937–38 and previewed as early as February 1938, and finally released as *Making Fashion* in 1939.[21] Jackson concludes that of the four films he mentions – *English Harvest, Farewell Topsails, The Farm* and *Design for Spring* – 'English Harvest is probably the best … a slight but beguiling study of farm work at harvest time which is Jennings' most direct treatment in filmic terms of that potent set of pastoral images – horse, plough, rural labourers – to which he returned again and again in his paintings'.[22] Jackson's argument regarding the persistence, and hence importance, of pastoral imagery in Jennings' paintings can be taken one crucial step further – pastoral imagery also permeates his films.

The pleasant scenes in *English Harvest* of rural life in the grain fields of pre-war East Anglia are accompanied by a soundtrack which features the music of Beethoven's *Pastoral Symphony* and a commentary spoken in quiet tones by A. G. Street, who at the time was known to listeners of the BBC as the 'Voice of the Country'. Street was a farmer as well as a popular writer and broadcaster and he generally attempted to depict rural life in ways which were devoid of nostalgia or the picturesque.[23] Nevertheless, in at least one of his broadcasts he drew heavily upon many of the tropes and themes of nostalgic revelry in his evocation of the idealised village of 'Sedgebury Wallop, Wessex'. The depiction includes a description of 'the old dairyman toddling along the lane behind his cows with his little grandson helping him to drive them into milking'. The village itself 'nestled serenely under the downs, its cottages rallying round the church and the inn as from time immemorial … Sparrows twittered in the thatch … [and] starlings gurgled on the roof of the barn'.[24] Features of Street's idealised arcadia were reflected in the commentary of *English Harvest*.

Roy Boulting's *Ripe Earth* (1938) covered similar ground to Jennings' film, with images of harvest time in the village of Thaxted, Essex. Boulting depicts the countryside in terms of 'ripeness' and an almost unlimited potential for exploitation – a point reinforced in the celebration in the film of a rich harvest. In these ways *Ripe Earth* evokes the notion of the land and the countryside as a cornucopia readily and 'naturally' available as a source of an uncomplicated form of production. Though he recognises the manual work required to produce an 'English harvest', Jennings also presents rural work in terms of unalienated labour. Street's narration for Jennings' film presents the work required to till the land in an idyllic way: 'Now for next year's harvest, ploughing, the king of jobs, the most charming disguise that work can wear'. *The Farm* similarly frames the countryside as a source that brings forth its 'bounty' with little effort. The film's images of farming and pastoral life reinforce the suggestion that the countryside is a space of 'natural abundance' and limitless regenerative capacities which seemingly exist outside or beyond history and complicated social experiences. Such allusions evoke central features of a pervasive and powerful rural myth, aspects of which frequently appear in later films by Jennings.

The so-called rural myth of Britain is a complex phenomenon. The historian Martin Wiener traces the origins of the myth to late nineteenth-century anxieties over industrialism and modernity, the very attitudes which Jennings documents in *Pandæmonium*.[25] The rural myth was promulgated in the late nineteenth century and early twentieth century in a variety of works, including architecture, garden design, literature, art, music, radio broadcasts and film. One expression of aspects of the myth contained within this range of sources is *In Search of England* (1927), a travelogue by the popular author H. V. Morton. Morton's description of rural England includes 'the smell of wood smoke lying in the still air ... little red birds singing in the blinds under the thatch ... church bells ... bats [starting] to flicker like little bits of burnt paper ... the slow jingle of a team coming home from the fields'.[26] Another book in the travelogue-survey genre, J. B. Priestley's *English Journey* (1934), refers to 'Old England', the 'country of the cathedrals and minsters, and manor houses and inns, of Parson and squire; ... we all know this England, which at its best cannot be improved upon in this world'.[27] Priestley's version of pastoral or regional lifestyles is temporally based, a nostalgic vision of a past England perpetuated into the present.

A variant of the myth frames it in spatial terms, specifically a 'Deep' England typically associated with gentle landscapes in southern England, or at least the Home Counties. Angus Calder summarises many of the features of the rural myth when he writes of:

> The ideal village – it may be in Sussex or in the Cotswolds, or in Jane Austen's Hampshire – [which] contains a pleasant Anglican vicar, an affable squire, assorted professionals, tradesmen and craftsmen, many of whom will be 'characters', plus a complement of sturdy yeomen and agricultural workers learned in old country lore. It has a green on which the village team plays cricket, with the squire or his son as captain.[28]

Another commentator adds that 'There is something for everyone in the countryside. Right- and left-wing versions of the [rural] myth were by no means mutually exclusive'.[29] By the early twentieth century the dream image of a rural idyll was projected as an essential component of national character (constructed in terms of 'Englishness' and not unproblematically translated as a feature of British identity). In these terms, the notion of 'Englishness' was closely identified with the countryside, and from these rural associations stemmed informing characteristics of solidity, peace and contentment, spirituality, responsibility and dependability, and a reverence for the time-honoured codes of tradition. It was assumed characteristics such as these which World War II threatened to destroy. Indeed, the fears generated by perceptions of industrialism's destruction of a rural way of life were exacerbated towards the end of the 1930s by the approach of technological warfare.

A sign of this reaction found form in the book *England Is a Village*, published in 1941 by the journalist C. Henry Green, in which he insisted that 'England's might is still in her fields and villages, and though the whole weight of mechanised armies roll over them to crush them, in the end they will triumph'.[30] The countryside as a mystical source of national regeneration, the repository of enduring and inalienable national characteristics, permeates British wartime representations. The 'naturalisation' of myth – the function of ideology, according to Barthes[31] – is, in the case of the rural myth, enacted in a form of auto-validation through which the myth represents its content (national identity) in the seemingly natural ideological terms of landscape and nature. The naturalisation of the rural myth is one of the undeniable 'propagandistic' functions of Jennings' films.

Representations of the rural are typically understood in relation to urban and suburban environments.[32] Jennings' inflection of the rural myth revises this point to the effect that the rural exits in tension with modern technology. Industrialism and technological modernity, the conditions implicitly contested within the circulation of the rural myth, are not banished or subsumed within Jennings' expression of the myth. In Jennings' films, industry and modern machinery, in the form of locomotives or technological warfare, are constantly deployed and contrasted with pastoral landscapes and rural life. The ambiguities inherent in the dichotomies of technology and nature, rural and urban, and the simultaneous expression of features of modernity and anti-modernity, productively inform a number of Jennings' later films.

'Colour won't stand dignity'

Contemporary critics writing on *English Harvest* and *The Farm* commented on the quality of the films' colour cinematography.[33] These two films, together with *Farewell Topsails* and *Design for Spring*, were shot in Dufaycolor, a British colour 'additive' process introduced in 1934.[34] During 1936 Jennings had briefly worked for Gasparcolor, another company producing colour film stock. *The Birth of the Robot* (1936), the film he made with his friend Len Lye, was shot using this film stock. Jennings is credited with 'colour direction and production' on *The Birth of the Robot*, though his contribution to the film extended beyond this role into directorial duties. In fact Jennings' contribution to the film in the form of assistant directorial duties may have surpassed his involvement as a colour consultant since, even granting Jennings the experience of working for Gasparcolor, Lye's expertise in the use of Gasparcolor in the production of his film *Rainbow Dance* (1936), for example, arguably already exceeded Jennings' skills in the area. *The Birth of the Robot* is an animated fantasy in which the heavenly figures of Mercury, Venus and Mars watch over a wayward motorist who careens across the desert, to be lost in a sandstorm. As the bones of the driver bleach in the desert sun, Venus sends drops of oil to earth, which transform the skeleton into a huge robot. Enacting the message of the film – which was produced as an advertisement for the Shell-Mex Oil Company – the robot spreads the benefits of well-oiled machinery across a landscape that was once desert.

Jennings' own films in colour were far-removed from Lye's avant-gardism, though through the use of colour he aligned himself with the innovative practices of certain works produced by the GPO Film Unit which exploited the expressive potential of colour, notably Lye's *A Colour Box* (1935), Norman McLaren's *Love on the Wing* (1938) and Lotte Reiniger's *Heavenly Post Office* (1938). Generally, however, the works of the British documentary film movement of the 1930s and 1940s were shot in black-and-white. The restricted use within these years of colour for documentary film resulted from institutional constraints and various theories concerning documentary realism. Grierson, for example, during his time at the GPO Film Unit, was willing to promote the use of colour in abstract films such as those made by Lye, 'but his cordiality did not extend to the live action subject. In Grierson's world, colour was art but not the art of the documentary'.[35] In contrast to Grierson, Ian Dalrymple of the Crown Film Unit, the successor of the GPO Film Unit, sought to promote the use of colour in wartime documentary films. Dalrymple noted, in a memorandum accompanying a proposal to the wartime Ministry of Information to film Pat Jackson's *Western Approaches* (1944) in colour, that 'Colour is still sufficiently a novelty to attract patronage. In other words, it sells propaganda ... [and] in addition colour automatically adds 100 per cent value – due to uniforms, flags and other patriotic insignia, etc'.[36] However, Dalrymple's arguments in favour of colour were denied by the Finances Division of the wartime Ministry of Information, which queried the costs associated with colour production.[37]

In terms of what was, in effect, an embargo during World War II on colour production within documentary filmmaking imposed by Jennings' future employer, the Ministry of Information, Jennings' abandonment of colour immediately prior to the war was fortuitous. Beyond this situation, Jennings' criticisms of colour reveal his commitment to a certain conception of realistic documentary practice. In contrast to the '100 per cent value' which Dalrymple argued accrued to colour, Jennings, who was to work closely with Dalrymple during World War II and who supported most of his decisions, argued in 1936 that colour subtracted from aspects of a film's effect. In a brief, thesis-driven review in the journal *World Film News* of Henry Hathaway's recently released *The Trail of the Lonesome Pine*, Jennings argued that '*Colour* and *Ideas* are fundamentally opposed; the black-and-white film has always lived on ideas; but colour depends upon *sensations*'.[38] The sensational effect of colour highlights objects. If the object is artificially constructed, such as a film set, or a film star, colour, by drawing attention to itself, ironically reveals imperfections in the object/body. The revelation of imperfection is less apparent in the case of objects and animals derived from the 'real' world beyond the fictional diegesis. Such phenomena connote a range of associations and sensations ungenerated by the misleading effects associated with colour. '[O]ne is satisfied with the sensation of dog', insists Jennings, 'one is not so satisfied with ... [the] sensation [of colour]'.[39]

It has been concluded from his arguments that Jennings' 'interest lies in the sensations and the spectacle of real things ..., not the spectacle of colour in its own right'.[40] In these terms colour is a central component of the spectacular, and – to follow the argument – that by denying colour the British documentary movement denied spectacle. Jennings' work revises this conclusion (thereby perhaps demonstrating his uneasy place within the British documentary movement). As his arguments in the film review make clear, Jennings' refusal of colour was a reaffirmation of documentary realism – to which, notably, he applied spectacle. One of Jennings' major achievements was the deployment of 'spectacular', in the sense of innovative, effects within documentary realist works in the form of reconstructed scenes of heightened emotionalism within a pronounced narrative (as exemplified in *Fires Were Started*). In another way Jennings applied 'spectacle' in the form of collage, a method he derived from Surrealism.

Surrealism/collage

In his biography of Jennings, Kevin Jackson argues that there is some credence to Jennings' claim that he read both *La Révolution surréalist* and *Le Surrealism au service de la révolution* on their first appearance, which would have meant that he read these founding manifestos of the artistic and political movement while in his late teens.[41] Jennings extended and informed this early interest in Surrealism throughout the 1930s through the publication of a number of Surrealist poems in English journals supportive of Surrealist ideas. In 1936 Jennings met and became friends with Paul Eluard, and he knew André Breton, to whom in 1937 he introduced Peggy Guggenheim, then embarking on compiling a collection of Surrealist art. Roland Penrose remembered Jennings as the active centre of the 'Surrealist Group' in London, which included Herbert Read, David Gascoyne, Henry Moore and Paul Nash.[42] In 1936 Jennings served as a member of the organising committee of the influential International Surrealist Exhibition held in the New Burlington Galleries in London during the summer of that year. Attended by Breton, Dali and other Surrealist luminaries, the exhibition featured the works of leading European Surrealists, among which hung a number of paintings by Jennings.

Jennings' Surrealism was further informed by his association in both the GPO Film Unit and the Crown Film Unit with Alberto Cavalcanti. While part of a group of young avant-garde filmmakers allied with Marcel l'Herbier and Louis Delluc in Paris in the 1920s, Cavalcanti mixed with members of Parisian Surrealism and applied some of their ideas in his early film *Rien que les heures* (*Nothing But the Hours*, 1926). As head of the GPO Film Unit during the years 1936–40 Cavalcanti's avant-gardism licensed Jennings' experimentation in documentary film form.[43] Searching for a way to explicate the relationship between such influences and his films, critics have reduced Jennings' informed understanding of Surrealism to certain unusual (though not necessarily extraordinary) shots in his films, such as the images in *Fires Were Started* of a one-legged man on a war-torn street and a stallion amidst fires started by a German incendiary raid. Techniques associated with the dream work of Surrealist cinema, such as superimposition, dissolves and slow motion, are largely absent from Jennings' films. Beyond superficial echoes of a denatured Surrealism identified in certain shots, Jennings' profound debt to Surrealism is evident within his films in the method of collage, a central strand of Surrealist aesthetics.

Collage, the appropriation and assemblage of disparate fragments reworked within and through juxtapositions, was widely practiced in Surrealist arts as varied as painting, poetry, drama, ballet, photography and film. Notably, Jennings employed collage within his work for Mass-Observation, a practice which itself owed much to Surrealism. The founders of Mass-Observation – who included, besides Jennings, the filmmaker Stuart Legg, the literary critic William Empson, and the poets Ruthven Todd, Kathleen Raine, Charles Madge and David Gascoyne – viewed the work of Mass-Observation as a way of creating new representational forms which held the potential to enact social change. The new forms transcended a pure documentarism by melding it to Surrealist approaches which were informed by the ideas of Gascoyne and Jennings.[44]

The first work produced by Mass-Observation was *May the Twelfth: Mass-Observation Day-Surveys 1937*, a study of social behaviour on the day George VI was crowned. Jennings and Madge edited the book and declared that they had arranged the various loosely connected contents 'in a simple documentary manner', a claim which demonstrated the degree to which Jennings by this time associated documentary with collage.[45] The central methodological practice of *May the Twelfth* was juxtaposition – official accounts of preparations for the coronation were, for example, placed alongside reports of strikes and the conditions of workers – through which the completed work constitutes a collage of observations on a date that simultaneously marked a historically significant event and everyday mundane occurrences. Jennings, disillusioned with the increasing reliance within Mass-Observation on a participant observation derived from classical anthropology, was soon to abandon the activities of Mass-Observation, though he continued to work in collage. Jennings' paintings and poetry juxtapose 'found' components in collagist forms, and the practice further informed his filmmaking.

As a filmic practice collage is often subsumed in critical estimations within the domain of montage, an inclusive word that has come to refer to any form of editorial assemblage. The film theorist Brian Henderson has noted that while the 'difference between montage and collage is a complex question, film critics generally use the term collage without elucidating its meaning nor even its difference from montage'. Henderson argues that '[t]here is sometimes the suggestion that the pieces of a collage are shorter or more fragmented than those of a montage, but this does not hold up. Modern film-makers rarely use any shot shorter than Eisenstein's average shot in *Potemkin*. Moreover, collage as practiced by moderns allows long takes and tracking shots; montage as practiced by Eisenstein did not'. [46] That being the case, '[i]t seems clear that the difference between montage and collage is to be found in the divergent ways in which they associate and order images, not in the length or nature of the images themselves. Montage fragments reality in order to reconstitute it in highly organized, synthetic emotional and intellectual patterns'. In contrast, collage 'collects or sticks its fragments together in a way that does not entirely overcome their fragmentation ... In regard to overall form, it seeks to bring out the internal relations of its pieces'.[47] The contributions of Jennings' editors, notably Stewart McAllister, are important to this process. Jennings' ideas on collage, and his collagist ideas, were matched, if not realised, within McAllister's associative montage. The practice of 'bring[ing] out the internal relations of [a work's] pieces' released shots and sourced footage from their original meanings, resulting in new meanings emerging from the recombination. The resultant collage is 'located in a space of unresolved tensions, on the one hand tending towards a new perceptual or intellectual unity, on the other hand foregrounding paradox', contradiction and ambiguity.[48]

All too often cast as a negative characteristic of the creative text, ambiguity, as demonstrated in the effects of collage, is a productive practice. Jennings' debt to Surrealism is traceable in his acceptance of a multiplicity of meaning, and the point is carried in his films, which are informed by productive ambiguities. The concerns within Jennings' filmmaking traced here – the locomotive as an agent and symbol of modernity, the rural myth, collaborative work practices (as demonstrated in his filmmaking with Len Lye), 'spectacular' formal methods and ambiguity – inform his later work. A number of the preoccupations referred to here – notably a move away from Mass-Observation and the presence of a productive ambiguity – are evident in his film *Spare Time*.

Notes

1 K. Jackson, *Humphrey Jennings* (London: Picador, 2004), p. 208.
2 Ibid., p. 152.
3 Jennings, 'Introduction', *Pandæmonium: 1660–1886*, p. vii.
4 Jennings, *Pandæmonium: 1660–1886*, p. 273.
5 R. Williams, 'Culture is Ordinary' [1958], in *Resources of Hope: Culture, Democracy, Socialism* (London: Verso, 1989), p. 4.
6 K. Robins and F. Webster, *Times of the Technoculture: From the Information Society to Virtual Life* (London: Routledge, 1999), p. 29.

7 Quoted in ibid., p. 25.
8 The engineer James Nasmyth, in his autobiography (1883). Jennings, *Pandæmonium: 1660–1886*, p. 348.
9 Ibid., p. 212.
10 Jackson, *Humphrey Jennings*, p. 205.
11 Ibid.
12 Quoted in A. Hodgkinson and R. Sheratsky, *Humphrey Jennings: More Than a Maker of Films* (Hanover: University Press of New England, 1982), p. 15.
13 J. Grierson, 'First Principles of Documentary (1932)', in I. Aitken (ed.), *The Documentary Film Movement: An Anthology* (Edinburgh: Edinburgh University Press, 1998), p. 88.
14 Ibid.
15 Quoted in Lovell and Hillier, *Studies in Documentary*, p. 15.
16 The dangerous race between a train and a bus in Hitchcock's *Number Seventeen* (1932) would have had more of a visceral effect if the train and bus weren't obviously scale models.
17 A. Kuhn, 'British Documentary in the 1930s and "Independence": Recontextualising a Film Movement', in D. Macpherson (ed.), *Traditions of Independence: British Cinema in the Thirties* (London: BFI Publishing, 1980), p. 31.
18 Quoted in M.-L. Jennings (ed.), *Humphrey Jennings: Film-Maker, Painter, Poet* (London: BFI in association with Riverside Studios, 1982), p. 22.
19 Jackson, *Humphrey Jennings*, p. 206.
20 Ibid. Jackson here follows Hodgkinson and Sheratsky who deduce from their studies of Jennings' early films that 'there is evidence to suggest that *English Harvest* was incorporated into – or possibly extracted from – a slightly longer film entitled *The Farm*'. Hodgkinson and Sheratsky, *Humphrey Jennings*, p. 19.
21 Jackson, *Humphrey Jennings*, p. 206.
22 Ibid., pp. 206–7.
23 S. Rose, *Which People's War: National Identity and Citizenship in Britain, 1939–1945* (Oxford: Oxford University Press, 2003), p. 201.
24 Quoted in ibid.
25 M. Wiener, *English Culture and the Decline of the Independent Spirit, 1850–1980* (Cambridge: Cambridge University Press, 1981).
26 H. V. Morton, *In Search of England* (Harmondsworth, Middlesex: Penguin, 1960 [1927]), pp. 13–14.
27 J. B. Priestley, *English Journey: Being a Rambling But Truthful Account of What One Man Saw and Heard and Felt and Thought During a Journey Through England During the Autumn of the Year 1933* (Harmondsworth, Middlesex: Penguin, 1984 [1934]), p. 210.
28 A. Calder, *The Myth of the Blitz* (London: Jonathan Cape, 1991), p. 188.
29 Ibid.
30 In J. Taylor, *A Dream of England: Landscape, Photography and the Tourists' Imagination* (Manchester: Manchester University Press, 1994), p. 199.
31 R. Barthes, *Mythologies* (New York: Hill and Wang, 1972).
32 D. Matless, *Landscape and Englishness* (London: Reaktion Books, 1998), p. 8.
33 Jackson, *Humphrey Jennings*, p. 207.
34 Though not capable of rendering the brighter, sharper colours available with 'subtractive' processes such as Technicolor from the US, Dufaycolor had the advantage of being cheaper to produce.
35 S. Brown, 'Dufaycolor: The Spectacle of Reality and British National Cinema', a report to the Centre for British Film and Television Studies [May 2006] (London: Birkbeck College, University of London) at www.bftv.ac.uk/projects/dufaycolor.htm (accessed 18/03/07).

36 Aldgate and Richards, *Britain Can Take It*, p. 250.

37 Ibid., p. 251.

38 H. Jennings, 'Colour Won't Stand Dignity', in D. Macpherson (ed.), *British Cinema: Traditions of Independence* (London: BFI Publishing, 1980), p. 183. Originally published in June 1936.

39 Ibid.

40 Brown, 'Dufaycolor' at www.bftv.ac.uk/projects/dufaycolor.htm.

41 Jackson, *Humphrey Jennings*, p. 164.

42 Ibid., p. 159.

43 The point is discussed in Aitken, *Alberto Cavalcanti*, p. 49.

44 J. MacClancy, 'Brief Encounter: The Meeting, in Mass-Observation, of British Surrealism and Popular Anthropology', *Journal of the Royal Anthropological Institute*, 1 (n.s): 3 (1995), 496.

45 H. Jennings and C. Madge (eds), with contributions by T. O. Beachcroft, J. Blackburn, W. Empson, S. Legg and K. Raine, *May the Twelfth: Mass-Observation Day-Surveys 1937 by Over Two Hundred Observers* (London: Faber and Faber, 1987 [1937]), p. v.

46 B. Henderson, 'Toward a Non-Bourgeois Camera Style', *Film Quarterly*, 24: 2 (winter 1970–71), 5.

47 Ibid.

48 Adamowicz, *Surrealist Collage in Text and Image*, p. 187.

Work and leisure: *Spare Time* 2

Alberto Cavalcanti, the film's producer, called *Spare Time* 'one of the best films the GPO ever made' and Dai Vaughan, in his portrait of Stewart McAllister, calls the film 'a curiously important [film] in the history of British documentary'.[1] Jennings rejoined the GPO Film Unit just prior to making *Spare Time*, which was his first major film and the last major film of the GPO Film Unit before it became the Crown Film Unit late in 1940 under the auspices of the Films Division of the Ministry of Information. This important though sometimes neglected work was one of two films produced by the GPO Film Unit for the Joint Committee of the British Council to be screened at the World's Fair in New York in 1939.[2] The theme of the fair, 'Building a World of Tomorrow' (a phrase rendered ironic on the eve of World War II) was alluded to in the joint title of the British documentary films submitted to the event: 'British Workers'. *The Times*, in its review of the films, played down references to any advances by labour and instead commented on certain characteristics within the collection of films sent to New York: '[The films are] in the first place [a] distinctly British contribution to the art of the moving pictures ... [T]hose who make films of fact ... go to New York to teach'.[3] Graham Greene was wary of emphasising pedagogic features of documentary; it was, he argued, one of the reasons why the word 'documentary' carries a 'dry-as-dust sound'. However, according to Greene, the 'best documentaries', including the ones bound for New York, 'have never been like that'; they contain a 'personal element – the lyrical and the ironic'.[4]

An internal memorandum which circulated within the GPO Film Unit prior to Jennings' association with the project stated that the 'general purpose' of the planned film was 'to show that workers of all grades have a secondary life, over and above their working life, in which colliers may become musicians, musicians may become engineers, engineers may become dog-fanciers and so on'.[5] The film that emerged from this initial suggestion is in three sections, each one devoted to an industrial city or region and associated leisure activities. The three industries are steel (Sheffield), cotton (Bolton and Manchester) and coal (Pontypridd). In the first section the narrator, Laurie Lee, states: 'Steel, there are three shifts, so spare time can be morning or afternoon'. Various shots illustrate the theme of leisure amidst the shifts: members of a brass band practice their music; scenes of factories (the site of work) and the interiors of houses (an important site of leisure); a man walks his dogs, another man attends to his pigeons; boys mend bicycles and cyclists ride through the countryside, stopping at a pub; a large crowd watches a football match. A similar pattern informs the next section on cotton, filmed in Bolton and Manchester. In Manchester a kazoo band plays the tune 'If You Knew Susie' on spare ground next to a gasometer. Shots of the interior of a house in Bolton depict a mother and her child, as children play outside in the street. The kazoo band performs 'Rule Britannia' as a member dressed as Britannia is raised on a homemade throne. The kazoo music continues across shots of Manchester's Belle Vue amusement park, including animals in their cages and a wrestling match. An amateur theatrical troupe rehearses a play and the segment concludes with the tune 'The Bells of St Mary's' and a shot of dancers in a ballroom. The final section dealing with coal reprises the relationship of work (in this case a mine) and the domestic space of leisure (rows of terraced homes). A choir sings Handel's 'Largo' as the scene cuts to a street scene of windows, house fronts, shops and pedestrians, and includes an interior in which a woman prepares a meal as a man reads a newspaper. The final shots focus on miners descending a pit to start a new shift, with chimneys silhouetted against the darkening sky.

The combined effect of the three sections is a reflection on aspects of English character and culture through a focus on region and leisure (with the latter contrasted to scenes and spaces related to work). *Spare Time* was not the first film of the British documentary movement to represent either leisure activities or regional areas. Varying geographic regions are included in a number of British documentary films of the 1930s: *The Horsey Mail* (1938) is set in the coastal village of Winterton, Norfolk; *The Islanders* (1937) is set on Eriksay, Guernsey and the Inner Farn Islands; *A Midsummer's Day's Work* (1939) is set in Amersham; and *Granton Trawler* (1934), *The Saving of Bill Blewitt* (1937) and *North Sea* (1938) are all set among Scottish fishing villages. In another way, the recreational activities of hiking, tennis and lounging are included within the images of Lye's *Rainbow Dance* (1936). Contrary to a critical focus on *Spare Time*'s representation of region and leisure, the break-through achievement of *Spare Time* in the field of documentary representation can be understood in terms of a series of innovations, which exceeded and revised extant documentary practices. The contemporary representational practices in question are those of Mass-Observation and the narrative conventions of the British documentary movement.

Mass-Observation and Humphrey Spender

What has become an almost universally accepted critical line argues that *Spare Time* was either produced by Mass-Observation or made in association with Mass-Observation. In this way Basil Wright insisted on various occasions that *Spare Time* was produced for the organisation, and Jim Hillier argues that *Spare Time* 'was made for the GPO Film Unit, but as a Mass Observation film'.[6] Anthony Hodgkinson and Rodney Sheratsky qualified the line in their argument that '*Spare Time*, made by Jennings for the GPO Film Unit, might just as well have been sponsored by Mass Observation'.[7] Dai Vaughan has pointed out that the complex and strict financial and administrative rules imposed on the GPO Film Unit by the Treasury were such that 'it is scarcely credible that [the Unit] should have been given leave to work for a totally independent organisation' such as Mass-Observation.[8] Nevertheless, having established this point, Vaughan does trace a link – 'through the character of the film's images' – between *Spare Time* and the work of Mass-Observation.[9] In light of such confusions a point of clarification is called for: *Spare Time* is not a Mass-Observation work. Jennings had openly abandoned Mass-Observation by the time he made *Spare Time*. Distinctions between Mass-Observation practices and Jennings' work at the time are evident within a contrast of the visual work of Mass-Observation – exemplified by Humphrey Spender's photographic assignment in Bolton in 1937–38 – and the photographic album that is *Spare Time*, a film which includes Bolton among its locations.

At the end of the 1920s, Humphrey Spender travelled with his older brother, the poet and novelist Stephen Spender, to Germany where he studied the emergent New Objectivity style of photography, a mode perceived by its practitioners to intersect with the images of certain films. Humphrey Spender was attracted to Mikhail Kaufman's film *Spring* (1930) as a source of imagery that could be replicated in his photographs. Similarly Walter Ruttmann's *Berlin* (1927) was another influence in his early years as a photographer. Spender associated Ruttmann's film with what he interpreted as the ability of newsreels to depict fleeting, impermanent moments.[10] It was such moments, derived from a basis in 'the news', which he sought out in his work as a press photographer in the mid-1930s, particularly as the 'Lensman' for the *Daily Mirror* and subsequently in his photographs for the *Picture Post.*

Spender joined Mass-Observation's so-called Worktown project in the spring of 1937. Though loosely conceived, the general idea of the project was to document the lives of local people as part of an on-going attempt to describe and understand essential activities and lifestyles characteristic of the nation. The northern post of this activity was the industrial city of Bolton where Spender replaced his 'Lensman' attention to newsworthy events with an ethnographic focus on the everyday ('Worktown' was adopted by the project to bestow a certain anonymity on Bolton). Mass-Observation's strategy in Bolton was a form of participant observation based on a detailed documentation of the minutiae of daily life. Subjects would occasionally be invited to describe their actions, though more commonly the 'fieldworker' collected details through unobtrusive observation. The raw data gathered by the observer comprised notes, reports, diaries and photographs. The guidelines for the working day issued to the Mass-Observation volunteers by Tom Harrisson, the adventurer-*cum*-anthropologist who oversaw Mass-Observation's Bolton work, emphasised serendipity and were far from those of a project organised along strict scientific lines. Spender noted that: 'There was a daily session which usually took the form of Tom seizing about half a dozen national newspapers, reading the headlines, getting us laughing and interested, and quite on the spur of the moment, impulsively, hitting on a theme that he thought would be productive. For instance, how people hold their hands, the number of sugar lumps that people pop into their mouths in restaurants, how much people stole things like teaspoons in restaurants, matches, bits of paper ... [Y]ou were working on your own, and one thing led to another'.[11] As he pointed out in later interviews, Spender was willing to follow Harrisson's eccentric Mass-Observation directives, even when he was only partially aware of the purposes or ends of many of his activities in Bolton.[12]

The notion of a study of life in a typical northern industrial town bore, as with Orwell's encounter with the North in *The Road to Wigan Pier* (1937), many of the marks of the 'Into Unknown England' tradition in which members of the London intelligentsia journeyed to the industrial North to record social conditions. The tradition in the 1930s extended the practices of so-called social investigators of the Victorian era who, motivated by reformist zeal, ventured into the *terra incognita* of 'darkest London' to document working-class conditions. In many ways Spender's activities in Bolton constitute a similar form of déclassé tourism and within this context, as Jessica Evans notes, 'much

has been written of the way in which Spender's photographs ... reproduced the structure of a colonial-bourgeois gaze on to the anthropological other. The very presumption of realism in these photographs
effaced the position of knower and thus rendered "the other" as savage
yet paradoxically impoverished threat'.[13] The charge is a serious one,
which Harrisson seemed to accept. When, looking back at his work
practices of the 1930s, he commented that 'We had the greatest difficulty in those days really looking at the working-class and ordinary situ-
ations without doing something to them ..., without thinking that they
had better be pastoralised, patronised, whatever you call it'.[14] In this
vein, the objectifying perspective evident in Spender's Bolton photographs has its basis in Harrisson's advice that Spender adopt the role
of a Western or imperial ethnographer in a foreign country.[15] Looking
at the photographs he took in Bolton the charge of 'colonialist gaze' in
Spender's work is difficult to avoid. One expression of such a gaze, and
the related distinction between self and other, is found in Spender's
anxiety and embarrassment in the presence of members of the working
class. Spender later admitted to being 'both scared in Worktown and
fascinated by the unknown'.[16] For Spender 'the whole landscape, the
townscape, was severe and made me apprehensive ... I always came
back to the factor that I was constantly being faced with – the class
distinction, the fact that I was someone from another planet, intruding
on another kind of life'.[17]

Rather than address this unease and thereby directly engage
subjects, the distance between Spender and his (working-class) subjects
was exacerbated by Harrisson's preference for practices of covert observation.[18] Graham Greene caricatured such practices in the actions of
Mr Muckerji in his 1939 novel *The Confidential Agent*, a character, a
'mass observer', who is always prying and spying.[19] The *Daily Mirror*
cast Tom Harrisson in the role of 'Public Busybody No. 1' for his willingness to employ such techniques.[20] Spender translated the emphasis
within Mass-Observation on surreptitious observation into the use
of a hidden camera. Concealed camerawork interested Spender, and
a covert photographic practice was made possible by newly available
small cameras such as the Leica and the Contax. In Bolton Spender
frequently took photographs with his camera hidden in his coat, and
often went to lengths to render himself inconspicuous. 'I believed
obsessively that truth would be revealed only when people were not
aware of being photographed. I had to be invisible', he said.[21] The aim
of 'invisibility' was not only to reveal 'truth' but to 'eliminate *all* relationship' with subjects.[22] The sought-after absence of empathy is reflected
in oblique views of subjects who are caught unaware in profile or seen

from behind retreating into the interiors of their houses. For example, Spender's photograph *Funeral, Davenport St. Bolton* (1938) depicts hearses parked in a street, and in the foreground a mourner in profile who is, it seems, unaware of Spender's camerawork. Anonymity and covert image-making is further exemplified in the fact that none of the workers depicted in another photograph leaving a mill demonstrates an awareness of the camera or the photographer.[23]

Covert camerawork not only resulted in oblique views of subjects; it also meant that subjects were rarely accorded the right to grant permission for their photograph to be taken. Another outcome of the practice was a lack of portraits in the 900 or so images Spender made in Bolton. In another way, hidden camerawork and anonymity meant that Spender was unable openly to enter the domestic spaces of his working-class subjects. Consequently, there is only one photograph in Spender's published work from Bolton of the interior of a house.[24] One of Spender's strategies to distance himself from his subjects was a preference for high-angle shots. His photograph *Lützowplatz, Berlin* (c. 1928–29), taken while he was still studying in Germany, looks down onto the place and thereby established a perspective he exploited in Bolton. The painter William Coldstream, who was aligned with Mass-Observation in Bolton at the time, similarly employed a high-angle view, from the roof of the Bolton Municipal Art Gallery, to paint his large-scale picture *Bolton* (1938). Whereas Coldstream used the angle to depict roofs, chimneys and smoke in the sky in an almost impressionistic way, Spender's high-angle photographs suggest an attitude of condescension towards subjects placed 'below' the photographer. Perhaps as a consequence of Spender's reluctance personally to confront his subjects, few of his outdoor scenes include human subjects. The emptiness of Spender's photographs is reminiscent of Atget's Parisian streetscapes, which Walter Benjamin famously described as resembling the scene of a crime.[25] The eeriness of Atget's deserted streets (evoking a feeling of the uncanny, which made Atget so appealing to the Surrealists) is, however, replaced in Spender's photographs by a sense of lifelessness.

More particularly, Spender's photographs lack an appropriate visual vocabulary and technique for a close or detailed representation of subjects. Don Macpherson has pointed to 'traces of the difficulty of establishing ... [a] relationship between the exoticism of the Northern working class (what Spender called "forbidden fruit") and the all-embracing cosiness of the photographer's frame'.[26] This ill-fit stems from the fact that photography was not integrated into Mass-Observation methods. In terms of an appropriate vocabulary of representation, Spender's photography 'appeared to lack a grammar or to be useful only

as the visual equivalent of a simple sentence, joining things together …
[Photographs] were too expensive for Mass-Observation to print them
in books; they were apparently more open to interpretation than factual
lists; they were only illustrations to the main published work, which
was drawn from the written accounts'.[27] It was not just the distance
Spender maintained from his subjects that resulted in a faulty representational grammar; the photographic image itself stood outside the
endless written reports that were at the centre of the Mass-Observation
method. In these terms filmmaking, like photography, would always be
unassimilable within the Mass-Observation project. The point is carried
in the fact that Jennings' approach in *Spare Time* to the representation
of the subjects of Bolton differs markedly from that adopted by Spender
in his attempt to meet the aims of a Mass-Observation assignment.

Re-writing Mass-Observation: *Spare Time* and its critics

Spare Time overturns the approaches and aesthetics of Spender's Mass-
Observation work. One example of this effect is found in the contrast of
Spender's high-angle photographs, which keep subjects at a distance,
and *Spare Time*'s opening high-angle shot of an industrial landscape.
The shot, which later proved popular with directors of the British New
Wave, establishes the scene, and it is from the original shot that the
camera moves in to construct an intimate engagement with the citizens
of Bolton.[28] A sense of intimacy is maintained in *Spare Time* with the
camera admitted to domestic spaces, which contrasts to Spender's
desire for anonymity, which resulted in his exclusion from the often
cramped interiors of Bolton homes. Orwell, in *The Road to Wigan Pier*,
his report on northern living conditions, remembered his excursions
into the 'working-class interior' in nostalgic terms of a glowing fire
with 'Father, in shirt-sleeves, [sitting] in the rocking chair at one side
of the fire reading the racing finals, and Mother [sitting] on the other
with her knitting'.[29] Though an almost unbearably sentimental vision
of a pre-World War I working class, Orwell's family portrait contested
to a degree the prevailing representation of the North as an exclusively
male space. Through the inclusion of interiors and women's presence
within such scenes, Jennings genders the everyday in terms far less
sentimental than Orwell's.

Jennings' approach in *Spare Time* also refuses to construct the
domestic interior as a space of defeat in poverty. The hearth that Orwell
depicted as the cosy site of family relationships was frequently used
in *Housing Problems* (1935), for example, as the location from which

a member of a working-class family addressed the camera to recount details of poor living conditions. In a similar way, Spender's 1938 photographs for a photo-essay in the *Picture Post* dealing with living conditions in Whitechapel depict decrepit domestic interiors within an accepted documentary representational form as evidence, he said, 'that bad living conditions contributed to juvenile crime and delinquency'.[30] Jennings resists both Orwell's nostalgia and a prevailing attitude to the representation of working-class living conditions in his depiction of domestic interiors as spaces capable of maintaining healthy families. Further, in contrast to Spender's Mass-Observation methods, Jennings openly confronts his subjects in ways that respect their privacy. Eschewing the objectifying, 'colonial' gaze of Spender's camera, Jennings' filming deferentially and sensitively depicts subjects in their leisure activities.

Such leisure activities include playing in a marching band, seen practising on a piece of disused land in Manchester. The idea for the scene originated in a draft memorandum, not written by Jennings, pertaining to an early version of the script for the film: 'A strange phenomenon of North East England is the popularity of kazoo bands for children. The children dress up in costume and competitions are arranged'.[31] A measure of the distinction between Spender's photographic practice and Jennings' film – and the critical expectations of each work – is found in the fact that Jennings' representation of the working class in the kazoo band scene opened *Spare Time* to criticisms not faced by Spender's oblique representations of the working class. Critical reaction to the scene followed an opinion expressed in the form of an annotation added to the draft of the film's script (one not included in the final version of the memorandum): 'This recreation is rather pathetic'.[32] Basil Wright upheld this interpretation when in 1950 he wrote that the material in *Spare Time* is 'brilliantly presented. But it is presented in terms of a cold disgust', adding that 'there is no sense of the human enthusiasm which must somewhere exist behind such a drab and pathetic spectacle'.[33] Wright maintained this position when as late as 1974 he declared that '*Spare Time* was a somewhat depressing picture of the British taking their pleasures sadly – the kazoo band sequence, with flimsy clad drum-majorettes shivering in the icy winds of the industrial North, was quite heartrending'.[34] Wright subsequently added that 'to all of us ... Humphrey seemed to show ... a patronising, sometimes almost sneering attitude towards the efforts of the lower-income groups to entertain themselves'.[35] Eric Rhode reinforced Wright's assessment, arguing that the 'scene of a band playing the National Anthem, escorted by a gauche Miss Britannia and some men in Union Jack waistcoats [is] filled with revulsion'.[36] Other commentators have argued that the kazoo performance of the Manchester Victorian Carnival Band was the 'most notorious' among the film's various scenes depicting musical performances by 'ordinary folk'.[37]

A scene featuring a kazoo marching band in *Get Carter* (Mike Hodges, 1971), a fiction film set in Newcastle, did not raise such critical ire (nor did a similar scene in *Stormy Monday* by Mike Figgis (1988), set in the same city). The difference in reception accorded *Get Carter* is not only attributable to the length of time that had elapsed since the release of *Spare Time*, providing in the interim an understanding of this particular form of musical performance. A variety of factors attended the critical reception of *Spare Time*, and these factors are highlighted by comparisons to subsequent films. For example, the band in *Get Carter* (and *Stormy Monday*) appears in a naturalistic setting, marching down a city street amid a parade. In *Spare Time* a familiar leisure activity in the North (a kazoo band) becomes unfamiliar as a result of a shift of perspective – from marching in a street to playing music on a wasteland. The unusual setting, and what is perceived to be the mood generated by the scene, reminds Dai Vaughan of scenes found in early Fellini films such as the carnival in *I Vitelloni* (1953) or the religious procession in *La Strada* (1954).[38] Other issues were implicated in the film's reception. It has been noted that the North 'is less a number of particular places with specific histories' than a 'place with an agreed iconography' typically depicted in the form of cloth caps and aprons, and also in terms of long-shots of chimneys and smoky streets crammed with terrace houses.[39] Jennings transcends the remoteness of the subject implicit in establishing long-shots by including within the array of techniques applied in the film an intimate focus on city streets, shop windows and the interiors of homes and pubs. Further, he rewrites the iconography of the North by replacing flat caps and aprons with, for example, the uniforms of a marching band, thereby upsetting patterns of expectation and reception. The representation of what was for most interpreters an unfamiliar and dislocated experience disturbed critics to the point that they misread the scene.

Another factor impinging on critical reactions to the scene may well have been contemporary responses to Americanisation. The fact that the band plays music commonly associated with the US (jazz, albeit in a denatured version in the form of the popular song 'If You Knew Susie') implicates or alludes to an anti-Americanisation, which was reasonably widespread within the English intelligentsia during the early decades of the twentieth century. Only a few years before Jennings' production of *Spare Time*, J. B. Priestley, for example, had travelled the roads of western and northern England and lamented the American face of modernity.[40] In a similar way, the 'American' appearance of the kazoo band was, perhaps, a cause of the anxiety that the scene aroused in certain critics. A deeper knowledge of the part played by music in northern communities may have tempered such criticisms. Band music – played by brass bands and kazoo bands – had long been a feature of northern life. Jennings' focus on the kazoo performance by the Manchester Victorian Carnival Band reflected this experience and recognised music not only as an aspect of northern leisure but also as a component of regional identity. Whereas a criticism of the American-style marching bands in the films *Get Carter* and *Stormy Monday* has argued that the practice is not meant to be seen as a genuine expression of a communal solidarity, Jennings effectively depicted the kazoo band as a valuable pastime and 'genuine expression' of communal feeling.[41] Thus criticisms of *Spare Time* failed to recognise that Jennings' depiction of working-class life was a sympathetic one, sensitively attuned to issues of communal solidarity and regional identity.

The pastoral and politics

The critical reaction to *Spare Time* contributed in certain quarters to its placement beyond the mainstream of British documentary. Such an effect was yet another sign of the distance between those members of the documentary film movement associated with Cavalcanti – including Jennings; Cavalcanti produced *Spare Time* – and those aligned with Grierson. This rift was fuelled from within the Griersonian camp by attitudes towards the representation of members of the working class as either victims (who are heroic in their adversity) or heroes (who often exist as such by transcending victimhood). In this way criticisms of the kazoo band sequence reflect the overriding perception that Jennings had failed to depict the working class in 'appropriately heroic' terms.[42] Such terms were set in place early in the history of the British documentary movement. Grierson's *Drifters* (1929) presents commercial fishermen bravely battling the torments of nature to land their catch. In works such as *Industrial Britain* (1933) and *Coalface* (1935), and numerous other documentary films produced by the Empire Marketing Board and the GPO Film Unit, the male body is depicted as a 'heroic figure' representative of 'the ardour and bravery of common labour'.[43] William Empson argued that the Griersonian documentary gave a 'pastoral feeling' to what Grierson referred to as the 'high bravery of upstanding labour'.[44] In an associated way, the central spaces in which working-class labour was typically exercised – industrial towns – were also presented as a version of this pastoral. Orwell's observation that 'even in the worst [industrial towns] one sees a great deal that is not ugly in the narrow aesthetic sense' summarises scenes in films such as *Industrial Britain* and *Coalface*, in which the camera lingers on chimney smoke merging with clouds at sunset, and high-angle shots of lines of narrow houses arranged artistically in geometric patterns.[45]

In many ways Jennings' work avoids the excesses implicit in the aesthetic orthodoxies subscribed to within the British documentary movement. His assessment of cities of the North, made in a letter to his wife during the production of *Spare Time*, does not ignore or unduly glamorise the industrial landscape:

> Buxton looking very smug: and then the beginning of Cotton at Stock-port. Cotton seems to produce a desolation greater – more extended – than any other industry. From Stockport it is really all streets through Manchester, Bolton, Preston – almost to the sea at Blackpool – about 60 miles. The desolation – the peculiar kind of human misery which it expresses comes from the fact that 'Cotton' simply means *work*.[46]

As an extension of this attitude to the industrial environment his representations of figures in this landscape are varied and non-reductive. In Jennings' films workers are human in ways which the stereotypes of 'victim' or 'hero' do not encompass.

Despite his refusal to deploy such stereotypes there are traces in *Spare Time* of a certain sentimentalisation of the working class, with its echoes of attitudes expressed within Griersonian documentaries. An early scenario for *Spare Time*, written in 1938 prior to Jennings' involvement with the project, outlined a number of ideas for the film: 'Female mill worker, machine tending or some such repetitive work, rehearsing her lines for a play in which she is to appear ... Pigeons might yield a sequence ... by a tie-up with a football match ... When a Tynesider stayed indoors for some weeks, he gave the explanation that his dog had died, and a man "looks daft without his dog."'[47] In the final version of the film themes such as the banality of manual labour are absent. The removal of reference to the emptiness of repetitive labour tends towards a certain sentimental impression of the working class as one composed of 'happy workers'. The suggestion is reinforced in Jennings' notion, included as a note accompanying a later draft of the scenario, that the film 'will attempt to show the natural gaiety of working people, and the varied expression which it finds'.[48]

In relation to this approach, certain commentators have debated what they identify as a political naïvety in the film concerning the condition of workers and an acceptance of the status quo.[49] Against such a charge is the recognition that, broadly, the representation of the working class in the 1930s was in itself a politicised act. A focus on an excluded class challenged the vested hegemonic drive to marginalise or silence certain voices within the public sphere. In other ways it is apparent that Jennings was not immune to contemporary politics, as demonstrated for example in the fact that he considered joining the Republicans in Spain and was a signatory to the 'Declaration on Spain' protesting the fascist assault on the fledgling Spanish democracy.[50] An awareness of prevailing political conditions is detectable in specific ways within the film, notably within the film's conclusion. The final words of *Spare Time*, read by Laurie Lee, recently returned from assisting the Spanish republic defend itself against fascism, declare that 'As things are, spare time is a time when we have a chance to do what we like, a chance to be most ourselves'. The implication that the status quo is not immutable ('as things are') carries with it the suggestion that social and political conditions could be organised very differently.

'Orthodox narrative construction'

The images that accompany the final words of the film – which depict an ongoing working routine in the form of a new shift entering a pithead cage to descend a mine – contrast with the intimation encoded in the words of the voice-over that working conditions and the nature of work will change. Contrast, contradiction and ambiguity set *Spare Time* apart from the films of a documentary movement which sought to impose a thematic consistency within its representations (as in the case of uniform stereotypical representations of workers) and a textual univocality which would banish polysemy. Reinforcing this point Geoffrey Nowell-Smith has noted the ways in which *Spare Time* 'neglects – even repudiates – the established codes of documentary narrative construction'. According to Nowell-Smith:

> [o]rthodox documentary narrative construction is formed around three elements: a seen object which attests to the 'documentary' reality of the film; codes of framing, lighting, etc., and also music, which add levels of connotation and emotivity; and a use of the spoken or written word, generally in the form of commentary, to establish meaning. Crudely, the object assures you that what you see is real; the music and *mise en scene* guide emotional response; and the commentary tells you what to think. Not all documentary films, fortunately, are quite so crude ..., but an overall shaping within these broad parameters is essential to the narrativised realism which is the hallmark of official documentary.

He adds, '[c]lumsily, and perhaps not always with full consciousness, *Spare Time* violates the codes'.[51]

The objects represented in *Spare Time* are presented as real, though in a form which resembles photographs – still snapshots that move. It is the 'uncinematic, snapshottish quality of the images that marks *Spare Time* as a different sort of documentary from the documentary model'.[52] The mise en scène is minimal and rudimentary, limited to a basic level of lighting which enables filming to take place, and the spoken-word commentary is also pared down, comprising only six sentences in total. Within this economy, according to Nowell-Smith, '[n]either the picture, nor (until the very end) the commentary, offers any guidance'.[53] However, the thrust of the open ending – with its reference to conditions 'as they are' – is to refuse to impose a firm or conclusive form of 'guidance'. Such a refusal admits a productive ambiguity to the film. In this relation, *Spare Time* 'is a film about the servitude and grandeur of working-class leisure under capitalism. But what is grand and what is servile is *left to be inferred*'.[54] The example points to the way in which the film's transcendence of extant documentary codes is profitably structured by contradictions and ambiguities which disrupt expectations. Another example of such a disruption occurs in the film's closing sequence, in which a woman prepares a meal at night for a man, who sits reading a newspaper. The image is that of Orwell's cosy working-class family, until it is revealed that the man isn't relaxing at the end of the day waiting for his evening meal, but is preparing to start work in the mine where he will eat the meal in the middle of his night-long shift.

The disruption of expectation and understanding is extended in the relationship of image and music within the film. The critical focus on the kazoo band sequence tends to reduce attention to one form of popularly produced music in a way that ignores the full range of music applied in the film. Just as the music produced by the kazoo band is played over an associated montage of disparate images of working-class leisure, so too Handel's 'Largo' is played over images of shop windows, the interior of a pub, a puppet show, further shots of shops, boys playing with a ball, and the domestic scene of a women preparing a meal. In these ways, a kazoo band playing 'Rule Britannia' and a male choir singing Handel both accompany images of everyday leisure activities. The result is an ambiguous interplay of 'high' and 'low' music – ambiguous since it denies a hierarchy of musical style and orchestration ('high' over 'low') within which both forms of music are productively applied as expressive, and exemplary, of working-class life. For Jennings, image, music and sound were components which, collage-like, structured and rearranged narrative expectations. The qualities in

Spare Time of contradiction and ambiguity issuing from the complex interaction of image and sound were extended and refined in Jennings' wartime films.

Notes

1 Vaughan, *Portrait of an Invisible Man*, p. 37.
2 There has been some confusion among film historians as to which films were included on the 'British Workers' programme. Richard Barsam notes that a debate, which became a controversy, ensued 'as the British Council and the Joint Film Committee argued over what aspects of British life to emphasize in films shown at the British Pavilion of the 1939 New York World's Fair'. Barsam adds that '[u]ltimately, the British showed many of the best films, particularly those featuring British workers, including *Night Mail*, *Spare Time*, *Men in Danger*, *British Made* and *Workers and Jobs*'. R. Barsam, *Non-Fiction Film: A Critical History* (Bloomington: Indiana University Press, 1992), p. 110. Few of these films were in fact taken to New York. As Grierson pointed out in the unpublished manuscript *Eyes of Democracy*, 'The British Council for "Cultural Relations Abroad" did not ... approve very much of showing Britain's ordinary man to the Americans'. The result of this approach was that in making its selection the British Council 'systematically ignored the films of the documentary Movement'. J. Grierson, *Eyes of Democracy*, edited with an introduction by Ian Lockerbie (Stirling: The John Grierson Archive, 1978). According to Kevin Jackson the films sent to the World's Fair under the joint title 'British Workers' were *Spare Time* and *British Made* (1939) by George Pearson. Jackson, *Humphrey Jennings*, p. 211. Pat Jackson includes the documentary film *Health in Industry*, later known as *Men in Danger*, among the films taken to New York. He adds that Jennings shot the film's opening sequence of the Waterloo shot tower. P. Jackson, *A Retake Please! Night Mail to Western Approaches* (Liverpool: Royal Navy Museum Publications and Liverpool University Press, 1999), p. 57.
3 Quoted in P. Rotha, *Documentary Film: The Use of the Film Medium to Interpret Creatively and in Social Terms the Life of the People as it Exists in Reality* (New York: Hastings House, 1970 [1935]), p. 191.
4 Quoted in V. Cunningham, *British Writers of the Thirties* (Oxford: Oxford University Press, 1989), p. 331.
5 Quoted in Jackson, *Humphrey Jennings*, p. 211.
6 B. Wright, *The Long View* (London: Secker and Warburg, 1974), and in an interview with Elizabeth Sussex, *The Rise and Fall of British Documentary*, p. 110; Jim Hillier in Lovell and Hillier, *Studies in Documentary*, p. 71.
7 Hodgkinson and Sheratsky, *Humphrey Jennings*, p. 40.
8 Vaughan, *Portrait of an Invisible Man*, p. 39.
9 Ibid.
10 D. Mellor, 'London-Berlin-London: A Cultural History: The Reception and Influence of the New German Photography in Britain, 1927–1933', in D. Mellor (ed.), *Germany: The New Photography, 1927–1933* (London: Arts Council of Great Britain, 1978), pp. 113–31.
11 Quoted in D. Frizzell, *Humphrey Spender's Humanist Landscapes: Photo-Documents, 1932–1942* (New Haven, Connecticut : Yale Center for British Art, 1997), p. 26.
12 H. Spender, *Worktown People: Photographs from Northern England, 1937–38*, ed. J.

Mulford (Bristol: Falling Wall Press, 1982), p. 15.

13 D. Macpherson and J. Evans, 'Introduction', to 'Nation, Mandate, Memory', in J. Evans (ed.), *The Camerawork Essays: Context and Meaning in Photography* (London: Rivers Oram Press, 1997), p. 145.

14 T. Harrisson, 'Films and the Home Front: The Evaluation of their Effectiveness by "Mass-Observation"', in N. Pronay and D. W. Spring (eds), *Propaganda, Politics and Film, 1918–45* (London: Macmillan, 1982), p. 243.

15 S. Edwards, 'Disastrous Documents', *Ten-8*, 15 (1984), 19.

16 Quoted in T. Kushner, *We Europeans? Mass-Observation, 'Race' and British Identity in the Twentieth Century* (Aldershot, Hampshire: Ashgate, 2004), p. 63.

17 Spender, *Worktown People*, p. 16.

18 On Harrisson's insistence on covert observation see J. Heimann, *The Most Offending Soul Alive: Tom Harrisson and His Remarkable Career* (London: Aurum Press, 2002), p. 142.

19 G. Greene, *The Confidential Agent* (Harmondsworth, Middlesex: Penguin, 1992 [1939]).

20 *Daily Mirror* (6 December 1938), p. 14. Reprinted in D. Mellor, 'Mass Observation: The Intellectual Climate', in J. Evans (ed.), *The Camerawork Essays: Context and Meaning in Photography* (London: Rivers Oram Press, 1997), p. 138.

21 H. Spender, *'Lensman' Photographs, 1932–52* (London: Chatto and Windus, 1987), p. 15.

22 Spender, *Worktown People*, p. 21.

23 The images of a funeral and of workers leaving a factory are reprinted in ibid., p. 121 and p. 50 respectively.

24 The photograph was taken as a result of an invitation by another Mass-Observation recruit, and was not initiated by Spender. The image is reproduced in Spender, *Worktown People*, p. 54.

25 W. Benjamin, 'The Work of Art in the Age of Mechanical Reproduction' [1936], in *Illuminations: Essays and Reflections* (New York: Schocken, 1969), p. 226.

26 Macpherson and Evans, 'Introduction', to 'Nation, Mandate, Memory', p. 149.

27 Taylor, *A Dream of England*, pp. 158–9.

28 See T. Lovell, 'Landscape and Stories in 1960s British Realism', in A. Higson (ed.), *Dissolving Views: Key Writings on British Cinema* (London: Cassell, 1996), pp. 157–77. In the same volume Andrew Higson refers to the technique within British New Wave films as 'That Long Shot of Our Town from That Hill'. A Higson, 'Space, Place, Spectacle: Landscape and Townscape in "Kitchen Sink" Films', in Higson (ed.), *Dissolving Views*, pp. 133–56.

29 G. Orwell, *The Road to Wigan Pier* (London: Penguin, 2001 [1937]), p. 108.

30 Quoted in G. Rose, 'Engendering the Slum: Photography in East London in the 1930s', *Gender, Place and Culture*, 4: 3 (1997), 286.

31 Quoted in Jackson, *Humphrey Jennings*, p. 211.

32 Ibid.

33 B. Wright, 'First Period, 1934–1940' in *Humphrey Jennings: A Tribute*, prepared by D. Powell, B. Wright and R. Manvell, (n.p.: The Humphrey Jennings Memorial Fund Committee, n.d.).

34 Wright, *The Long View*, p. 201.

35 Wright quoted in Sussex, *The Rise and Fall of British Documentary*, p. 110. In the same interview Wright admits that 'I've revised my opinion on that. I think we were a bit too doctrinaire in our attitude in those days ... I think we may have perhaps missed the point', p. 110.

36 Rhode, *A History of the Cinema*, p. 378.

37 Hodgkinson and Sheratsky, *Humphrey Jennings*, p. 41.

38 Vaughan, *Portrait of an Invisible Man*, p. 37.

39 P. Dodd, 'Lowryscapes: Recent Writings About "the North"', *Critical Quarterly*, 32: 2 (1990), 17.

40 Priestley, *English Journey*.

41 P. Hutchings, '"When the Going Gets Tough ...": Representations of the North-East in Films and Television', in T. E. Faulkner (ed.), *Northumbrian Panorama: Studies in the History and Culture of North East England* (London: Octavian Press, 1996), p. 277.

42 Edgar Anstey quoted in Vaughan, *Portrait of an Invisible Man*, p. 41.

43 Edgar Anstey and Forsythe Hardy quoted in K. Dodd and P. Dodd, 'Engendering the Nation: British Documentary Film, 1930–1939', in A. Higson (ed.), *Dissolving Views: Key Writings on British Cinema* (London: Cassell, 1996), p. 43.

44 W. Empson, *Some Versions of Pastoral: A Study of the Pastoral Form in Literature* (Harmondsworth, Middlesex: Penguin, 1966 [1935]), p. 14; Grierson, 'First Principles of Documentary (1932)', p. 88.

45 Orwell, *The Road to Wigan Pier*, p. 53.

46 Quoted in 'Chronology and Documents' compiled by Mary-Lou Jennings, in M.-L. Jennings (ed.), *Humphrey Jennings*, p. 22.

47 These particular ideas were proposed by Alberto Cavalcanti in a note appended to an undated memorandum outlining a proposed production which was to become *Spare Time*. Quoted in Vaughan, *Portrait of an Invisible Man*, p. 43.

48 Quoted in ibid., p. 44.

49 See, for example, D. Berry, *Wales and Cinema: The First Hundred Years* (Cardiff: University of Wales Press, 1994), p. 181.

50 The declaration was originally published in *Contemporary Poetry and Prose* in 1936. It is reprinted in M. Remy, *Surrealism in Britain* (Aldershot, Hampshire: Ashgate, 1999), p. 105.

51 Nowell-Smith, 'Humphrey Jennings', p. 325.

52 Ibid p. 326.

53 Nowell-Smith, 'Humphrey Jennings', p. 326.

54 Ibid. Italics added.

George Orwell's Blitz-inspired ruminations on the conditions of the 'English character' in his essay 'The Lion and the Unicorn' (1941) are prefaced by a pervasive anxiety of terror from the skies: 'As I write, highly civilised human beings are flying overhead, trying to kill me'.[1] The connection in his depiction between national identity and the experience of war – and the essay form of that representation – forces a question relevant to all home-front accounts of World War II: how to adequately portray a nation at war? The question centrally motivates *Words for Battle* (1941) and *Listen to Britain* (1942), and in addressing this question Jennings constructed representations which departed radically from extant practices characteristic of the nonfictional forms of newsreels.

An attempt to revise the depictions of war in newsreels informs *London Can Take It!*, a film produced at the beginning of the Blitz in September 1940 by the GPO Film Unit, with input from Jennings. The film's chief director, Harry Watt, charged Jack Beddington, head of the Films Division within the Ministry of Information (who in this role oversaw the transformation of the GPO Film Unit into the Crown Film Unit in October 1940), with giving preferential treatment to newsreel production. Beddington, according to Watt, was keen to be 'in with the newsreels'.[2] It was Beddington's position that 'the newsreels were very important for propaganda and so on'.[3] The first director of the Ministry of Information Films Division, Joseph Ball, had earlier decided that newsreels would constitute the central feature of British wartime film propaganda.[4] In line with this policy, Beddington and Sidney Bernstein of the Granada cinema chain, and an important honorary adviser to the Films Division, were supportive of a proposal by G.B. News to produce a short for American distribution on the effects of the Blitz on London, to be compiled from newsreel footage.[5] Watt, who in his own words 'felt pretty superior to the newsreels', suggested to Beddington and

Bernstein that the newly formed Crown Film Unit make the film, an idea which Beddington eventually accepted.[6]

Watt objected to the way in which newsreel footage focused maximally on devastation. According to Watt, 'This wasn't the cameraman's fault. He wasn't making propaganda, but just showing the facts the best way he could. But the two hours of [newsreel] film I saw [prior to making *London Can Take It!*] would have convinced anyone that the whole of London was completely flattened'.[7] Jennings felt that while newsreels could depict a historical event, or fortuitously capture a newsworthy issue as it was unfolding, they failed to offer any contextualisation of events.[8] For Jennings a crucial difference between newsreels and documentary films was one of focus and emphasis. Jennings argued that newsreels are concerned with depicting the event in certain accepted ways, with little thought to 'set up'. Speaking on behalf of documentary filmmakers he argued that 'we are ... in a position, when shooting a scene, to take greater pains to think of the background and the ideas which have produced the scene we are photographing ... Our business is to say that the background in this street is not exactly right, that the event would be better presented in a slightly smarter street or a slightly dingier street, or if it were shot in a better light. The news-reel man cannot choose in that way, whereas we have to'.[9] Jennings' notions of selectivity and emphasis connect with Watt's approach to 'making propaganda', the basis of Watt's distinction between newsreels and documentary film.[10]

In keeping with the practice of making propaganda, Watt, in association with Jennings and the editor Stewart McAllister, sought to depict the fortitude displayed by Londoners in the face of massive aerial bombardment. Joe Mendoza, who worked as an assistant editor within both the GPO Film Unit and the Crown Film Unit, remembered making *London Can Take It!*:

> The film was in two parts. The first part Harry directed, and the second part Humphrey and McAllister directed ... It was designed for [the well-known American journalist] Quentin Reynolds, who was due to go to New York in a fortnight. The idea was that he would take [the film] to New York under his arm, and this is what happened. And the film, when it was shown in New York, was such a success that the [Ministry of Information] thought, we've got something here which is much more significant than we reckoned – it's not just making advertising films for the Post Office. Because the general feeling was that Britain really wouldn't last two or three weeks after the Blitz began, that London was being destroyed and we were pretty much finished – that was the feeling the Germans were trying to put over. So *London Can Take It* was really quite an important piece of propaganda.[11]

London Can Take It! was shot over two weeks and depicts conditions in the capital during the winter following the Battle of Britain. The film opens with a shot of St Paul's cathedral, after which Reynolds' introduces himself, 'speaking from London', over shots of people heading home after a day's work. As darkness approaches preparations are made for another night's air attack. As if on cue, German bombers appear in the sky and ground-based anti-aircraft guns commence firing. Bombs descend on London, as inside air-raid shelters people attempt to sleep. With the new day sirens announce the end of the raid, and people head to work amid the bomb damage. The Queen visits a bombed site, and workmen clear the streets of rubble. The tenor of the film then changes, moving from images of fortitude to images of retaliation. A headline scribbled in chalk on a board by a newspaper vendor announces that Berlin has been bombed, followed by images of an RAF bomber being loaded with munitions, and taking off on a mission. Reynolds' commentary continues to celebrate London's resolve – 'a bomb has its limitations, it can only destroy buildings and kill people. It cannot kill the unconquerable spirit and courage of the people of London'. A jaunty Civil Defence man cadges a cigarette from a passing milk van on his way home, and the final shot is of a statue near Westminster Palace of Richard I, appearing appropriately aggressive with sword raised. Reynolds' final words announce that 'London can take it!'

Despite the collaborative process involved in the making of the film – Watt working with Jennings, who for the first time was assisted by Stewart McAllister as editor – the original impetus for its production was Watt's desire to move away from newsreel coverage. It is ironic, then, that *London Can Take It!* is similar in a number of ways to newsreel journalism. Reynolds, a print journalist for the US news magazine *Collier's*, provides a voice-over which, with American audiences in mind, resembles certain tones and emphases (and accent) of the narration by Westbrook Van Voorhis for the US newsreel series *The March of Time* (1935–51). Beyond the voice-over, *London Can Take It!* is composed of a series of 'sights' or views of war-ravaged London which are not dissimilar to those of newsreel or photojournalistic practice (for example, shots of smashed windows on Oxford Street are reminiscent of George Rodger's press photographs of the same war-torn scene[12]). Jennings subsequently largely abandoned features of newsreels such as a stentorian voice-over and a journalistic observation of sensational scenes within a radical revision of documentary forms.

Heart of Britain

In order to dispel the suggestion implicit in *London Can Take It!* that the war was felt only in the capital, another film was conceived as its counterpart to highlight the effects of the war in the North. Jennings described the new project, still at the time titled *Backbone of Britain*, as a 'kind of *Spare Time* assignment', thereby stressing the focus shared by the two films on northern locales and cities such as Manchester.[13] The completed film, renamed in a twist of anatomical reference to *Heart of Britain* (1941), opens with the sounds of Elgar and shots of rural regions (including Yorkshire, Derbyshire and the Lakes District). Interestingly, the narrative soon eschews allusions to the rural myth associated with such bucolic scenes and turns to a construction of industrial and urban centres as the true 'heart' of the nation.

In such a centre George Good, a furnace worker in Sheffield, talks directly to the camera of his daily routine, which involves a shift in the factory followed by service as an air-raid warden. Scenes in Lancashire depict readiness for air attack, and female workers from the cotton mills play games in an air-raid shelter. In Manchester Malcolm Sargent conducts the Hallé Orchestra in a performance of Beethoven's Fifth Symphony, which continues to play as the sequence shifts to include scenes of the bombed streets of Coventry. Here among the wreckage a member of the Women's Volunteer Service addresses the camera and speaks of her attempts to assist those injured in air raids and her feelings of helplessness and distress as she hands out cups of tea as members of the ARP remove corpses from the rubble. She adds, relieving the tension of the word picture, that she is often praised by those she helps for a cup of tea that 'washes the blood and dust out of my mouth'. In the final sequence the Huddersfield Choir sings the 'Hallelujah Chorus' from Handel's *Messiah*, and the scene depicts the ruined centre of Coventry and the bombed cathedral. As the narrator talks of the people's resistance and the 'power to hit back' a cut depicts the interior of an aircraft factory, with workers assembling bombers. While the 'Hallelujah Chorus' swells on the soundtrack a Whitley bomber takes off at dusk on its way to attack the enemy. The final shot of the film is a return to the rural scenes of the film's opening.

The structural core of the film is the sequence filmed in Coventry. The devastating raid on the city on the night of 14–15 November 1940 led to a change in plans for the film. Prior to the raid of mid–November, which destroyed the cathedral, Jennings and his crew had filmed footage of air-raid damage in the city. He returned after the massive raid to shoot scenes of the devastation and the rescue work being conducted in the wake of the attack. As a result, Coventry displaced the other locations as the geographical and moral focus of the film, with the raid on the city serving as the point at which the narrative leads to – and justifies – the argument of the propaganda of the film's ending. The reworked film that stemmed from the raid on Coventry also incorporated an increased use of music, with the effect that music becomes, together with the focus on Coventry, a central structuring device for the film.[14] From the opening refrains of Elgar to the closing rendition of Handel, music – and references in the commentary to music and singing, and the partial displacement of commentary by music – serves as a theme, or notation, running throughout the film. The effect presages the rigorous integration of sound and image subsequently achieved in *Words for Battle* and *Listen to Britain*.

The *Documentary News Letter*, however, disliked what it called the 'usual defensive commentary' used for *Heart of Britain*.[15] The reviewer for the journal criticised what was interpreted as redundant comments used to reinforce the meaning of images.[16] The commentary delivered by J. B. (Jack) Holmes, taking time out from his own filmmaking, is in places patronising and it is difficult to dispute the criticism that not all scenes require an obvious and over-stated explanation.[17] In his following film, *Words for Battle*, Jennings would use extracts from literature and other texts as the basis of a commentary that cues images which expand the meanings and metaphorical connotations inherent in the texts. In *Listen to Britain* the commentary is replaced by the masterful juxtaposition of sounds and images as the vehicle for narrative. The problems inherent in the commentary of *Heart of Britain* are pronounced in the final voice-over, the most blatant piece of propaganda in all of Jennings' films. The ending of the film suffers as a result of its propagandistic aims from an emptying of metaphor. As the 'Hallelujah Chorus' sung by the Huddersfield Choir surges on the soundtrack the narrator states: 'People who sing like that in times like these cannot be beaten. These people are slow to anger, not easily roused ... But these people have the power to hit back – and they are going to hit back, with all the skill of their hands, the tradition of their crafts, and the fire in their hearts'. A Whitley bomber takes off, the scene changes from Coventry to a rural landscape, and the commentary continues with a grim warning: 'Out of the valleys of power and the rivers of industry will come the answer to the German challenge – and the Nazis will learn, once and for all, that no one with impunity troubles the heart of Britain'.

In the final scenes and the accompanying commentary the rich meanings and the potential for productive ambiguities inherent in the 'heart of Britain' – a phrase informed by the variety of connotations derived from the rural myth, and expanded in the film through reference to the cities of the Midlands and the North to encompass geographical and other allusions to the core of a nation's 'character' – are reduced in the film's ending to 'military might' which will avenge the Coventry raids. In his use of the 'Hallelujah Chorus' in the closing shots Jennings was accused by members of the documentary movement of 'going religious'.[18] In reply Jennings decried what he interpreted as overblown Griersonian notions of 'pure documentary'.[19] Ironically, in the matching of words and images in the final scenes of *Heart of Britain*, Jennings replicates the didactic expository methods of numerous Griersonian documentaries. The success of the film's move away from Griersonian documentary resides in Jennings' use of music as a narrative device which embodies the potential to inform images with emotional and referential resonances and meanings. In these terms *Heart of Britain* was a precursor to the far more elaborate, sophisticated and subtle approaches to the question of 'how to represent a nation at war?' undertaken in the reworking of commentary in the words and images of *Words for Battle* and the complex relationship of sounds and images in *Listen to Britain*.

Words for Battle: 'In England Now'

In August 1940 the head producer of the GPO Film Unit, Alberto Cavalcanti, who had been so influential in Jennings' career up to that point, left the Unit to join Michael Balcon at Ealing Studios. Cavalcanti was replaced that month as supervisor of the Unit by Ian Dalrymple, who, as a film editor early in the 1930s, had maintained strong links with Balcon, then at Gaumont-British studios. Jennings struck an immediate friendship with the unassuming 'Dal'. Dalrymple, who reported to Jack Beddington in the Ministry of Information Films Division, was responsible for the practical arrangements associated with the establishment of the new Crown Film Unit.[20] It was through Dalrymple's activities in this area that the new Unit was able to relocate from its small and ill-equipped facilities in central London to Denham Studios and then to Pinewood Studios, where it had access to wider resources, including a fully equipped sound stage. Within its new quarters the Crown Film Unit 'was the single most important source of wartime documentary film production', even though 'in terms of numbers its output represented little more than 5 per cent of the 1400 or so official documentaries that were produced during the war'.[21] Audience exposure to documentary films was increased during the war when, as of the summer of 1940, cinemas reluctantly accepted a proposal from the Ministry of Information to screen short official films.[22] *Words for Battle* was included in this scheme.

The working title of the production that became *Words for Battle* was 'In England Now', a work which was conceived as a companion to a film to be called 'In Germany Now'. The second film was to include quotations from Goethe, Schiller and Heine, among other German authors and poets, which would be used contrapuntally with contemporary images of Nazi Germany culled from sources such as Leni Riefenstahl's *Triumph des Willens* (*Triumph of the Will*, 1936). In contrast to the planned opposition of word and image in the companion film, a draft treatment of 'In England Now' demonstrates that, as with *Words for Battle*, extracts from stirring well-known poems and political speeches were to be used in a complementary and mutually enforcing way. An early treatment of 'In England Now' includes reference to extracts from Milton, Blake, Shelley, Browning, Kipling, Churchill and Lincoln, to be used in association with images of Britain at war.[23] A shooting script of 'In England Now' follows this general outline, opening with a spoken commentary: 'Among the most precious memorials of England, now nightly threatened by fire-bombs, is Westminster Abbey. Here lie the tombs ... of kings and queens, the statues of statesmen, the monuments of ancient victory ... [H]ere too the much humbler shrines of English poetry'.[24] The commentary introduces Milton, whose words are to be spoken in the second sequence, accompanied by images of the countryside and other locations. The fourth sequence of the treatment – featuring extracts from Shelley's radical poem 'The Mask of Anarchy' and images of a man ploughing, factory work, an AFS (Auxiliary Fire Service) man, RAF recruits and soldiers marching – does not appear in *Words for Battle*. (Shelley's call to revolutionary arms may have been deemed by the Ministry of Information as inappropriate to the current military situation.) The treatment is a general outline of shots, with reference to some of the source footage to be included in the film, including close-ups from *Triumph of the Will*, footage of evacuated children shot by Arthur Elton, together with newsreel and Army footage. The outline includes eight sequences, which would have resulted in a film shorter than the brief eight minutes of *Words for Battle*.

The final edited version of the script incorporates certain of these elements within an expanded work which includes extracts from William Camden's *Britannia* (1588), Milton's *Areopagitica*, Blake's 'Jerusalem', Robert Browning's 'Home-Thoughts, from the Sea', Kipling's 'The Beginnings', Churchill's 'We shall never surrender' speech of 4 June 1940, and Lincoln's 'Gettysburg Address'. The selected passages are supported and interpreted by images recycled from a range of sources, together with footage shot specifically for the film. In certain scenes images 'introduce' the commentary – for example, a shot of a bust of Milton appears prior to Milton's words – and in other scenes the commentary links, and narrativises, the images – as in Churchill's 'Fight on the beaches' speech, which threads together images as varied as shots of mending a city street and footage of ANZAC troops. In his reference to the film Dai Vaughan is critical of aspects of the editorial relationship of word and image. For Vaughan the complementary association of word and image is, in a number of cases, overly literal or inappropriate in terms of the metaphorical intent of the quoted poetry.

> Thus Milton may liken the nation's spirit to an eagle, drawing upon the metaphorical associations of splendour, sovereignty and soaring flight; and a Hurricane may be likened to an eagle in its physical grace and in the similarity whereby it swoops upon its enemy out of the sun: but to set the Milton quotation against shots of Hurricanes is not to enrich the symbolism but – since the similes are of radically different kinds – to confuse it.[25]

Vaughan cites other examples, and criticises the alignment of Blake's reference to building Jerusalem in England with shots of children in a wood, 'where the effect can only be to limit rather than expand the sense. Likewise, to set the line "… full in face Trafalgar lay" over a cut to a full-face shot of Nelson can do neither words nor images any good'.[26] Indeed, the matching of images of waves on a shoreline with Churchill's words, 'we shall fight them on the beaches', is banal. However, while in certain places the relationship of word and image may result in simplistic associations, to reduce the film to such moments is to overlook or deny the overall effect of a subtle arrangement of elements. In this way *Words for Battle* constructs its object – 'Britain at war' – within a dense interaction of temporality and spatiality.

The temporal axis

A temporal dimension, a meeting of the past and the present, is achieved in the film through a presentation of extracts from texts (which, with the exception of Lincoln's words, are chronologically arranged in order of the authors' dates of birth) associated with the iconography of war.[27] The effect of the selection of texts is to move chronologically through a literary and cultural heritage and thus through time. Simultaneously, the emphasis in the quotations on a fighting, heroic heritage in effect constructs aspects of national identity which, in the totality of components, suggest a staunchly democratic people steadfast in a green and pleasant land against an aggressive enemy. Thus, through the application of a simple temporal device *Words for Battle* performs part of the complex ideological work of evoking a unified nation.

The simplicity and utility of the effect in *Words for Battle* is underlined through reference to David Macdonald's *This England*, a fiction film released the same year as Jennings' film. *This England* (also known as *Our Heritage*) seeks to evoke a unified nation through a temporal structure of episodes presented in chronological order from a past to the present. Macdonald's film opens with a poem in which the 'autumn mists', 'brambleberry flame' and 'tangled, rain-soaked grass' of an 'old, old earth' predate human habitation. According to the poem 'the earth of England' has existed throughout a 'time out of mind'. The poem situates 'the past' within the terms of the rural myth which, in turn, contextualises the subsequent action. The rural myth and its temporal associations are deployed in the opening narration, which emphasises the place of rural life and work within the history of the nation: 'This England, among whose hills and valleys since the beginning of time have stood old farms and villages. The story of the Rookebys' farm and the village of Clevely is the story of them all'. The film, with its 'air of a glorified village pageant', traces the experiences of the Rookeby family of farmers (all played by John Clements) and the Appleyard family of farm workers (all played by Emlyn Williams) across various generations, stressing four key moments of adversity and war: the Norman conquest, the Spanish armada, the Napoleonic wars and World War I.[28] A naïve American journalist (Constance Cummings) visiting Clevely is the device through which Rookeby and Appleyard narrate each event as a way of informing her of the wars endured by their ancestors in defence of their land. The film ends with Rookeby reciting the 'This England' soliloquy from Shakespeare's *Richard II*.

While most critics would probably agree with Jeffrey Richards that '*This England* was not a very good film', James Chapman argues that the film 'is significant in so far as it represents the first attempt during the war to mobilise the past in order to address social divisions and to promote the need for social unity'.[29] Contradicting Chapman's claim is the fact that Jennings' film (which was filmed during the Blitz in the autumn of 1940) was released prior to *This England*, thereby making *Words for Battle* the first wartime film to rely on the past to promote national unity, and it does so in ways which are infinitely more subtle than the array of plot and narrative devices deployed in Macdonald's film. Such devices within *This England* include an introductory commentary, the presence of the character of a journalist to function as the butt of the storytelling by Rookeby and Appleyard, various characters from the Rookeby and Appleyard clans who narrate their yarns, and a series of 'historical' highlights.

In contrast, the narrative techniques of *Words for Battle* are minimal and effective. The film's narrative economy is exemplified within the inclusion of a sixteenth-century map of the nation, from Camden's *Britannia*, in the opening frames of the film. The nation – the critical focus of the film – is established at the outset through the map's figurative representation. Details of the nation are provided through the voice-over, eloquently spoken by Laurence Olivier, who reads a description of the landscape from *Britannia*. Thus the old map foregrounds the concept of a historical (temporally grounded) nation and establishes a visual basis of the film's evocation of the past to complement the aurally based temporality constructed in and through the progression of spoken extracts. In these ways the sixteenth-century nation depicted by the map is the point of origin of references to national characteristics which, when accumulated, constitute the present nation in its time of war.

The spatial axis

The map is also a spatial representation of nation. Indeed, extending and informing the temporal axis is an extensively constructed spatial axis to the narrative, which further specifies and 'grounds' the concept of a unified nation. In doing so, *Words for Battle* effectively constructs a narrative of nation which, as with any narrative, is based in time and space. A testy, anonymous review of *Words for Battle* in the *Documentary News Letter* at the time of the film's release failed to recognise the film's form of narrativisation; in fact it failed to detect any trace of narrative in its reference to the film as 'an illustrated lantern-slide lecture'.[30] In other ways analyses of forms of narrativisation in documentary have tended to feature only one component of the temporality/spatiality couplet. For example, Brian Winston's detailed explication of the formal features of British documentaries of the 1930s and 1940s emphasises 'chronologic', the temporal basis of narrative.[31] Complementing such an analysis is the presence within narrative of a 'spatial logic' (spatiologic, perhaps), which is as central as the slight 'chronologic', if not more so, to the construction of narrative in *Words for Battle*. Recognising what is a complex 'spatiologic' operative in *Words for Battle* points to a sophisticated form of narrativisation in a film which Winston criticises as lacking a narrative trajectory.[32]

In a related way Dai Vaughan concludes from his study of the editorial relationship of image and what he considers to be rarefied words within each shot and scene, that there is 'very little scope for visual manoeuvre' in the film.[33] In other words, the language of the selected texts imposes limitations on the range of images and associated narrative emphases that can be used in the film. However, looking beyond the narrow focus of particular shots to the combined seven sections of the film it can be noted that Jennings and the editor McAllister do establish room (or space) to visually manoeuvre within the narrative, primarily in a reworking of the wartime tropes of 'looking up' and 'looking down', and in the productive ambiguity which is established in the relationship of countryside and city. The ambiguity is resolved in an outcome that suggests the emergence from war of a new, rebuilt and reinvigorated nation.

Looking up and looking down

In the terms set out here, *Words for Battle* is organised according to the lines of a dramatic narrative structure with the citizens of Britain as the protagonists. The film opens with a scene of (rural) stability, which is dramatically interrupted (by the presence of war), though in turn the disruption is resolved (or at least addressed, by the protagonists' heroism and fortitude), to end in a satisfying conclusion (that looks to a better future for the nation).[34] Within the film's narrative progression the temporal and spatial dimensions – or axes – inform each other, often in direct ways, as in the image of the map, its historically based temporality complemented and extended through its function as a marker of geographical space.

The markers of geographical space are extended within a revision of images of citizens and military personnel looking to the skies. The image appears in the second section of the film; against Milton's words from *Areopagitica* ('Methinks I see her as an Eagle ...'), members of an RAF ground crew scan the skies. The image of 'looking up' functioned as a central representational form of the Blitz. As John Taylor notes, 'such imagery represents a wartime "new line of sight" of vigilance, resilience and optimism, eyes looking not only for potential bombs and death but into a brighter future'.[35] Images of figures looking to the skies featured prominently in films and print publications of the era, including the cover of the *Picture Post* for 23 September 1944, which featured an image of a mother and her small son looking skyward through the window of a cosy cottage, used to accompany a story on the home-front effects of the war.[36] The notion of a brighter future encoded in 'looking up' was evident even in the early years of the war, as demonstrated by Jennings and Watt in *London Can Take It!*. A scene halfway through the film depicts the morning after an air raid and includes a woman with wavy Jane Morris, pre-Raphaelite hair looking out and upwards from a window with a broken pane, as the voice-over states that 'London looks upwards towards the dawn'.[37] The notion of a peaceful future inherent in the image addressed, if not to a degree assuaged, the anxiety of the early war years associated with a sky perpetually filled with enemy aircraft.

The image of 'looking up' had as its corollary aerial shots of the landscape, the perspective of 'looking down'. The device was popularised in wartime Britain in news magazines and newsreels through reference to aerial shots of targets. The currency of such a device led the *Picture Post* in May 1943 to publish a number of 'before' and 'after' photographs of an Allied bombing raid under the title, 'How to Interpret an Aerial Photograph'.[38] In *Triumph of the Will*, a film Jennings knew well, Riefenstahl used the 'looking down' image to heroise Hitler, as he descends god-like through the clouds in his aeroplane to the adoration of the German military amassed at Nuremberg. In contrast to Riefenstahl's deployment of the 'looking down' shot in the service of Hitler and a militarised Germany, Jennings uses the technique in *Words for Battle* to provide an opening aerial shot of clouds and long shots of the English landscape, from where the camera moves into close contact with local civilians. In this way the shot is a variant of the 'pan in from the top of that hill' shot at the beginning of *Spare Time*. Jennings' 'looking down', unlike the use of the landscape in aerial bombing photographs or in Riefenstahl's film, depicts the landscapes of city and countryside, though in places war-torn, as accommodating as the skies from which the perspective was filmed. The evocation of the nation resulting from such spatial perspectives and orientations is extended within the film's mobilisation of a spatial dialectic of city and country.

The city and the country

Each of the seven sections of *Words for Battle* encompasses a representation of a range of environments which feature urban and rural landscapes. The opening section depicts rural scenes. Westminster Abbey opens the second section, which includes an aerial shot of urban and rural locales. The third section links city and country as it follows children evacuated from London to the countryside. The fourth section (with words from Kipling's 'The Beginnings') depicts a war-damaged London. The fifth section serves as an interlude from the landscapes of Britain and replaces urban and rural scenes with shots of the Mediterranean Sea (against words from Browning's 'Home-Thoughts, from the Sea'). The sixth section (accompanied in part by Lincoln's 'Gettysburg Address') returns to a focus on London, and the film ends with images of city streets filled with military personnel. Myths of city and country are at play in these scenes, though through the informing presence of ambiguity, the film refuses the limited meanings inscribed in such myths.

In this way, a productive ambiguity is present within the first three sections of the film. The opening section encodes many of the foundational meanings of the rural idyll or myth: the countryside as a site of tranquillity, community and stability. Against such a presence the second section introduces the city – London's streets and Westminster Abbey – which, via shots of fighter planes, is associated with war. The notion of a 'dangerous city' that emerges from this association is enlarged in images of the evacuation of children from the city to the safety of the countryside. The following scenes – of children at play in their rural haven – reinforce allusions within the rural myth to the countryside as an 'accommodating' place of safety and peace. However, meanings opened in these scenes cannot be reduced or contained by the common inscription of a rural myth. The evacuation of the city during wartime points to a return to the city once peace has been restored. The future evoked through such associations is further intimated through the fact that the evacuees are children, the nation's future. The scenes, then, refuse a retreat into the past commonly associated with the rural myth (the countryside as site of the values and features of 'yesteryear'). In these terms the countryside is both (temporary) refuge from contemporary experiences and a site that augurs the future.

In a similar way meanings ascribed to the city in wartime are rendered ambiguous, and through that ambiguity are resolved, within a potent appeal to the nation's victorious future. Sections five, six and seven (accompanied in turn by extracts from the words of Kipling, Churchill and Lincoln) simultaneously establish the city as a place of destruction and death and a site of rebuilding, renewal and future order. The former meanings are openly represented in images of destroyed houses, the removal of a body on a stretcher from the rubble of a bombed house, and shots of a hearse moving in procession along a bombed street. These scenes carry an undeniable emotional power and to achieve this effect Jennings was willing to contravene an earlier proscription in wartime imagery on the representation of death to suggest the extent of destruction and suffering experienced during the Blitz.[39] However, the effect of these images is superseded by another set of meanings – those associated with regeneration – which pervasively evoke the nation's path.

Signs of rebuilding are apparent in the sixth section, which is accompanied by Churchill's words and which includes a shot of a team of workers repairing a bomb-damaged footpath, which in terms of the theme of renewal is followed by the more significant shot of St Paul's cathedral looming above the rubble. Photojournalism played a major role in situating the cathedral within the public imagination in specific ways. The archive of such images includes Bill Brandt's photograph, 'St Paul's Cathedral in the Moonlight' (1940), which features the cathedral in stark silhouette against rubble in the foreground, Cecil Beaton's image of smoke encircling the cathedral's bell towers after an incendiary raid on London on 29 December 1940, and George Rodger's deep-focus photograph of Fleet Street with a news seller in the foreground ('Latest From All Battlefronts') and St Paul's aloof and stately in the background.[40] In each of these images St Paul's is deployed as an indication of the damage inflicted by the enemy, and via its 'eternal' (seemingly indestructible) nature functions as a symbol of home-front fortitude and hope. Such meanings were informed within what the front page of the *Daily Mail* newspaper of 29 December 1940 called 'War's greatest picture': a photograph of the cathedral wreathed in flames and smoke, the effects of the same air raid depicted in Beaton's photograph. The *Daily Mail* printed comments by the photographer, H. A. Mason, which add another layer of meaning to the image: 'I focused at intervals as the great dome loomed up through the smoke. Glares of many fires sweeping clouds of smoke kept hiding the shape. Then a wind sprang up. Suddenly, the shining cross, dome and towers stood out like a symbol in the inferno. The scene was unbelievable. In that moment or two I released my shutter'.[41] Mason's account echoes descriptions from the Judaeo-Christian tradition of apocalypse and the site of final judgement, references which were overt in the commentary of a live BBC radio broadcast of the London raids of 7 September 1940: 'The flames are leaping up in the air now. St. Paul's, the dome of St. Paul's Cathedral, is silhouetted blackly against it … The smoke is going up very slowly now and it's just illuminated faintly. It's almost like the Days of Judgment as pictured in some of the old books'.[42] Allusions to an infernal end of the world gave way to other meanings evoked via the image of St Paul's as a symbol of Britain's indomitable spirit and a people's resistance to the Nazi onslaught. In this set of meanings St Paul's features as the cornerstone of the People's War and is expressive of the stance that 'London can take it'. The position, circulated in Jennings' film of that name, is extended and highlighted in *Words for Battle* in a shot of St Paul's, which is accompanied by Churchill's declaration that 'We shall never surrender'.

The emphasis on a people's perseverance connects in *Words for Battle* with the notion of national renewal, a concept reinforced within the evocation of a 'new world'; a condition variously alluded to in the film. The effect of the deletion from the film's draft script of an extract from Shelley's poem 'The Mask of Anarchy' was to deny any suggestion that the new world to come would be the result of social revolution. Within the film a 'new world' is evoked in the sixth section within images of British allies from Australia and New Zealand, and more readily in Churchill's reference to the New World of the US, which will enter the war and come to Britain's aid. From such allusions to the New World the notion of a post-war 'new world' is evoked in the form of a rebuilt, regenerated and unified British nation. This emergent condition – a future social landscape – ties together the temporal and spatial axes as the rhetorical focus of the film. The result of the film's productive ambiguities produced within and through the meeting of temporal and spatial features is an 'extraordinary bravura' work.[43] Jennings would exceed this achievement in *Listen to Britain*.

Listen to Britain: collaboration and collage

The question Jennings addressed in *Listen to Britain* was the same as that taken up in *Words for Battle*: how to depict a nation at war? The question involves a historical trauma which threatened to exceed many of the extant forms of representation. In the case of *Listen to Britain*, as with *Words for Battle*, the question implicates the role of narrative structure. The temporal and spatial features of the slight narrative of *Listen to Britain* are informed by a range of formal influences, including that of avant-gardist 'city symphonies' of the 1920s. More particularly, the central structural features through which *Listen to Britain* effectively represents the nation at war derive from a revision of the expanded application of the sonic and visual capacities of documentary film.

Listen to Britain began in the spring of 1941 as a script idea dealing with military music (the draft was tentatively titled 'Men on the March').[44] By mid-1941, by which time the filming of scenes had commenced, the working script (titled in places 'Tin Hat Concerto') was focused on a lunch-time performance of Mozart in the National Gallery.[45] Filming recommenced in August and continued until October 1941 using an

expanded treatment of the 'Tin Hat Concerto' as the script. During these months shooting included many of the key locations which would be included in *Listen to Britain*: a school playground, a Gillette's factory (a scene that was to be accompanied in the completed film by the BBC radio programme 'Music While You Work'), and the Tower Ballroom in Blackpool.[46] Following a common practice within the Crown Film Unit, further footage was provided by reusing stock footage. In a letter to his wife in September 1941 Jennings referred to his current project as a film 'about music', thereby emphasising the focus of a film which includes a range of sounds and music.[47] The scenes filmed throughout the summer and autumn of 1941 and a number of the sonic features are evident in the post-production script of the film. The script, reproduced in full here, provides an adequate summary of *Listen to Britain*.[48]

Opening titles	trumpet, drums, crowd noise
tree tops sway in the afternoon wind	sound of aeroplanes
fields of grain	
two Spitfires fly past	
grain in breeze	
field labourers digging potatoes	
air watchers, looking skywards	
four Spitfires overhead	
wheat field, with observation bunker	sound of threshing machine
threshing machine in wheat field	
six planes overhead	sound of aeroplanes
exterior of country home	BBC pips/ 'This is the BBC Home and Forces Programmes'
evening: woman places a lamp in window, draws curtains	
sea lapping a shore at sunset	aeroplanes (fading)/dance music
two soldiers on a bench overlooking the sea at sunset	
air wardens in a bunker overlooking the sea	
sign: 'Members of H.M. Forces in uniform, ½ price'	dance music
interior: dance hall [Tower Ballroom, Blackpool]	
crowd of people dancing	dance music/people whistling and talking/singing to the music
people sitting out the dance, a woman hides photographs from her inquisitive friends	muffled talk
dancers on the dance floor	'Roll Out the Barrel'/voices singing along to the music

air raid wardens overlooking the sea	'Roll Out the Barrel' (fading)
miners descending a pit	talking/sound of machines
coal mine	clanging as cage is lowered into the mine/talk
chimney and village	
pit head winch	
railway signal	clank of signal
night sky, train crosses scene from left to right	
train stops	
Canadian troops in railway compartment singing	'Home on the Range'
troops in compartment talking	talk/'Home on the Range' – singing and yodelling
railway signals, train starts	clank of signal/sound of steam
train departs, signals change	
interior: aircraft factory, with workers assembling a Lancaster bomber	train sounds fading/factory noises
bomber taking off against a night sky	aeroplane sounds
sign: 'Ambulance Station 76'	singing
interior: statue of Charles I in high-ceiled room	singing
woman at piano, female ambulance workers	singing 'The Ash Grove'
Big Ben silhouetted against the night sky	bells of Big Ben
radio masts	'The is London calling...'
Thames and Battersea power station	music
Thames	'London calling' [roster of various locations, in various languages]
radio tubes aglow	
clouded sky, radio tubes	
sun rising over sea	
new day: tree tops	bird calls
trees silhouetted on the horizon against morning sky	
morning sky, pan from left to right	horse hooves on stone
factory chimneys and smoke, two horses in foreground	
workers arriving at factory gates	voices/factory noise
aerial shot of city (pan from left to right)	singing and music, voice of dance instructor
man walking on damaged city street	
Battersea power station	factory noise

factory chimneys emitting steam and smoke	
tree top in breeze	piano music
interior: woman with teacups looks out window	
children in nearby school yard dancing	piano music, sounds of children dancing
interior: woman with photograph of Scots soldier	
children dancing in school yard	
tanks and military vehicles in village street	sound of vehicles
aerial shot of villages and countryside	'Calling all Workers'
road underpass, with train on the line	
cityscape, with barrage balloons	
interior: female factory workers at lathes	'Music While You Work'
Tannoy in factory, workers at lathes	singing 'Yes, My Darling Daughter'
workers at lathes	
exterior: cityscape	
interior: railway station	train whistle
soldiers and others on platform	
tea van with customers	singing
worker painting exterior of building	
food being served in a factory canteen	
sign: 'In the Canteen To-day at 12.15 – Flanagan and Allen'	singing 'Round the Back of the Arches'
Flanagan and Allen on stage	
blackboard menu: 'Scotch broth, fried cod and chips' etc.	
Flanagan and Allen on stage	singing
wide shot: interior canteen	
Flanagan and Allen on stage with piano and orchestra	
audience members	'Underneath the Arches', audience whistling along
Flanagan and Allen on stage, audience [clock on far wall reads 1.10]	
exterior: National Gallery, orchestra playing on stage, before an audience	Mozart's concerto for pianoforte in C major
sign: 'Lunchtime Concerts'	orchestral music
sign: 'Fri June 13 1 o'clock The Orchestra of the Central Band, H.M. Royal Air Force.	

Myra Hess Pianoforte'
orchestra playing
people entering the National Gallery
high ceiling and windows in gallery
blackout curtains hanging across
     broken glass in upper windows
audience members standing and
     seated before copy of Uccello's
     'Battle of San Remo'
printed concert programme lists   orchestral music
     'Concerto for Pianoforte in
     C Major: Myra Hess'
orchestra playing
people entering the gallery through
     swinging doors
women eating lunch on steps inside
     the gallery
sign: 'War Artists' Exhibition'
people viewing war art
a woman views gallery postcards
people eating lunch on steps inside
     the gallery
sailor admiring war art painting:
     maritime battle scene
interior of concert hall, orchestra on
     stage with audience
Myra Hess at piano
audience members, including
     the Queen   Myra Hess playing Mozart
interior of concert hall
high-angle interior shot of empty
     gallery: sandbagged windows,
     bare walls, an empty frame on
     the wall
fire pails, sandbagged windows
audience members before print of
     Gainsborough's 'The Painter's
     Daughters'
audience members, Queen in
     audience
exterior of National Gallery
woman on the Gallery's portico looking
     into Trafalgar Square
leaves on tree in breeze, trees in
     Trafalgar Square
exterior of gallery

barrage balloon viewed through arch of portico	
St Martin's in the Field and the Strand from the gallery	
facade of St Martin's in the Field	
buses in the Strand	
rooftops, Nelson column and Big Ben in the distance	
Nelson column	
sailor looking into Trafalgar Square from gallery portico	
facade of National Gallery	
barrage balloon, derricks and masts of ships	
interior of factory	Mozart (fading)/factory sounds
workers assembling tanks	(hammering/drilling)
military band playing and troops marching in city street	military band music ('A Life on the Ocean Waves')
interior of iron smelter	military music (fading)/factory sounds
interior of factory	factory sounds (fading)/choral music
factory chimney	
wheat field in breeze	choral singing of 'Rule Britannia'
factory chimneys	
aerial shot through clouds of countryside	

End title

Thinking that audiences would require it, the Ministry of Informa-tion appended a spoken introduction to *Listen to Britain*. The segment is introduced with the title 'Foreword by Leonard Brockington, K.C.', who is seated in a regal-looking chair and who proceeds to state the obvious, namely, that *Listen to Britain* is concerned with the 'sound of [British] life by day and night'. Over a map of Britain Brockington states that 'you too [as you watch the film] will hear [the heart of Britain] beating'. He adds that this is a 'great sound picture', which blends 'together in one great symphony the music of Britain at war'. Brockington then refers to many of the sounds in the film ('the BBC sending truth on its journey around the world', and so on). The intri-cate editorial relationship of the film's sonic and visual components is recognised in the credits, which acknowledge both Jennings and Stewart McAllister as 'directors'. Interestingly, commentators have emphasised this credit to redress McAllister's previously underesti-

mated role in the production of Jennings' films, and in doing so have
at times overplayed McAllister's contribution to the film. For example,
in stressing McAllister's role in *Listen to Britain*, Ken Cameron, a
sound recordist who worked on a number of wartime documentaries
before a lengthy post-war career in filmmaking, tends to characterise
McAllister as the director in charge of the production, including the
division of labour on the project: '[T]here is no doubt that Mac made
a tremendous contribution to [*Listen to Britain*]. He told Humphrey
what he needed – "Humphrey, go out and shoot this" – and Humphrey
did it'.[49] More appropriate to the situation is Dalrymple's claim that
McAllister received the on-screen credit in recognition of the importance of his editorial contributions.[50]

Working collaboratively, Jennings and McAllister produced a film
which is a collage of images and sounds of Britain (or England) in late
1941. The subject that informs this collage is the everyday life of the
nation. As in *Words for Battle*, the war is not represented. While the
war's presence is felt (in the form of coast watchers, for example), the
focus in *Listen to Britain* is on 'normal' life; not as an anxious response
to external threat but as daily routine. The representation of everyday
life is constructed through narrative components of place, time and
space, which are contained within the prominent relationship of sound
and image.

Space and time

It has been argued that *Listen to Britain* displays an 'insistence on place',
namely London.[51] However, the capital is not the only locale depicted in
the film. In another way, any 'insistence' on place is attenuated since the
places that are featured in the film are not always clearly designated. In
contrast to the film's nebulous allusions to places is a rigorous specification of spaces, as exemplified in particular within the careful delineation
of the spaces of the National Gallery. Thus a weak 'insistence on place'
is superseded within the scenes in the National Gallery, which 'insist on
... spatial coherence'.[52] The focus of these scenes is a lunchtime concert
within the gallery of Mozart's Piano Concerto No. 17 in G major, K453,
performed by the RAF orchestra, accompanied by Myra Hess as soloist.
The audience for the performance includes the Queen, Kenneth Clark,
the director of the National Gallery (who earlier in the war had served as
head of the Films Division within the Ministry of Information), armed
services personnel, and civilians. However, the National Gallery scenes
are not reducible to the interior space of the concert performance. In

particular, the National Gallery sequence involves an expressive inter-play of interior and exterior scenes.

These scenes include shots of various architectural features of the gallery, among them the entrance vestibule, occupied by visitors to the gallery. Other views in the sequence include shots of empty frames on the gallery walls (the paintings having been removed to safety, beyond the potential for damage by aerial bombardment), the portico at the front of the gallery, and a panorama of the streets adjacent to the gallery and Trafalgar Square. James Merralls uses the word 'glide' to refer to the smooth, seemingly effortless movement of the camera within and through these scenes: 'During the concert the camera glides away from the pianist, first lingering on the audience, entranced by a Mozart concerto, then gliding around the Gallery, along the sandbagged walls, where the paintings ought to be hanging, then outside to the noble clas-sical portico, out into a bright London spring day until the rumble of the traffic drowns the music and the image fades'.[53] In Merralls' account the interior and exterior spaces are unified and equivalent in terms of their representation as rational, apprehensible space. William Guynn informs this point by arguing that the scenes also function 'according to a principle of opposition, which is in the first instance spatial, but which is ultimately figurative'.[54] These scenes contribute to a pattern throughout the film in which interior and exterior spaces are posed as contrasting and antithetical: interiors bespeak domesticity, integra-tion and continuity and exteriors connote diversity, discontinuity and dislocation. Within the references to dislocation and disruption the 'text proposes the familial community of the concert hall: Myra Hess, the last in a chain of maternal figures, commands the attention of her children. The text undertakes a symbolic work of this incorporation: to annex all Britain to this domestic sanctuary'.[55] In his dense reading of the film, Guynn notes that the scenes maintain a 'certain coherence of space' and are abetted in this function via the concert music, which 'anchors' the scenes, serving as a directional marker. Even as the camera moves around the interiors and exteriors of the gallery, 'we have not gone very far from the sound source'.[56]

Notably, too, the role of sound as a component of spatial orientation is, ironically, complemented in these scenes by the absence of paint-ings from the walls of the gallery. Paintings serve certain functions in films, their presence carrying a host of connotations. Such associations may include 'sophistication' for example, and allude to the economic – a painting is, in effect, surplus value on display. Paintings also perform narrative functions, illuminating character and their relations in space, as Stephen Heath's analysis of 'narrative space' in the fiction film points out. In Hitchcock's *Suspicion* (1941), for example, various characters acknowledge a painting on the wall of a protagonist's home. For Heath the painting is a marker of the characters' point of view, as they look at or away from the painting. Further, the painting is a point of reference within the scene, from which the characters' positions to each other within the physical space of the room can be determined.[57] In both functions the painting is the focus of diegetic attention in the sense of serving as the centre of narrative space. In the case of *Listen to Britain* an absence of paintings evokes spatial relations in ways that differ to the presence of paintings in Heath's example. The absence of paintings in the gallery permits a close examination of interior and exterior spaces. Given the gallery's empty walls the camera does not dwell, as it would otherwise, on paintings, and locations in space are not registered against a fixed point – such as a painting on a wall. Instead, spaces are registered in the free-floating movements of the camera as it 'glides' around the interior of the gallery, and, transcending interior space, as it roams and surveys nearby streets.

As with space, time is marked within a narrative, 'conceived' as one commentator puts it, 'around time', as is apparent in an early script treatment: 'It is half past nine – the children are already at school ... and at 10.30 [from] the BBC comes "Calling All Workers" ... At half past twelve, the chatter of typing in the Ministries and offices in London lessens'.[58] As the temporal progression here suggests, the narrative is inscribed within a diurnal cycle (from afternoon to afternoon). The 'day in the life of a city' format was the basic temporal pattern of the European avant-gardist 'city symphony' of the 1920s and 1930s, a term which resonates with Jennings' symphony of sounds in the daily life of wartime London. In his criticism of one of the central works of the city symphony genre – Walter Ruttmann's *Berlin* (1927) – Grierson argued that the film was an exercise in formalist experimentation that lacks the aim of 'fulfil[ling] the best ends of citizenship'.[59] In addressing this task Grierson proposed that films should exploit the figure of the individual at (industrial) work. Reduced to a cipher for labour, Grierson denies the 'figure' humanity. Jennings' 'symphony' avoids such a depiction within its emphasis on individuality. As with Cavalcanti's city film, *Rien que les heures*, *Listen to Britain* evokes a sense of character through a focus on the faces of subjects.

Conversation and speech are the usual vehicles of character in film. The constant disruption of intelligible speech by other sounds in *Listen to Britain* adds purpose to the film's attention to faces. The subjectivity of individuals is reinforced through the use of point-of-view editing which implicates a 'spectator's viewing [and draws] this viewing into the "social subjectivity" that supposedly grows out of the experience of living in wartime Britain'.[60] Such a positioning is in certain ways the result of a mimetic function of the identification with faces. Such shots constitute a '*scene of empathy*, we see a character's face ... either for a single shot of long duration or as an element of a point-of-view structure alternating between shots of the character's face and shots of what she or he sees. In either case, the prolonged concentration on the character's face is not warranted by the simple communication of information about character emotion. Such scenes are also intended to elicit emotion in the spectator'.[61] Spectatorial empathy and identification with the fortitude, courage and social bonds of the people depicted is one way in which the film functions in the service of its propagandistic purpose of evoking and reinforcing such attributes within the audience. Beyond the narrative markers of place, space, time and character the quotidian experience of (a unified) society is innovatively represented via sound and music.

Sound and music

Jennings' one-time colleague Basil Wright argued that the 'use of sound imagistically, the cross-cutting of sound and visuals (counter-point) can undoubtedly be effective, but this does not mean to say that good visuals could not get the same effect more legitimately – in fact I begin to wonder if sound has any advantage at all'.[62] It is a curious statement from a director who, in the same year as he made the comment, had experimented with the disjunctive relationship of sound and image in his film *Song of Ceylon* (1934). Wright's comments may reflect his frustrations with making his film, though many of his additional statements on sound have the ring of declarations intended to guide, or rule, creative practice: '[W]e must not forget that the film is visual, so much so that the perfect film should be satisfactory from every point of view without sound and, therefore, shown in complete silence'.[63] As if acting the devil's advocate critical of the sonic innovations of his film *Night Mail* (1936) he asserts that 'If you put any natural sound which doesn't correspond with the visual action you make a dull highbrow film!'[64]

Such views, with their echoes of Grierson's disparagement of 'art' and the 'aesthetic' in documentary, were not necessarily prevalent within the documentary movement.[65] Cavalcanti, for example, encouraged a willingness among those he instructed, including Jennings, to experiment with sound and image relations, and Wright's statements can be contrasted to the sonic practices of Len Lye's films. Lye, with whom Jennings collaborated on *The Birth of the Robot,* was not included in the group that Jennings referred to bitterly as 'Grierson's boys'.[66] As with Jennings, Lye's filmmaking was not easily assimilated into characteristic Griersonian documentary forms. While 'Mickey-mouse-editing' (editing according to the rhythm of music) had been introduced in Disney's 'Silly Symphonies' cartoons, Lye's syncopation of sound and image in animated films such as *Colour Box* (1935) and *Rainbow Dance* (1936) preceded Disney's experiments in this field in *Fantasia* (1940).

Jennings' innovative application of film sound resolutely returned sonic experimentation to documentary film where it revised traditional documentary codes, among them spoken commentary. Voice-over narration functions in a particular way within the documentary text. Voice-over narration, cut loose from the subjectivity of an identified presenter, asserts itself from an impersonal, and universal, position of dominance. This function is reflected in references to narration in terms of the 'voice of God', with its implicit suggestion of an all-seeing, all-knowing narrational perspective. As such, images are subservient to, or presented as supportive illustrations of, voice-over. Within a reliance on voice-over the evidentiary capacities of images are not self-apparent, but instead rest on the guiding, authoritative role of a commentator. In *Listen to Britain* the absence of extradiegetic narration is filled by diegetic sound. Such a shift avoids the textual dominance of narration; sound and image relations are not prescribed in a hierarchical system involving precedence and subservience of codes (sound over image). Instead, sound in *Listen to Britain* is multiple and multivalent, 'bespeaking' a variety of experiences not constrained by the dominant and domineering function of narration.

In its sonic register the film replaces the sound of war with everyday sounds and noise. Sounds of children playing, snatches of muffled conversation, laughter, and the sounds of machinery are part of a broad palette of sound which also includes a variety of musical sources and forms, among them marching bands, dance bands, orchestra concerts, canteen concerts, radio programmes (notably the BBC's 'Music While You Work'), small groups of singers (Canadian soldiers) and individual singers (a girl at her machine in a factory singing 'Yes, My Darling Daughter' and a woman at a piano in an ambulance station singing 'The Ash Grove'). This variety of sounds and music is deployed in varying ways. In one way the use of sound in *Listen to Britain* conforms to what Michel Chion calls acousmatics, a 'sound that is heard without its cause or source being seen'.[67] Typically in *Listen to Britain* such a practice operates within what has been identified as a 'process of misapprehension-correction, the spectator attributes a sound to one source when it belongs, the film then clarifies, to a second'.[68] In other cases two sounds reflect each other across scenes, as in the example in which the rhythmic noise of a locomotive is replicated by the rhythm of a marching band. In a third case 'two sounds blend in an acoustic dissolve in an opposing movement of crescendo-descendo, one sound fading-in, the other fading out'.[69] In each case sounds – the music and noise of everyday life – are linked to, and complemented by, images similarly derived from various contexts.

The image and 'doink'

The images in the film include purpose-shot footage and recon-structed scenes (for example, the scene of the woman singing 'The Ash Grove' was staged for Jennings' camera[70]). Further, up to a quarter of the footage is derived from archival sources. Deferring to shortages of film stock, time constraints and a precedent operative within the documentary film movement, the recycling of footage was a regular practice employed within wartime documentary filmmaking. Jennings frequently ransacked his own work and the work of other directors for appropriate images. As Ken Cameron of the Crown Film Unit noted, 'Humphrey used whatever he wanted'.[71] The point is further exempli-fied by Pat Jackson who, in his memoir of the era, recounts how he was disturbed to see shots from his film *Ferry Pilot* (1941) included without his permission in *Words for Battle*.[72] Jennings' image acquisition may have been more rigorous than that of other directors but, as Malcolm Smith notes, '[t]here is nothing unusual about this [practice] in wartime documentary, or in the British documentary tradition, which time and again used stock-shot material. What is unusual in *Listen to Britain* is that the material is not used for continuity purposes, as was normally the case. Indeed, it is discontinuity which becomes the point in the selection of the visual material'.[73]

Smith's comment draws attention to the expressive function of editing, and the close collaborative relationship of Jennings and his editor Stewart McAllister. Ian Dalrymple recalled that within their symbiotic relationship 'Humphrey and McAllister had a strange effect upon one another':

> Humphrey was frightfully well-organised in shooting. He'd have the most marvellous luck, too, because he'd been a painter and in fact was still daubing with paint when he had a moment, but he has a wonderful gift for choosing the exact place to put the camera. So he'd go out and shoot madly and all the stuff would come in to McAllister, and McAl-

lister would brood over it on the Movieola. When Humphrey had finished shooting, he would join McAllister in the cutting room and nothing would happen for weeks, apparently. You wondered when the hell anything was going to emerge ... Then all of a sudden, overnight. Somehow everything went together – doink. And there was what I thought a mini-masterpiece in each case.[74]

Within the editorial process – a mixture, as Dalrymple points out, of hard work, skill and serendipity – the range of sounds and images were married to each other in particular ways.

The relationship of sound and image

The practice of acousmatics prominently 'directs' images in *Listen to Britain*. The introduction of the singing duo of Flanagan and Allen exemplifies this process. The voices are heard, softly at first, over shots of passengers on Waterloo station, and as the sound of the singing increases, across shots of firemen at a mobile tea canteen and a man painting a factory wall, to people at a serving hatch in a factory canteen, to a poster announcing a performance by Flanagan and Allen, and then, in a way that unifies the preceding scenes, to Flanagan and Allen on stage in the factory canteen. The process is repeated in what the contemporary director Michael Grigsby has called 'two of the greatest aural dissolves ... in the history of cinema'.[75] In an extension of the scenes described here Flanagan and Allen, singing 'Round the Back of the Arches' on stage in a factory canteen, hit a note which is used to connect to the next scene, in which Myra Hess plays the same note in a lunchtime concert of a Mozart piano concerto.[76] From there, in turn, the film dissolves from Mozart into the sound of machinery in a factory. In these examples a source sound precedes and 'introduces' images that then accompany the continuing sound.

However, not all sound in *Listen to Britain* is synchronous with the images. Asynchronism, a disjunction of sound and image, is a feature of Jennings' film. Writing in 1929, V. I. Pudovkin claimed that asynchronous sound enriches rather than depletes or neutralises an image.[77] A similar point was made by Alberto Cavalcanti who, writing in 1939, while he was working with Jennings during the last days of the GPO Film Unit, advocated the use of asynchronous sound as a method of achieving an otherwise unattainable rendering of reality.[78] Cavalcanti's ideas on the relationship of the sonic and visual components of a film were applied within *Night Mail*, a film directed by Harry Watt and Basil Wright. Cavalcanti is credited as 'general supervisor of the soundtrack' on *Night Mail*, though he argued that his contribution to the film was much broader and that his ideas on sound and image relationships permeate the film.[79] Cavalcanti noted four factors which contributed to the successful relationship of sound and image in the film. Apart from the 'preoccupation with sound perspective, the selection of the dominant sounds, and the study of punctuation', a fourth, crucial factor in the relationship of sound and image was 'counterpoint', the asynchronous contrast of images and sounds.[80] Jennings, perhaps having heeded the effect of Cavalcanti's advice and practices, applies sounds in places in *Listen to Britain* in ways which are in disjunction to, or not completely integrated with, images. In this effect, as Dai Vaughan notes, 'What is distinctive about [the disjunction of sound and image in *Listen to Britain*] is the delicacy with which the disjunctive method is employed'.[81] The introduction of Flanagan and Allen who, before they appear on screen are heard over shots of Waterloo station, is a case in point.

The disjunctive alignment of sound and image is most pronounced in relation to those shots and scenes that include the presence of a radio. Radio sound is always identified as such, though radio sounds and on-screen images are not always in direct relationship to each other. For example, the 'Music While You Work' radio programme is, after a lengthy introduction, eventually identified as emanating from speakers in a factory. Elsewhere the disjunction is not fully resolved: the sound of the pips marking the time on the radio 'may or may not be' associated with a cottage with darkened windows, the ostensible source of the sound.[82] Asynchronism, as this latter example illustrates, is the site of ambiguity within *Listen to Britain*. Further to this point, William Guynn identifies the crux of ambiguity in the film as the 'gap between the specificity of the image and the [plenitude] of sound [through which] the [film achieves] a certain pluralism: a confusion of sources, a reinterpretation [of its material]'.[83] He elaborates this idea when he sets out two aspects of the textuality of *Listen to Britain* as, firstly, 'that elements of the sound track can have an independent textual activity ... not defined or ... only partially defined in relation to the image and, secondly, that a textual plurality is possible based on the "rediscovered" separateness of the materials of expression'.[84] An example of such separate, unaligned, moments occurs in the sequence: waves meeting on a shoreline; coast watchers; speech from a BBC broadcast; noise of aircraft; and the music of 'Roll Out the Barrel'. The elements 'coexist without coalescing' and thus produce a plurality of meanings which, when unresolved or incompletely resolved, result in a productive ambiguity.[85]

Ambiguity and the everyday

What has been called the 'rule of ambiguity' structures and informs
Listen to Britain.[86] One way in which ambiguity is expressed in the film
is via and through segues from one scene to another, in which material
in one scene is not fully resolved or emptied of meaning before the
scene cuts to another similarly open-ended scene. In another way ambiguity is inherent in the visual realm of the close-up:

> Jennings plays with the ambiguity inherent in the close-up. A close-up
> shot on its own, without any contextualising shots to explain it, can
> be extremely disorienting. The close-up of a cottage, the close-up of a
> window, the close-up of waves ... they could be anywhere, any place, any
> time – and by using sound as an umbrella, Jennings is able to move
> freely through space, leaving it to the spectator's imagination to fill in
> the ellipses that he is deliberately creating.[87]

One commentator argues that the mixing of sound and image produces
a 'rich ambiguity' within *Listen to Britain*, and another interpreter
suggests that this effect 'is, perhaps [the film's] most important political
achievement'.[88] 'Politics' is here linked to propaganda, and Jennings's
ambiguities – and the resultant 'open', polysemic text – reflect a wartime
propaganda policy which refused to denigrate its audience. According to
Nicholas Reeves, '[t]he essence of the [Ministry of Information's] propaganda strategy was that the people of Britain deserved to be treated as
intelligent and sophisticated democratic citizens [capable of accepting
and negotiating sound and image disjunctions], and nowhere was that
confidence vindicated more than in the response that *Listen to Britain*
provoked from its audience'.[89]

However, for certain critics any propaganda benefit was lost within
the presence of ambiguity, which has been interpreted in terms of an
absence within *Listen to Britain* of an 'ideologically prominent meta-
discourse'.[90] An attempt to 'stabilise' the work resulted in the addition
of the spoken introduction to versions of the film. The seeming lack
of a defining and guiding 'meta-discourse', and the impact of such a
perception on the effectiveness of the film as propaganda, led to Edgar
Anstey's notorious criticism, made at the time of the film's release, that
Listen to Britain is 'an aesthetic enough conception in all conscience, but
[it remains] the rarest piece of fiddling since the days of Nero', which
'will not encourage anyone to do anything at all'.[91] That is, as Andrew
Higson astutely points out, Anstey's criticism rests on the assessment
that *Listen to Britain* is 'good art, but bad propaganda!'[92] Anstey was
subsequently to modify his impression of the film though he maintained that the method of *Listen to Britain* resulted in a work that was

'too indirect and oblique'.[93] For Anstey, propaganda was conceived in a specific way, as a form of universal directive guaranteed to result in a certain ideological (and political) outcome. In these terms, multiple meanings and ambiguous representations such as those in *Listen to Britain* were anathema.

Beyond such a position is the understanding that ambiguity does not equate to textual 'chaos', a point which can be accompanied by the recognition that *Listen to Britain* does possess a structural metadiscourse – that of the everyday. Constructed within and through a disjunctive relationship of sound and image – and the associated plural, and ambiguous, meanings – the everyday experience of the nation's people is depicted as varied and complex. Indeed, the film stresses the rich diversity of the everyday life of the nation while also emphasising that the social unity of the nation is the outcome of that diversity. In this way, though the nation is represented as divided, or inflected, by differences of class, culture, region and occupation, an 'essential' unity holds the variety in place. Andrew Higson offers an extended analysis of this point:

> National identity is proposed as the sum of this productive variety: the contemporary coexists with tradition (two uniformed women eat sandwiches under a classical statue; a barrage balloon is visible through the arches of the National Gallery); the rural coexists with the industrial (Army vehicles rumbling through the street of a Tudor village; aircraft spotters work on in an idyllic setting); popular culture coexists with high culture (Flanagan and Allen sing in a factory canteen, while Myra Hess plays Beethoven [sic] to the Queen).[94]

Many of these oppositions are unified in the film's final montage, which includes a variety of sounds and images within approximately one minute of screen time: a Royal Marines marching band plays 'A Life on the Ocean Waves', with the sound of the music fading into the rhythmic sounds of a steel mill. A worker in a steel mill eases a molten ingot from a furnace, where it is hammered into shape. Another ingot is carried to an anvil, where it too is recast. Workers use welding equipment which produces sparks, and on the soundtrack the industrial sounds of the steel mill merge with those of a choir singing 'Rule Britannia'. Steelworkers stand on a balcony in the furnace room, followed by an exterior shot of the mill and its smoking chimneys. Shots of a field of wheat rustling in the wind merge into images of industrial towers and a factory chimney. In a reprise of the shot that opens *Words for Battle*, the final shot is an aerial view through clouds of the countryside, as 'Rule Britannia' comes to an end on the soundtrack. The sequence brings together a series of separate allusions – to industry, the military (an earlier scene showed tanks on a production line, the finished products of the work in the furnace), and a rural landscape – all unified by refrains from 'Rule Britannia'.

Annette Kuhn notes that images of fire and sparks recur within the closing montage – welders producing sparks, the furnace gates emitting flames, sparks produced when the steel is pounded. '[T]his perhaps [is] the film's consummate moment ... [Fire] figures as a desire, a hope, that what we value of the past will survive the flames and be renewed for the future in the ashes of destruction'.[95] Importantly, the connotation of the war is achieved within scenes of everyday work. The war's presence is felt, though the everyday dominates, and in this way 'the effect is one of the continuing saga of everyday life, with the disruption of the war being assumed as outside the text'.[96] Thus the everyday life of the nation is presented as a sequence of contrasting relationships – city and country, industry and military, and so on – in which the image of the nation which emerges is one of diversity, complexity, paradox and ambiguity – a set of relationships and experiences which ultimately are unified in the everyday nature of those experiences.

Notes

1 G. Orwell, 'The Lion and the Unicorn', in *George Orwell: Essays* (London: Penguin Books in association with Martin Secker and Warburg, 2000), p. 138.

2 Quoted in Aldgate and Richards, *Britain Can Take It*, p. 8.

3 Ibid.

4 P. Taylor, *British Propaganda in the Twentieth Century: Selling Democracy* (Edinburgh: Edinburgh University Press, 1999), p. 182. The Films Division, under a director and deputy director, administered the Crown Film Unit and independent production companies working on contract to the Ministry of Information. The Films Division also handled theatrical and nontheatrical distribution of government films within Great Britain and internationally. The Arts Enquiry, *The Factual Film: A Survey Sponsored by the Darlington Hall Trustees* (London: Oxford University Press, 1947), p. 64.

5 Watt, *Don't Look at the Camera*, p. 137. Watt mistakenly identified the proposal as coming from *Movietone News*. Quoted in Vaughan, *Portrait of an Invisible Man*, p. 63.

6 Watt, *Don't Look at the Camera*.

7 Ibid., p. 138.

8 Taylor, *British Propaganda in the Twentieth Century*, pp. 2–3. Reflecting on the situation many years later Ian Dalrymple, Jennings' colleague and the head of the wartime Crown Film Unit, felt that newsreel coverage of events in the early part of the war had been 'haphazard'. Dalrymple, 'The Crown Film Unit, 1940–43', pp. 209–20.

9 Humphrey Jennings and Jack Holmes, 'The Documentary Film' [n.d], a typescript in the Humphrey Jennings Collection, BFI Special Collections, the British Film Institute.

10 Interestingly, Jennings here reinforces a position originally espoused by his

nemesis, John Grierson. Central to Grierson's definition of documentary film is that it is separate from the 'lower forms', that is nonfiction works which include newsreels. Grierson, 'First Principles of Documentary (1932)', p. 82.

11 In Jackson, *Humphrey Jennings*, p. 232. Quentin Reynolds states in his autobiography that it was Sidney Bernstein who approached him to narrate a film which at the time carried the title 'London in the Blitz'. Reynolds claims that he suggested that the film should be titled *London Can Take It*. Q. Reynolds, *By Quentin Reynolds* (London: William Heinemann Ltd., 1964), p. 186. Reynolds added extra commentary to *Britain Can Take It*, a version of the film intended for British release. The production file for *London Can Take It!*, including a reference by the Ministry of Information, 14 October 1940 on *Britain Can Take It*, is located at The National Archives, INF 6/328.

12 See *The Blitz: The Photographs of George Rodger*, introduced by T. Hopkinson (Harmondsworth, Middlesex: Penguin, 1994).

13 In a letter to his wife Cicely, reprinted in K. Jackson (ed.), *The Humphrey Jennings Film Reader* (Manchester: Carcanet Press, 1993), p. 7.

14 Earlier, untitled, drafts of the script from 20 October 1940 are held by The National Archives, INF 5/77. Early versions of the script are discussed in Vaughan, *Portrait of an Invisible Man*, p. 73. The film's production history is examined in A. Smith, 'Humphrey Jennings' *Heart of Britain* (1941): A Reassessment', *Historical Journal of Film, Radio and Television*, 23: 2 (2003), 133–51.

15 *Documentary News Letter* was produced by the Film Centre, an organisation established in 1936 by John Grierson to promote non-government sponsorship of documentary films. The journal commenced publication in January 1940 and in many ways it filled a space in film criticism left by the earlier cessation of the journal *World Film News* (1936–38). *Documentary News Letter* was initially produced as a typescript and demand for the first issue led to the newsletter going into print form. The journal became influential during the war years within the documentary filmmaking community, and beyond. It ceased publication in 1947.

16 Extracts from the review are reprinted in Vaughan, *Portrait of an Invisible Man*, p. 72.

17 Before the war Jack Holmes specialised in making instructional and education films (such as *How to Cook*, 1937). Holmes was appointed production supervisor of the GPO Film Unit after Grierson's resignation from the Unit in 1937. He was soon replaced as senior producer by Alberto Cavalcanti, though he remained influential within the administration of the Unit and an important figure in the Unit's successor, the Crown Film Unit. Holmes was an assistant producer on Jennings' film *Welfare of the Workers* (1940) and producer of Jennings' *The True Story of Lili Marlene* (1944). In 1941 he directed the story-documentary *Coastal Command* for the Crown Film Unit.

18 Letter to Cicely Jennings, Easter Monday 1941, reprinted in Jackson (ed.), *The Humphrey Jennings Film Reader*, p. 15.

19 Ibid., p. 16.

20 According to Dalrymple, Harry Watt, Jack Holmes and Jennings enticed him away from the commercial film industry to replace Alberto Cavalcanti as leading producer with the GPO Film Unit. Dalrymple, 'The Crown Film Unit, 1940–43', p. 21. It was Dalrymple who suggested that a reorganised GPO Film Unit should be called the Crown Film Unit. His idea was approved and the CFU was created in October 1940 within the Films Division of the Ministry of Information headed by Beddington. A. Harding, 'The Closure of the Crown Film Unit in 1952: Artistic Decline or Political Machinations?', *Contemporary British History*, 18: 4 (winter 2004), 24.

21 Reeves, *The Power of Film Propaganda*, p. 156. Reeves points out that 'Many documentaries were made by independent documentary production companies and in certain cases by commercial film studios'.

22 Ibid.

23 Reprinted in Jackson (ed.), *The Humphrey Jennings Film Reader*, pp. 117–18.

24 Ibid., p. 20.

25 Vaughan, *Portrait of an Invisible Man*, pp. 74–5.

26 Ibid.

27 There is a residual snobbery evident in critical reactions to Jennings' inclusion of so-called high culture texts. Clive Coultass, for example, exhibits a certain condescension towards the ability of what he calls 'ordinary people' to understand the quotations. C. Coultass, *Images for Battle: British Film and the Second World War, 1939–1945* (Newark: University of Delaware Press, 1989), p. 74.

28 J. Richards, *Films and British National Identity: From Dickens to Dad's Army* (Manchester: Manchester University Press, 1997), p. 99. Murphy similarly calls *This England* a 'historical pageant'. R. Murphy, *Realism and Tinsel: Cinema and Society in Britain, 1939–1949* (London: Routledge, 1992), p. 29.

29 Richards, *Films and British National Identity*, p. 100. Chapman, *Past and Present*, p. 91.

30 Quoted in J. Chapman, *The British at War: Cinema, State and Propaganda, 1939–1945* (London: I. B. Tauris, 1998), p. 239.

31 Winston, *Claiming the Real*, pp. 104–12.

32 Winston refers to *Words for Battle* as a 'non-narrative'. Ibid., p. 112.

33 Vaughan, *Portrait of an Invisible Man*, p. 75.

34 The structure follows that identified by Gustav Freytag in his studies of dramatic structure.

35 Taylor, *A Dream of England*, pp. 205–6.

36 The image is reproduced in J. Taylor, *War Photography: Realism in the British Press* (London: Routledge, 1991), p. 87.

37 The image and the words of the commentary for *Britain Can Talk It* are reproduced in Q. Reynolds (commentary), *Britain Can Take It: The Book of the Film* (London: John Murray, 1941) [n.p].

38 Reprinted in Taylor, *War Photography*, p. 59.

39 Audiences objected to images of corpses on the home front. J. Fox, *Film Propaganda in Britain and Nazi Germany: World War II Cinema* (Oxford: Berg, 2007), p. 115.

40 See P. Delany, *Bill Brandt: A Life* (Stanford, California: Stanford University Press, 2004), p. 167; *Cecil Beaton: War Photographs, 1939–45*, introduction by G. Buckland (London: Imperial War Museum and Jane's Publishing Co., 1981), p. 26, and *The Blitz: The Photography of George Rodger*, p. 152.

41 Quoted in M. Smith, *Britain and 1940: History, Myth and Popular Memory* (London: Routledge, 2000), p. 82. Smith reproduces the photograph on p. 81.

42 Ibid., p. 80.

43 Nowell-Smith, 'Humphrey Jennings', p. 330.

44 Vaughan, *Portrait of an Invisible Man*, p. 84.

45 Ibid., p. 85.

46 Ibid., p. 86.

47 The letter is reprinted in Jackson (ed.), *The Humphrey Jennings Film Reader*, p. 31.

48 The print used for this transcription is held by the National Film and Television Archive. The print does not include a foreword appended to the film by the Ministry of Information.

49 Quoted in Vaughan, *Portrait of an Invisible Man*, p. 83.

50 Quoted in ibid., p. 87.

51 A. Kuhn, *Family Secrets: Acts of Memory and Imagination* (London: Verso, 1995), p. 118.

52 W. Guynn, *A Cinema of Nonfiction* (Rutherford, New Jersey: Fairleigh Dickinson University Press, 1990), p. 138.

53 J. Merralls, 'Humphrey Jennings: A Biographical Sketch', *Film Quarterly*, 15: 2 (winter 1961–62), 31.

54 Guynn, *A Cinema of Nonfiction*, p. 141.

55 Ibid.

56 Ibid., p. 127.

57 S. Heath, *Questions of Cinema* (Bloomington: Indiana University Press, 1981), p. 24.

58 Winston, *Claiming the Real*, p. 105.

59 Grierson, 'First Principles of Documentary (1932)', p. 87.

60 Leach, 'The Poetics of Propaganda', p. 159.

61 C. Plantinga, 'The Scene of Empathy and the Human Face on Film', in C. Plantinga and G. Smith (eds), *Film, Cognition, and Emotion* (Baltimore: Johns Hopkins University Press, 1999), p. 239.

62 B. Wright and B. V. Brown, 'Manifesto: Dialogue on Sound', *Film Art*, 3 (spring 1934), reprinted in D. Macpherson (ed.), *Traditions of Independence: British Cinema in the Thirties* (London: BFI Publishing, 1980), p. 178.

63 Ibid.

64 Ibid., pp. 178–9.

65 See J. Grierson, 'The Documentary Idea (1942)', in I. Aitken (ed.), *The Documentary Film Movement: An Anthology* (Edinburgh: Edinburgh University Press, 1998), pp. 103–14.

66 In a letter to his wife, reprinted in Jackson (ed.), *The Humphrey Jennings Film Reader*, p. 16.

67 M. Chion, *The Voice in Cinema*, trans. C. Gorman (New York: Columbia University Press, 1999), p. 18.

68 Guynn, *A Cinema of Nonfiction*, p. 120.

69 Ibid.

70 See Vaughan, *Portrait of an Invisible Man*, p. 83.

71 Quoted in Drazin, *The Finest Years*, p. 154.

72 Jackson, *A Retake Please!*, p. 83.

73 M. Smith, 'Narrative and Ideology in *Listen to Britain*', in J. Hawthorn (ed.), *Narrative: From Malory to Motion Pictures* (London: Edward Arnold, 1985), p. 148.

74 Quoted in Sussex, *The Rise and Fall of British Documentary*, p. 144.

75 At www.bfi.org.uk/features/interviews/grigsby.html (accessed 17/04/07).

76 The scene depicting the factory performances of Flanagan and Allen was echoed in *Millions Like Us* (1943), made a year after *Listen to Britain*. *Millions Like Us* includes a sing-along in a workers' canteen, in a scene that combines documentary and fictional footage. In a related way the high-angle shot in *Listen to Britain* of couples dancing at Liverpool's Tower Ballroom was reworked in similar dance-hall scenes in *Millions Like Us* and *The Happy Breed* (1944).

77 V. I. Pudovkin, 'Asynchronism as a Principle of Sound Film', in E. Weis and J. Belton (eds), *Film Sound: Theory and Practice* (New York: Columbia University Press, 1985), pp. 86–91.

78 See A. Cavalcanti, 'Sound in Films', in Weis and Belton (eds), *Film Sound*, pp. 98–111.

79 Aitken, *Alberto Cavalcanti*, p. 53.

80 Quoted in E. Monegal, 'Alberto Cavalcanti', in R. Barsam (ed.), *Nonfiction Film Theory and Criticism* (New York: Dutton, 1976), p. 240.

81 Vaughan, *Portrait of an Invisible Man*, p. 90.

82 Ibid., p. 92.

83 Guynn, *A Cinema of Nonfiction*, p. 93.

84 Ibid., p. 103.

85 Ibid.

86 Leach, 'The Poetics of Propaganda', p. 108.

87 Ibid., p. 111.

88 J. Hillier in Lovell and Hillier, *Studies in Documentary*, p. 87; Reeves, *The Power of Film Propaganda*, p. 169.

89 Reeves, *The Power of Film Propaganda*.

90 A. Higson, 'Five Films', in G. Hurd (ed.), *National Fictions: World War Two in British Films and Television* (London: BFI Publishing, 1984), p. 24.

91 Quoted in ibid.

92 Higson, 'Five Films', p. 24.

93 Quoted Sussex, *The Rise and Fall of British Documentary*, p. 145.

94 Higson, *Waving the Flag*, p. 202.

95 Kuhn, *Family Secrets*, p. 117.

96 Higson, *Waving the Flag*, p. 203.

Documentary reconstruction and prognostication: *Fires Were Started* and *The Silent Village*

4

After the experiments with sound and image relations in *Listen to Britain*, Jennings' next films, *Fires Were Started* and *The Silent Village*, involved a different variety of experimentation in the form of dramatisation and re-enactment. Such practices were ingrained within the British documentary movement, though a heightened degree of dramatisation, especially in *Fires Were Started*, raised issues of authenticity.[1] The question of authenticity in representation received further attention within considerations of the nature of wartime propaganda and its connection to experience. Studies of authenticity in literature have identified the concept in relation to a sense of legitimacy, sincerity, the genuine and the 'concrete'.[2] Such issues were at stake within the contemporary criticism published in the *Documentary News Letter* that Jennings had 'gone all arty' in *Fires Were Started* by including snippets of Raleigh and Shakespeare within a speech by one of his characters.[3] For Jennings, whose understanding of national character and personal experience was informed by the words of Milton, Shakespeare, Blake and other prominent poets and writers, the literary extracts were 'natural' components of everyday life. Brian Winston argues that the reading of a literary text permits Jennings to convey the heightened situation of the calm before an air raid. 'Using the most cerebral of the [cast] (and a Scotsman) to read Raleigh solves the problem at least as well as having the men express their fears, or indeed anything deep, in their own words. That would, perhaps, have been even more unlikely than showing one of them reading aloud'.[4] What the 'arty' criticism of Jennings' inclusion of poetry ignores is that a person quoting poetry or literature may in itself be authentic. In this way the criticisms were condescending in the inference that 'Englishmen' of whatever class are shy of poetry and literature. More particularly, the issue of 'going all arty' has relevance beyond the immediate example – it points to broader, more profound, questions of authenticity raised within *Fires Were Started*.

Fires Were Started: scripting the real

Questions of authenticity surrounding the documentary representation of *Fires Were Started* were not compromised by the fact that the film involves a degree of scripted fictionalisation. The poet William Sansom (who plays the character of Barrett in *Fires Were Started*) insisted that Jennings had '[n]o script. A general scheme, of course, which we did not know about. The film was shot both on and off the cuff. Dialogue was always made up on the spot – and was of course the more genuine for that – and Jennings collected details of all kinds on the way, on the day, on the spot'.[5] Sansom's impression captures Jennings' ability to give reign to his actors to fill in aspects of the action, but misinterprets the degree of scripting which Jennings brought to the filming of *Fires Were Started*. The special collections section of the British Film Institute holds research notes and outlines heavily annotated by Jennings of six drafts of what would become a script for *Fires Were Started*, written between October 1941 and January 1942.[6] The notes and synopses constitute a script in progress and the dates of the treatments demonstrate that Jennings rapidly developed the ideas that would, together with the sort of ad hoc inclusions referred to by Sansom, be used in the final version of *Fires Were Started*. Jennings complemented the scripting by making notes on possible cast members and their on-camera presence during rehearsals. From this process Jennings arrived at the final cast: the Scottish sculptor Loris Rey became Rumbold ('the Colonel'), and William Sansom played Mike Barrett. Fred Griffiths (Johnny), T. P. Smith (B. A.), John Barker (Joe Vallance), Johnny Houghton (Sidney 'Jacko' Jackson), Philip Wilson-Dickson (Section Officer Walters) and George Gravett (Dykes) were all members of the volunteer Auxiliary Fire Service. Relying on 'real' firemen to enact the script was a central component of an authenticity inscribed in the film.

The script – which deals with the activities of a team of AFS firemen in London's dock area during the nightly air raids on London during the winter of 1940–41 – reinforced its authenticity through the inclusion of aspects of historical experience. By situating *Fires Were Started* among the docks of the East End Jennings located the action among the historically verifiable targets of German air raids during the first phase of the Blitz (from late August to early September 1940). Later raids widened the target area beyond the East End boroughs, though the docks continued to be heavily bombed.[7] During production Jennings wrote to his wife Cicely that he had 'never worked so hard at anything or I think thrown myself into anything so completely', and he recognised that *Fires Were Started* was an 'advance' in his filmmaking.[8] He described the advancement in his filmmaking practice in terms of gaining and applying 'real' or authentic insights into people and 'not just looking at them and lecturing or pitying them'.[9]

Halfway through shooting *Fires Were Started* Jennings described the film in terms of an unlikely mixture of 'slapstick and macabre blitz reconstruction'.[10] The fire-fighting scenes were reconstructed on St Katherine's Dock on the lower Thames and filming was finished by October 1942. An opening credit announces that the events of the film occurred during the winter of 1940–41, prior to the integration of the AFS into a National Fire Service. The completed film has three distinct sections: before, during and after a fire in a warehouse caused by a heavy night-time raid. The first section employs a simple narrative device to introduce each of the characters. A new recruit to the AFS, Barrett, arrives at fire sub-station 14Y and is assigned to the fire-fighting device Heavy Unit One. As he is introduced to his fellow crew members so too each character is introduced to the audience: Johnny, Jacko, Rumbold, B. A., Vallance and Walters.

Johnny is assigned to show Barrett the fire station's area of operations, a region adjoining the docks at Trinidad Street, where a munitions ship is moored. The brief expedition is a simple yet effective device through which Jennings specifies the geographical location of the fire-fighting team. Spatial specificity is reinforced throughout the film. In the second section scenes in the fire-fighting operations room frequently feature a map of the area. Telephone calls to and from the command centre continually refer to the Trinidad Street dock area. Various point-of-view shots contribute further to spatial orientation. In one such shot crew members of a ship anchored in the Thames look back to shore and the flames of the warehouse fire. Jennings paid close attention to the geography of the area in his research for the script, walking the streets near the docks scouting for suitable locations, and, as he put it in a letter to his wife, 'living in Stepney the whole time' of the shoot.[11] While the 'One Man Went to Mow' scene – in which, on entry to the fire station's recreation room, each member of the fire crew is accompanied by Barrett playing the song on the piano – is important to the narrative emphasis on group spirit and communal feeling, in its specification of spatial location the script takes on metonymic associations. In this way, one small patch of land – the area of operations – becomes exemplary of national experience. Importantly, this specific area is isolated yet not cut off from other regions. It is integrated through the device of constant telephone communications from the command centre to other centres, and the connections between specific and wider locations is underlined in the arrival of a fire engine from 'sixty miles away'.

The second section centres on two events, the need to quell flames in a burning warehouse before they spread to an ammunitions ship anchored nearby, and Jacko's death in the warehouse fire. The night-time filming of the scenes resulted in outstanding images of silhouetted forms framed against smoke and fire. During the night bombs continue to fall, and Jacko and Dykes ascend to the roof of the blazing warehouse in an attempt to stem the fire. The water pressure in the hoses drops and hoses are diverted to a nearby sunken barge, which serves as a reservoir. Barrett is ordered to the rooftop to retrieve Jacko and Dykes. As flames engulf the stairs to the warehouse roof an exploding incendiary knocks Dykes unconscious. Barrett descends from the roof on a turntable ladder, as Dykes, still unconscious, is lowered down via a rope steadied by Jacko. The flames spread, and Jacko falls to his death into the inferno of the blazing warehouse. The third section depicts the morning after the fire, a time in which relief at saving the munitions ship is tempered by mourning for Jacko. Workers arrive on the docks as the firemen depart the scene of destruction, though as Johnny points out, the munitions ship is untouched. In a piece of bitter irony, Jacko's wife, unaware of her husband's death, listens to a radio report that announces that though 'fires were started' casualties are likely to be few. Shots of members of the crew at Jacko's funeral are intercut with shots of the munitions ship heading down the Thames – with the clear and unmistakable implication that Jacko's death was not on vain.

Propaganda and authenticity: the price to be paid

One commentator has found the sum of the three parts of the film's structure less than convincing in terms of authenticity, and argued that the depiction of the Blitz 'in this supposed documentary' is 'utterly and grotesquely unreal'.[12] Other commentators have argued that authenticity suffered as a result of the strictures of the Ministry of Information propaganda policy and the resultant mythical interpretation of the Blitz that, by the time the film was made, a year after the events depicted, was hardening and conflicting with history.[13] Indeed, elements within *Fires Were Started* of an official propaganda policy are revealed within a comparison of *Fires Were Started* and the booklet *Front Line, 1940–41*, the Ministry of Information's 'Official Story of Civil Defence in Britain' published in 1942. *Front Line* includes many of the details of fire-fighting contained in Jennings' film – water supply and water pressure were constant problems; flying embers were a particular hazard; bombs fell all night, often rekindling fires that had been quelled; and '[m]any fires were started [though] none got right out of hand'.[14] The imagery of this particular document, in the form of numerous black-and-white photographs, also bears a close resemblance to the mise en scène of *Fires Were Started*: night-time shots of blazing buildings with the silhouetted figures of fire fighters aiming hoses into the flames and smoke, London's auxiliary firemen carrying hoses, firemen on extension ladders above flaming buildings, fire-ravaged buildings collapsing into the street, a tangle of hoses amid rubble in the street, and flaming and gutted warehouses on St Katherine's Dock (on the night of 11 September 1940). Throughout the representations of *Front Line* London is depicted in organic, corporeal terms: '[t]he enemy sought to destroy the bodily life of the capital: to cut the nerves, pierce the veins, sever the muscles'.[15] The body metaphor displaces the literal depiction of bodies; death and images of the dead are absent from *Front Line*. 'Sacrifice' is aligned in the text with the characteristics of fortitude and hard work in the face of persistent fires and continual air raids, and exemplified in repeated images of Londoners 'taking it'.

The prohibition on images of death within the Ministry of Information's publication was reflected in the Ministry's propaganda policy for film. Aspects of the Ministry's film policy were set out in 1940 by Kenneth Clark in a committee paper entitled 'Programme for Film Propaganda'. In this paper Clark, who at the time was director of the Ministry's Films Division, codified the three central planks of the Ministry of Information's propaganda policy: 'What Britain is fighting for', 'How Britain fights' and 'The need for sacrifice if the fight is to be won'.[16] The demand to represent the latter point, arguably the most contentious of the three strands of the policy, had to negotiate an understandable aversion by viewers to images of death and dying. In this way a study of wartime films by Mass-Observation noted that footage and films of the Blitz 'tended to be popular when they did not include horrific scenes of the dead or the physically mutilated'.[17] Within this context an effective way for film to fulfil the notion of the 'ultimate sacrifice' is through fictionalised devices. Such a device was employed in *Fires Were Started* in the form of Jacko's death, and indeed that 'one of the characters should die was deemed intrinsic to the project by the Ministry of Information; it was vital to demonstrate that sacrifice was necessary. Thus a note that one of the firemen was "going to get killed" [is included] in Jennings' earliest plans for the film'.[18] In these terms Jacko's death is the price paid for the Ministry of Information's propaganda policy, and while the fictional death accords with the literal loss of life in the raids it is, in terms of its heavy-handed and melodramatic rendering, an inauthentic element within the film.

'Other irons in the fire': the story-documentary and fiction film

As crucial as it was to aspects of wartime representation, the Ministry of Information's propaganda policy did not necessarily 'determine' textual or formal outcomes. The scene of Jacko's death was in one way a response to the implementation of official policy. In another way the death scene – in which references to home-front casualties are expressed within and through components of fictionalised drama – reflects the film's investment in the form of the so-called story-documentary, a product of various factors within the film industry at the time. In certain estimations the meeting of fictional and documentary elements characteristic of the story-documentary has been interpreted in relation to the 'wartime wedding' or 'wartime marriage' of documentary realism and fictional film which, it is argued, resulted from staff exchanges between the documentary sector and film studios such as Ealing.[19] The exchange – which was somewhat one-sided, marked by the exodus from documentary production of people such as Harry Watt and Cavalcanti to Ealing (Jennings considered the move on more than one occasion) – contributed to a renewed emphasis on realism within British wartime cinema. According to Paul Rotha, Jack Beddington, as head of the Ministry of Information's Film Division, actively encouraged closer cooperation and exchange between fiction film producers and documentary filmmakers.[20] In making this case Rotha suggests that the creation of the story-documentary and its wedding or mixing of elements of fictional film and documentary was the result of Beddington's official policy directives. However, in terms of fiction filmmaking, the 'wartime wedding' may have had more to do with a process of differentiation of national cinemas – a pronounced realism as a response by the British film industry to the fantasy of Hollywood film then beginning to seriously encroach on British markets – than with Ministry of Information policy on staff exchange. (Indeed, staff movements between sectors of the wartime film industry were in all probability motivated by expanded opportunities for realist fictional filmmaking).

Within the documentary sector, on the other hand, the impetus for the 'story-documentary' was the result of conditions within the sector, as opposed to any response to official policy. Harry Watt, who first applied the so-called story-documentary form in *North Sea* (1938) and who extended its applications in *Target for Tonight* (1941), described the development of the form in relation to a split in the mid-1930s between Grierson and his followers who favoured non-theatrical exhibition of documentary, and Cavalcanti, Jennings, Pat Jackson, Jack Lee and himself who felt that theatrical distribution was the most viable way to reach a large audience for their work.[21] Watt described the form in terms of '"taking true events", using real people, but also using "dramatic licence" to heighten the tension and the story-line'.[22] Jennings' application of the story-documentary form tended in *Fires Were Started* towards an emphasis in the first half of the film on 'classic' documentary sequences, and the use of 'dramatic licence' in the film's second half. The first part of the film, with its traditional frame, involves Barrett's arrival at the substation, where he is introduced by Johnny to the station's organisation and operating procedures. Johnny's instructions to Barrett and the voice of a controller on the telephone checking the condition of fire-fighting appliances serve a function similar to that of expository voice-over narration. Within these sequences specific items of fire-fighting paraphernalia are identified, as are the routines of the substation.

The film's distributors, General Films Distributors, attuned to the audience expectations of fictional texts, wanted the first half of the film, with its expository sequences, cut. Representatives of General Films Distributors argued that the opening sequences lacked dramatic tension and that the first half-hour was very slow, thereby detracting from the film's effect as entertainment and propaganda.[23] Jack Beddington, who succeeded Kenneth Clark as director of the Films Division, agreed with the estimation and wrote to Ian Dalrymple within the Crown Film Unit on 26 November 1942 to say that judicious editorial cuts would improve the film from a 'propaganda and an entertainment point of view'.[24] Jennings was, understandably, irate. In reaction to the criticisms made by General Films Distributors he wrote to his wife that:

> All sorts of people – official and otherwise – who apparently had not had the courage to speak out before, suddenly discovered ... that the picture was much too long and much too slow and that really instead of being the finest picture we had ever produced (which was the general opinion till then) it was a hopeless muddle which would only be 'saved' by being cut right down and so on ... All of this arising out of the criticisms of one or two people in Wardour Street, who had other irons in the fire anyway and who fight every inch against us trespassing on what they pretend is their field'.[25]

A compromise was reached whereby eight minutes were cut from the opening and the title changed from *I Was a Fireman* to *Fires Were Started*.

The move into theatrical distribution was not, then, without problems for the story-documentary. Jennings may have been correct in his impression that the 'other irons in the fire' – the commercial fiction film industry, with the commercial distributors and producers of Wardour Street – resented and resisted the incursion on 'their field' by the story-documentary. In turn, the story-documentary was compromised: its moves to authenticity were besieged and denatured by the expectations associated with fictional film, which led to the demand that editorial cuts be made to the first half of the film. The differing expectations of fiction film and documentary are inscribed in the story-documentary form of *Fires Were Started* as a tension between a narrative focus on spectacle and sensation – including the climactic fire scene and the heavy-handed death scene – and the authentic details of the operations and procedures of the volunteer fire service.

Distinctions between fiction and nonfiction, and the place of authenticity within such distinctions and dichotomies, were further highlighted by the impending release of the fictional *The Bells Go Down* (1943). Much of the unease felt by the distributors of *Fires Were Started* was related to their desire to compete with *The Bells Go Down*, a film that is strikingly similar in content to *Fires Were Started*. Both films focus on a fire crew in the London docks area. The daily routines of a fire station are common to both films, as is a dramatic engagement with a major fire. In both *Fires Were Started* and *The Bells Go Down* a central character dies in the fire fighting, and both films end with a funeral. However, though similar in content the fictional film and the documentary are dissimilar in their varying approaches. The fiction film is clearly marked as such within its emphasis on the lives and personal background of each of the central characters. In contrast, there are few revelations of the personal lives of Jennings' characters. In another way, the tone of *Fires Were Started* is that of the traditional documentary, a 'discourse of sobriety', to use Bill Nichols' phrase.[26] In contrast, *The Bells Go Down* indulges in comedic sequences, at the centre of which is the film's star, Tommy Trinder, a well-known vaudevillian comic. Editing style is another difference between the two films. The editing of *Fires Were Started* is directed in the main at providing information about the fire service, rather than constructing drama, and the film maintains this stance even during the final, climactic scenes involving the fire. Most notably distinctions between *The Bells Go Down* and *Fires Were Started* are pronounced within the function of re-enactment. Rather than collapsing the representation into a fictional mode, re-enactment within a documentary frame validates the depiction as documentary. The point is central to Vaughan's analysis of the 'One Man Went to Mow' scene. In this sequence Barrett is seated at a piano in the recreation room playing a tune, when Johnny enters the room, recognises the music and begins to sing. 'Thereafter, the six others have to enter precisely on cue for their respective verses; and for a bonus, the air-raid siren begins just as the last chord is fading. Such a device would ... register as contrived and unconvincing in any normal feature film ... If we find this sequence acceptable in *Fires Were Started*, it is because we are not responding strictly within the conventions of narrative realism, but are seeing it as a re-enactment in which the world is granted a certain licence for its self-representation'.[27]

Witness and re-enactment

Vaughan's example indicates the ways in which re-enactment within the frame of documentary authenticates fictional scenes. The point is clarified through reference to the range of possible re-enacted performances. Brian Winston's elaborate typology of the interventions and types of performances characteristic of re-enactment or reconstruction is valuable here. Winston's continuum includes, at one extreme, non-intervention by the filmmaker in the profilmic scene – the filming of natural disasters is such an example – and total intervention at the other – as in completely fictional representations of people, places and events. From non-intervention '[w]e can move on this continuum [to] unfilmed interaction between filmmaker and subject (the asking of permission to film, for example)', and from there through 'specific unfilmed requests made without prior research to repeat or delay action, to specific requests to re-enact actions witnessed during the research process, to specific requests to re-enact actions witnessed by the subject or others in the past (what may be called history), to specific requests to re-enact actions witnessed elsewhere during the research process performed by other people of the same type as the subjects (what may be called typical), to specific requests to enact actions which are possible but unwitnessed, to specific requests to "act" (that is, to perform before the cameras at the request of the filmmaker without reliance on any witness in ways unrelated to the subject's actual behaviour and personality)'.[28] Thus, the steps within the continuum are: non-intervention; permissions; delays and repetitions; re-enactment of witnessed action; re-enactment of history; re-enactment of the typical; enactment of the possible; acting; total intervention.[29]

According to the continuum, *Fires Were Started* involves re-enactment of witnessed events (by non-professional actors). In these terms authenticity is conveyed within and through re-enactments, which are endorsed by the fact that they are based on prior realities. 'The claim on the real in these circumstances was not that the camera filmed things as they were happening, but that it filmed things as they had happened and been witnessed'.[30] Examples of this process in the film include, among others, the 'One Man Went to Mow' sequence. Writing to his wife in October 1940 of the effects of the Blitz, Jennings commented on '[p]eople in the north singing in public shelters: "One man went to mow – went to mow a meadow."' In the same letter he notes another image that was to reappear in *Fires Were Started*: the presence of 'WVS girls serving hot drinks to firefighters'.[31] In May 1941 he included among the Whitmanesque lines of his poem 'I See London', a series of observations of the capital in the time of the Blitz, the line 'I see a one-legged man crossing the fire on crutches', an image which is reproduced in *Fires Were Started* after the film's climactic fire. Such witnessed events were bolstered by the research trips conducted by Jennings in the process of writing the film's script. The quality of the research is reflected in the fact that commentators praised the film's authenticity. According to a Mass-Observation survey that asked respondents to list their six favourite films of 1943, 'never have ordinary people been more convincingly documented' than in *Fires Were Started*.[32]

Summarising the form of re-enactment undertaken in *Fires Were Started*, Winston refers to the practice as 'people acting themselves'.[33] The practice can be located on his continuum of re-enacted action and closely approximates the form he identified as a filmmaker's request to subjects to re-enact witnessed actions. More particularly, however, a sense of authenticity is achieved in *Fires Were Started* via people *being* themselves during extended sequences within a documentary frame. Such a condition within the context of reconstruction, though, falls outside the continuum of re-enactment. In a direct way the practice draws on prior reality – the habitual routines of lived reality – as the source of authenticity.

'With tired firemen'[34]

Jennings' particular method of arriving at a situation in which people 'are themselves' is via repeated rehearsals. Fred Griffiths, who plays Johnny Houghton, recalled his rehearsals for his part in the 'One Man Went to Mow' scene: 'I've started at half past eight in the morning and we go on singing all the way through. A break – half an hour, forty minutes for lunch. Start again. At 5 o'clock – cut! [Jennings] comes over to me, he says: "I think your voice is going." I'd been singing for 9 hours and he said: "Your voice is going"'.[35] In one way such a technique was intended to overcome the shyness and awkwardness of cast members who, in their fatigue, would forget the presence of the camera. More particularly, seemingly endless rehearsals reduced his cast members to fatigue, which was the authentic condition of over-worked fire fighters in the midst of the Blitz. In these terms, his cast members were not 'acting tired', they were tired before the camera. The method is, clearly, extreme. The irony of an endless artificial rehearsal to achieve an authentic condition does not hide the insensitivity, even cruelty, of the technique or dispel the suggestion of Jennings' 'imagi-native disengagement' from people.[36] The outcome tends to a degree to contradict Jennings' assertion in a letter to his wife that during the making of *Fires Were Started* he was 'really beginning to understand people'.[37] However, despite such contradictions, what remains is his commitment to questions of authenticity – often to the point of overly long, exhausting rehearsals of his cast.

What has been called the 'deeper truth' of *Fires Were Started* is revealed via Jennings' close observation of 'real' personnel filmed within the reality of non-studio locations.[38] Jennings depicts people from varying classes (Barrett, played by William Sansom, is clearly marked as from a different class to, say, Johnny and Jacko) in ways which refuse a reduction to stereotypes and which eschew characterisations involving, for example, positions of working-class deference or middle-class smugness. Further, the rehearsal process and Jennings' observational attention to his subjects was capable of revealing 'flickers of authen-ticity' – moments when re-enactment broke down or was substituted by the revelation of real selves.[39] Sixty years after Jennings' film this process has become the subject of critical attention in relation to its operation within televisual 'popular factual entertainment'. In *Fires Were Started* a mood of complete authenticity is maintained through a range of strategies. The effect, as William Sansom commented in the early 1960s, is 'true to life in every respect'.[40]

The Silent Village: 'It could happen here'

The Silent Village is motivated by a simple though ingenious conceit: the Nazi massacre of the inhabitants of the mining village of Lidice in Czechoslovakia is transposed to south Wales. Implicit in this approach is the much more complex question of how to represent the unimagi-nable that is atrocity. Jennings' contemporary, W. H. Auden, reflected on poetry's capacity to represent human suffering in his essay 'Squares and Oblongs' (1948) and in the course of doing so referred to Lidice: 'There are events which arouse such simple and obvious emotions that an AP cable or a photograph in *Life* magazine are enough and

poetic comment is impossible. If one reads through the mass of versi-
fied trash inspired, for instance, by the Lidice Massacre, one cannot
avoid the conclusion that what was really bothering the versifiers was a
feeling of guilt at not feeling horrorstruck enough. Could a good poem
have been written on such a subject?'[41] Auden queries poetry's ability
to function as *documentary*, and to rival or outstrip other forms such
as war reportage ('an AP cable') and photojournalism (a 'photograph
in *Life* magazine'). Elsewhere he concludes that the inventiveness of
poetry can transcend documentary visual techniques to depict atrocity.
In his poem 'Memorial for the City', which concerns the civilian toll of
aerial bombardment, he writes that 'The steady eyes of the crow and the
camera's candid eye/see as honestly as they know how, but they lie'.[42] In
a different conclusion, Jennings upholds the ability of documentary to
represent the atrocity of Lidice. However, Jennings the 'cinematic poet',
like the poet Auden, does so through a major revision of documentary
forms. Eschewing reportage (and first-person testimony) and the voice-
over commentary employed in numerous wartime documentaries,
Jennings extends the reconstructive technique applied in *Fires Were
Started*. The structural ambiguity between fact and fiction at the core
of re-enactment and reconstruction is further reworked by Jennings in
The Silent Village. In this film Jennings not only reconstructs history
– what happened – but also deploys a 'preconstructive' mode characterised by supposition and speculation – what might happen.[43]

The idea for a documentary film commemorating Lidice and
alerting the world to the Nazi atrocity arose with a letter received by
Jennings in July 1942 from émigré poet Viktor Fischl, then working
for the Czech Ministry of Information in London. Fischl's letter was
headed, 'A village in Bohemia: the first draft of a synopsis for a short
film on Lidice'.[44] Jennings immediately saw the possibility of realising
the idea and a year later recalled that he thought it 'really one of the
most brilliant ideas for a short film that we'd ever come across'.[45] The
British Ministry of Information agreed and Jennings commenced work
on the project in the summer of 1942. Fischl's proposal drew comparisons between the coal-mining village of Lidice and a representative
mining village in Wales. Jennings set about inspecting potential Welsh
locations for such a village. To this end, on the advice of his friend
Allen Hutt, he contacted Arthur Horner, president of the South Wales
Miners' Federation, who in turn introduced Jennings to D. D. Evans,
the miners' agent for the village of Ystalyfera. Evans suggested to
Jennings he reconnoitre the valleys towards Swansea. Before heading
off Jennings found in Ystalyfera a postcard depicting a nearby village,
Cwmgiedd. Having surveyed the village – with its white-washed Meth-

odist church, a stream and the surrounding hills – Jennings decided to make his film in the village and the local area. As with *Fires Were Started*, though for different reasons, a suitable location was crucial to the project's desired representational effect. Jennings and his crew spent six months filming in and around Cwmgiedd and the unit of a dozen people stayed with local villagers for the duration of filming. He enlisted the entire population of the village in aspects of the production process and various villagers play themselves in the film, using their own names. In a letter to his wife and children on 10 September 1942 Jennings expressed his deep admiration for the local people (a feeling that seems to have been reciprocated) and describes the film that was to become *The Silent Village* as a 'reconstruction of the Lidice story' in which he is filming the inhabitants of the village 'as honestly as possible – neither like *How Green* [*Was My Valley*] – too theatrical – or *The Grapes of Wrath* – too poverty-stricken'.[46]

Fischl's proposal called for a straightforward documentary depiction of a Welsh locale and a reconstructed Lidice. The idea was simplified as a drama set in a single Welsh village, recasting the German invasion of Czechoslovakia as a German occupation of Britain. The approach results in a film that fulfils a dual function – it represents the events of Lidice within a re-enactment by the villagers of Cwmgiedd, while it also depicts the everyday culture of the working people of a south Wales mining community during wartime. It is in the dual representation – the re-enactment of events in Lidice and the life of Cwmgiedd, and the interaction and tension of these two components – that the film gains much of its effect. Within this framework *The Silent Village* is divided into two parts: life in the village prior to the arrival of the Germans, and life under Nazi rule. The first part presents the landscape and locations of Cwmgiedd, including the town's chapel, houses and shops with the chimneys and winches of the pit in the background. The daily life of the people of the village is depicted within a range of activities: singing in the chapel, workers in the mine, children in their schoolroom, domestic chores, a man in his garden and customers in a shop. The day progresses, a shift finishes and the children are let out of school. The evening activities are signalled by the miners returning home. Children enjoy cartoons at the cinema, men talk in a pub and the Miners' Federation holds a meeting in town to discuss silicosis – a reminder that life in the village is based on a '*double* image' of zest for life and poor working conditions.[47]

The second part of the film is introduced by a title, 'Such is life at Cwmgiedd, and such too was life in Lidice until the coming of the Nazis'. The Nazi occupation is introduced through the arrival in the village of a car mounted with a loudspeaker, ordering the people to obey Deputy Reich Protector Heydrich. The villagers immediately band together to resist the intrusion. Members of a quickly organised resistance movement meet in the ruins of a nearby castle, and an underground newspaper is printed. A sniper shoots a German and the villagers sabotage machinery. The occupiers announce that there has been an attempt on Heydrich's life, and the villagers are ordered to register with the authorities. As villagers' names, ages and occupations are listed a radio announces that a family has been sentenced to death. 'She only just laughed at them', says a villager. The Germans set an ultimatum – the assassin must be turned over to them by midnight. The deadline passes and the next morning women and children are separated and marched out of town and the men are lined up against a stone wall surrounding the cemetery next to the chapel. Sounds of gunfire and shots of the school burning follow. A title in Gothic script reads: 'All the male adults of the village have been shot, the women have been sent to a concentration camp, the children have been handed over to the authorities. The buildings of the locality have been levelled to the ground and the name of the community has been obliterated'. A final scene depicts Cwmgiedd in the present – a shepherd and his flock, children playing in the school grounds. Villagers read the proclamation which appeared in the title and a union leader states, 'No, comrades, the Nazis are wrong. The name of the community has not been obliterated – the name of the community lives on ... We have the power, knowledge, and understanding to hasten the coming of victory – to liberate oppressed humanity, to make sure there are no more Lidices'. A poster advertises a 'Mass Meeting: Lidice Shall Live Again', miners return from a shift, and a long shot shows Cwmgiedd in its valley.

Memory and mapping

The re-enactment undertaken in *The Silent Village* involves a process of memory – of events in Lidice – which is mapped onto the landscape of Cwmgiedd. In this way the site of a barbaric act is mapped on to a landscape which Jennings invests with a travel-brochure lustre. His introduction to Cwmgiedd, in the form of a picture postcard found in a stationer's shop in Ystalyfera, set the frame for Jennings' filmic depiction. In a talk broadcast on the BBC Home Service he described the postcard image as a 'very striking photo of a beautiful little chapel with a long wall and a cluster of miners' houses round it, and a little stream, and a hillside in the background'.[48] The terms of this description of an image – 'beautiful', and the associations of the compact and the cosy in 'little' – resonate in his description of his first sight of the village:

> [u]p in a little valley ... is the village of Cwmgiedd, with a little straight street that goes up into the hill and on each side – charming, beautiful little stone houses and down the middle, parallel to the street, is a mountain stream that comes running down ... [There] is a grocer's shop on the right ... and on the left, a beautiful white Methodist Chapel ... There is a very turbulent river running down this valley and this extraordinarily beautiful group of cottages and then the rest of the street going up ... into the farms and mountains.[49]

This peaceful and Edenic image is replicated in the opening scenes of *The Silent Village*, thus rendering the violent actions and events of the second half of the film all the more disruptive and shocking. A reviewer for *The New York Times* captured some of this effect in a review at the time of the film's release in the US by stating that 'because one comes to love this village as one's own, one feels its death more deeply'.[50] However, even before the realisation of events in the second half of the film the memory of Lidice hovers over the imagery and, ironically, the picturesque adds to the memorialisation process – the beauty on screen inevitably evokes the horror which was undertaken off screen. In turn the Nazi atrocities call forth and reinstitute an image of the peaceful countryside, endearing and enduring, a protective place to be protected.

Lyrical descriptions of the village are absent from a 'book of the film' published in 1943. The focus of Noel Joseph's *The Silent Village: A Story of Wales and Lidice Based on the Crown Film Unit Production* is the miner, who is turned into a figure of 'Liberty' in the pan-European fight against fascism.[51]

> When Mussolini threw his unwilling peasants and eager generals against the spearmen of Abyssinia, secure in the knowledge that gas would decide the issue in his favour if battle did occur, the miner had no ear for the sweetly reasonable voices which explained how well the neat blue-prints of a caesarean culture would fit the wild wastes of the Ethiopias ... [And in Spain, at Guadalajara] and on the banks of the Ebro, men from these coalfields had died among the first volunteers for Liberty ... now these miners who had seen Fascism blight and wither the flowering hopes of nation after nation, were to hear one of their leaders tell them their own fate, tell them that their hour had struck.[52]

The film does not rely on such unconcealed propagandistic rhetoric. The miners play a crucial role in Jennings' film, though their heroism is based on fortitude and a quiet courage as opposed to the overly eager 'volunteers for Liberty' of the book's narrative. In *The Silent Village* the miners are heroic in their resistance to occupation – and as such the figure in Jennings' film abandons the Griersonian image of the coal miner in *Coalface* (1935) and other films from the British documentary movement of the 1930s wherein the miner is either a victim or a heroised agent of state-endorsed labour.

Rather than such restricted depictions, or equally limiting representations of the miner as a worker in various relations to the means of production, Jennings in *The Silent Village* is more concerned with the evocation of a sense of what is essentially a romanticised image of the miners' characteristics. It was this image which he repeated in a letter to his wife, in which he talked of the miners' 'honest Christian and Communist principles daily acted on as a matter of course … Not merely honesty, culture, manners, practical socialism, but real life: with passion and tenderness and comradeship and heartiness all combined'.[53] Jennings' description of the countryside and his depiction of its inhabitants show signs of the rural myth that pervades much of his work. The combination of countryside and nation is deployed here, as in works such as *Spare Time*, *Heart of Britain* and *Listen to Britain*, to suggest essential national characteristics. However, unlike the films mentioned here, *The Silent Village* pursues such a representation within and through a preconstructive mode.

The preconstructive mode and the future

The preconstruction of *The Silent Village* involves re-enactment of historical events intended to signal the possibility of varieties of action in the future. Such a category is beyond the continuum of forms of re-enactment devised by Winston. As with *Fires Were Started*, the re-enactment in *The Silent Village* is of actions witnessed by the subjects or others in the past, though it supersedes this function in its implicit exhortation to action intended to avert future possible outcomes. In these terms the re-enactment of historical events begs the assessment that 'it could happen here if fascism is not stopped'. The preconstructive mode is also applied in the film *Went the Day Well?*, directed at Ealing Studios a few months before *The Silent Village* by Jennings' old friend Alberto Cavalcanti. The story of *Went the Day Well?* concerns a group of Nazi soldiers who, disguised as British troops, infiltrate an English village as the first step towards a wider occupation of Britain.[54] The film historian Clive Coultass argues that 'By the time the film was released [October 1942], there was scarcely any danger of an invasion of Britain and the story is presented as a retrospective look at fictional events'.[55] While the fear of invasion may have passed, historical context – in the form of anxieties over invasion – no doubt informed the production of both *Went the Day Well?* and *The Silent Village*. However, to reduce *Went the Day Well?* to this perspective misses the point of the film. *Went the Day Well?* is not directed to the past; it is a preconstructive looking forward, not necessarily to a Nazi invasion of Britain but to the pressing need to conquer fascism in order to preclude such a situation. Like *The Silent Village*, Cavalcanti's film has a hard propagandistic edge, which functions as a warning to act to secure the British way of life now and into the future.

However, within its mediation of entertainment values the allusions to the British way of life in *Went the Day Well?* tend to be muted, or displaced within a plot which continually emphasises suspense in its move towards climactic action. In contrast *The Silent Village* clarifies its appeal to the British way of life within its consistent evocation of a rural myth that embodies landscape as the 'heart of Britain' and which encapsulates the essential decency of those who are sustained by such a landscape. In these terms the cogency of the message of *The Silent Village* exceeds that of *Went the Day Well?*, and Jennings' film more effectively serves as a call to protect the British way of life. While *Went the Day Well?* pays attention to the nefarious Nazis, Jennings' film rarely depicts the enemy invaders in its attention to the countryside and its inhabitants. In contrast, then, to *Went the Day Well?*, where the narrative focus is on 'who we are fighting', *The Silent Village* emphasises 'what we are fighting for'. In another way, unlike *Went the Day Well?*, a fictional plot based on a short story by Graham Greene, *The Silent Village* roots its exhortation to action in the memory of historical events. The form of memorialisation operative within and via the preconstructive mode in *The Silent Village* thus has a dual function. It is a call to military action to stop fascism, and it is also a conservationist call to action on the home front. The latter feature, which is linked to the first, emphasises that the way of life and the landscape represented by Cwmgiedd should not be lost. In this way the film uses the past to motivate future action: to erase fascism, and in so doing maintain the British way of life.

According to certain critical assessments, the event that motivated this representation – World War II – was intricately associated with the story-documentary form through which the event was represented. Andrew Higson has elaborated this point in an analysis of the story-documentary, which stresses a focus within the form on the role of social groups in wartime (such as the firemen in *Fires Were Started*, or in an example not cited by Higson, the villagers of *The Silent Village*). The ideological effect of this emphasis, he argues, is 'an articulation of nation as responsible community *and* individual desire, an articulation which finds a place for both the public and the private'.[56] This mediation of the public and private spheres within wartime story-documentaries coincided with, and functioned in support of, a war effort that conscripted the private sphere into the national public domain. Higson contextualises the economic and policy conditions within the film industry which led to the creation of the story-documentary by arguing that the 'ideological conditions of World War II ... established the possibility of a remarkable convergence of documentary and narrative fiction modes'.[57]

Higson's analysis valuably draws attention to the ways in which the concept of the nation during wartime included existing understandings of its relationship to the public and expanded to encompass individual desire, wants and hopes. However, the conclusion drawn from this situation – that the enlarged concept of the nation laid the ideological groundwork for the meeting of documentary and fiction modes – is problematic. The distinction in this analysis between 'documentary' and 'narrative fiction modes' runs contrary to Grierson's foundational definition of documentary as the 'creative treatment of actuality', an interpretation that accepts a degree of fictionalisation within the practices referred to as documentary. Following Grierson, the early British documentary movement frequently produced works referred to as documentaries (among them some of the best-known works of the movement such as *Night Mail*, 1936, and Grierson's own *Drifters*, 1929), which licence multiple fictional elements, including scripted acting, point-of-view shots, and forms of editing which permitted narrative movement in time and space. Jennings innovatively revised this approach by including within his creative treatment of the Lidice story a preconstructive mode through which he effectively raised questions concerning Britain's future by marrying the story-documentary with the preconstructive mode. In a connected way, *The Silent Village* and *A Diary for Timothy*, both of which are linked via context and narrative with events during World War II, deploy the preconstructive mode to evoke possible future conditions and, in the case of *A Diary for Timothy*, explicitly to look forward to and beyond the end of the war.

Notes

1 The correct title of the film is '*Fires Were Started* – ', which is simplified here to *Fires Were Started*. After the images of fire which closed *Listen to Britain*, Jennings' focused on fire, and fire-fighting, as a theme of home-front experience during the Blitz. Regular references in broadcasts and newsprint to the fact that 'fires were started' as a result of German incendiary raids reinforced the centrality of fire within the Blitz.

2 See L. Trilling, *Sincerity and Authenticity* (London: Oxford University Press, 1972).

3 *Documentary News Letter*, 4 (1942), 200. Quoted in Winston, 'Fires Were Started – ', p. 53.

4 Ibid.

5 W. Sansom, 'The Making of *Fires Were Started*', *Film Quarterly*, 15: 2 (winter 1961–62), 27.

6 Box 1, Humphrey Jennings Collection, BFI Special Collections, British Film Institute, London.

7 S. Inwood, *A History of London* (London: Macmillan, 1998), pp. 788–9.

8 Letter by Humphrey Jennings to Cicely Jennings, 12 April 1942 reprinted in Jackson (ed.), *The Humphrey Jennings Film Reader*, p. 58.

9 Ibid.

10 Ibid.

11 Ibid.

12 A. Britton, 'Their Finest Hour: Humphrey Jennings and the British Imperial Myth of World War II', *CineAction!* 18 (fall 1989), 40.

13 R. Colls and P. Dodd, 'Representing the Nation: British Documentary Film, 1930–45', *Screen*, 26: 1 (January–February 1985), 27.

14 Ministry of Information, *Front Line, 1940–41: The Official Story of the Civil Defence in Britain* (London: HMSO, 1942), p. 24.

15 Ibid., p. 39

16 Quoted in J. Chapman, 'Cinema, Propaganda and National Identity: Film and the Second World War', in J. Ashby and A. Higson (eds), *British Cinema, Past and Present* (London: Routledge, 2000), p. 198. In other ways official policy stressed references to historical events and past times as elements of wartime propaganda. After 1941 MoI film policy shifted emphasis. In 1942 the *Kinematograph Weekly* noted that the MoI sought films 'which were not nostalgic about the old ways and old days ... but realistic films of everyday life'. Quoted in S. Harper, 'The Years of Total War: Propaganda and Entertainment', in C. Gledhill and G. Swanson (eds), *Nationalising Femininity: Culture, Sexuality and British Cinema in the Second World War* (Manchester: Manchester University Press, 1996), p. 195. The near contemporary setting of *Fires Were Started* (it deals with events from the beginning of the Blitz, a year before production) fits within the MoI's new policy requirements. The overriding theme of MoI film policy remained that of patriotism, a theme reinforced in *Fires Were Started* in the 'national service' role of the Auxiliary Fire Service. On emphases within propaganda policy see chapter 6, 'Adaptation to War' of M. Dickinson and S. Street, *Cinema and State: The Film Industry and the Government, 1927–84* (London: BFI Publishing, 1985), and the Introduction to F. Thorpe and N. Pronay, with C. Coultass, *British Official Films in the Second World War* (Oxford: Clio Press, 1980).

17 Quoted in Fox, *Film Propaganda in Britain and Nazi Germany*, p. 115.

18 Winston, 'Fires Were Started – ', p. 21.

19 Chapman, 'Cinema, Propaganda and National Identity', p. 199. Other sources on the 'wartime wedding' include Murphy, *Realism and Tinsel*, chapter 2, and C. Barr, 'The National Health: Pat Jackson's *White Corridors*', in I. MacKillop and N. Sinyard (eds), *British Cinema of the 1950s: A Celebration* (Manchester: Manchester University Press, 2005), pp. 64–73. According to James Chapman the term 'wartime wedding' appears to have originated with John Shearman in his article 'Wartime Wedding', *Documentary News Letter*, 6: 54 (November–December 1946), 53. J. Chapman, 'British Cinema and "the People's War"', in N. Hayes and J. Hill (eds), *'Millions Like Us?' British Culture in the Second World War* (Liverpool: Liverpool University Press, 1999), p. 35. Chapman argues elsewhere that the 'fiction-documentary formula' was the 'characteristic mode of representation in most 1950s war films which were based on actual wartime events'. He cites in

this relation *The Colditz Story* (1950), *The Wooden Horse* (1950), and *The Dam Busters* (1956), among other titles. J. Chapman, 'Our Finest Hour: The Second World War in British Feature Film since 1945', *Journal of Popular British Cinema*, 1 (1998), 69. Andrew Higson argues that a conjunction of fiction and documentary elements characteristic of the story-documentary constituted a core of Britain's contribution to wartime and immediate post-war cinema. A. Higson, '"Britain's Outstanding Contribution to the Film": The Documentary-Realist Tradition', in C. Barr (ed.), *All Our Yesterdays: 90 Years of British Cinema* (London: BFI Publishing, 1986), pp. 81–8.

20 Quoted in Chapman, 'Cinema, Propaganda and National Identity', p. 199.

21 'NFT Programme Notes (n.d)' by Harry Watt, appended to G. Lambert, 'Interview: Alberto Cavalcanti and Gavin Lambert', *Screen*, 143: 2 (1972), 48.

22 Ibid.

23 Letter from Colonel A. C. Bromhead of General Films Distributors to Jack Beddington, director of the Films Division of the Ministry of Information, 27 November 1942. The National Archives INF 1/212.

24 Memorandum from Jack Beddington, director of the Films Division, to Ian Dalrymple, head of the Crown Film Unit, 26 November 1942. The National Archives INF 1/212.

25 Reprinted in Jennings (ed.), *Humphrey Jennings*, p. 35.

26 B. Nichols, *Representing Reality: Issues and Concepts in Documentary* (Bloomington: Indiana University Press, 1991).

27 Vaughan, *Portrait of an Invisible Man*, p. 107.

28 B. Winston, '"Honest, Straightforward Re-enactment": The Staging of Reality', in K. Bakker (ed.), *Joris Ivens and the Documentary Context* (Amsterdam: Amsterdam University Press, 1999), p. 163.

29 Ibid.

30 Winston, '*Fires Were Started* – ', p. 20.

31 Reprinted in Jackson (ed.), *The Humphrey Jennings Film Reader*, p. 8.

32 J. Richards and D. Sheridan (eds), *Mass-Observation at the Movies* (London: Routledge and Kegan Paul, 1987), p. 225.

33 Winston, '*Fires Were Started* – ', p. 68.

34 The phrase is by Jennings in a letter to his wife during the making of *Fires Were Started*: 'But what one learns at midnight with tired firemen...'. Reprinted in Jackson (ed.), *The Humphrey Jennings Film Reader*, p. 8.

35 Quoted in Winston, '*Fires Were Started* – ', p. 33.

36 Britton, 'Their Finest Hour', 40.

37 Reprinted in Jackson (ed.), *The Humphrey Jennings Film Reader*, p. 58.

38 Winston refers to the 'deeper truth' of *Fires Were Started* a number of times in his analysis of the film. Winston, '*Fires Were Started* – '. See, for example, pp. 34, 64, 69.

39 J. Roscoe, 'Real Entertainment: New Factual Hybrid Television', *Media International Australia*, 100 (August 2001), 14.

40 Sansom, 'The Making of *Fires Were Started*', p. 29.

41 W. H. Auden, 'Squares and Oblongs', in C. Abbott (ed.), *Poets at Work* (New York: Harcourt, 1948), pp. 163–81.

42 Quoted in M. Bryant, *Auden and Documentary in the 1930s* (Charlottesville, Virginia: University Press of Virginia, 1971), p. 173.

43 The preconstructive mode expresses and embodies the conditional mood of the grammatical tense of the subjunctive – what might have been, could be or would be.

44 Jennings discussed the origins of *The Silent Village* in a talk on the BBC Home Service, 26 May 1943. A rough transcript of the broadcast is printed in Jackson

(ed.), *The Humphrey Jennings Film Reader*, pp. 67–75. The reference to Fischl's letter is on p. 67.

45 Ibid., p. 67.

46 Reprinted in Jackson (ed.), *The Humphrey Jennings Film Reader*, p. 62.

47 Ibid.

48 Reprinted in Jackson (ed.), *The Humphrey Jennings Film Reader*, p. 70.

49 Ibid.

50 T. S. 'At the World', *New York Times* (2 October 1943), at http://movies2. nytimes.com/mem/movies/review.html?_r=1&title1=silent%20village (accessed 15/04/07).

51 N. Joseph, *The Silent Village: A Story of Wales and Lidice Based on the Crown Film Production* (London: The Pilot Press Ltd., 1943).

52 Ibid., p. 31.

53 Letter of 10 September 1942, reprinted in Jackson (ed.), *The Humphrey Jennings Film Reader*, p. 62.

54 *The Silver Fleet* (1943) returned to the theme of Nazi invasion and occupation, begging the question in its representation of resistance in Nazi-occupied Holland, 'How should we behave if the Nazis ran the country?', C. Geraghty, 'Disguises and Betrayals: Negotiating Nationality and Femininity in Three Wartime Films', in Gledhill and Swanson (eds), *Nationalising Femininity*, p. 234.

55 C. Coultass, 'British Feature Films and the Second World War', *Journal of Contemporary History*, 19: 1 (January 1994), 14.

56 Higson, '"Britain's Outstanding Contribution to the Film"', in Barr (ed.), *All Our Yesterdays*, pp. 72–97.

57 Ibid., p. 88.

'What will befall Britain?'
A Diary for Timothy

5

Jennings began location work on *A Diary for Timothy* in the autumn of 1944 and shooting was complete in April of 1945. During this time Basil Wright had joined the project as producer and was bewildered by Jennings' filming methods and concerned by what he perceived to be a lack of structure to the film. According to Wright, when he queried Jennings on these matters Jennings replied that 'when we've finished shooting we'll find out what it's all about, won't we?'.[1] The off-hand remark – in all likelihood intended as a way of keeping an anxious producer from interfering with the filming – and similar comments made at the time by Jennings, led Wright to conclude that the film was scriptless. According to Wright, 'There was no script ... and you didn't know how the rushes were going to fit with anything else, it was an awful job for the old producer. And Humphrey was never available, because he was always out shooting again!'[2]

Jennings did have a conception of the overall work and early in the shooting schedule he worked to a detailed handwritten outline of the film.[3] However, despite the attention to specifics in the draft description, Jennings recognised that a rapidly changing military situation – with its impact on details he hoped to include in the film – demanded ongoing changes to the outline of the film as filming progressed. The film focuses on the first year in the life of Timothy Jenkins, born on the fifth anniversary of the outbreak of World War II. The film's six sections, each of which are marked by a fade out to a black screen, relate events in the European war and incidents in Timothy's life. A further structural pattern is established through reference to the activities of Alan, a farmer, Goronwy, a miner, Bill, a train driver, and Peter, a wounded RAF pilot. A voice-over commentary, spoken by Michael Redgrave, narrates events and action and poses questions of the future in store for Timothy and the nation in the wake of the war.

In the first section of the film the BBC Home Service announces that it is the fifth anniversary of the commencement of the war. On this day – 3 September 1944 – Timothy James Jenkins is born, amidst the 'worst war ever known', as the commentary puts it, in a hospital near Oxford. The radio announces German defeats on the battlefield. Good and bad news from the war is a theme running throughout the film. The theme is employed not so much as a way of building narrative suspense as an evocation of emotion – of the resignation required to see the war through, even in the face of defeats with victory in sight. The four characters – Alan, Goronwy, Bill and Peter – are introduced, 'all fighting [the war] in their ways'. The second section opens with Redgrave stating in his patrician tones, 'And now Tim we will show you a little of the history of your first days on earth – the start of your life, the end of our war in Europe'. Land mines are cleared from beaches and Timothy comes home from hospital on the 'very Sunday that our bombers were out towing the gliders to Arnhem – this we thought was the final stroke of victory'. The radio announces that Allied troops are in Holland, and Alan watches home movies of his land being cleared at the beginning of the war. The third section is dominated by bad news. The radio announces defeat at Arnhem: 'It's the middle of October now and the war certainly won't be over by Christmas', says the narrator. Timothy is baptised and Peter, the injured airman, is on the road to recovery. The thematic movement in which anticipation of the war's end is thwarted by military set-backs is mirrored here in the fate of the characters: as Peter recovers, Goronwy is injured in a mining accident.

The mood established by the news from Holland and Goronwy's accident is carried into the fourth section, which depicts London in wartime. 'Things are chancy here', states Redgrave. Rockets land on London and people sleep in the Underground, though routine life continues with a production of *Hamlet*. In the fifth section, set in December, more bad news from the front is balanced by preparations for Christmas. While the narrator mentions that 'death came to many of us by telegram on Christmas eve', a letter seen arriving for Timothy is from his father stationed in the Far East, wishing him a merry Christmas. A sense of renewal is extended in the final scene of the segment, in which Peter, now mobile, attends a dance to celebrate the New Year. The sixth section opens at the beginning of 1945 and the commentary introduces the first of a number of pointed rhetorical questions, among them: 'What's going to happen in 1945 and the years to follow?' The radio announces a Soviet offensive and on the home front Goronwy recovers from his accident. As he does so he reflects on the past, raising another pointed question: 'The last war, unemployed, broken homes, scattered families and then I thought, has all this really got to happen again?' The battlefield victories are celebrated by a children's choir which performs on stage before the Soviet flag and the banner 'Greetings to the Red Army'. Peter returns to his fighter plane, and Goronwy goes back to the mine as the narrator asks of Timothy: 'What are you going to do?'

Basil Wright, who was so confused by Jennings' working methods during the film's production, called the completed film a 'stroke of cinematic genius', and indeed the film includes scenes and effects that are among Jennings' most outstanding work.[4] The interplay of dialogue in a scene involving a worker in a canteen explaining to his co-workers the velocity and distance travelled by a V2 rocket and John Gielgud on stage as Hamlet in the play's graveyard scene is masterful. 'How long does it take to reach the objective?' asks the worker explaining a rocket's trajectory, 'Nay, I know not' is Hamlet's reply. The scene ends with the dramatic intrusion of the subject of discussion – a V2 explodes nearby sending the workers in the canteen scurrying for cover. Jennings replaces the Shakespearean graveyard scene with war's constant intimations of mortality, which on a broader level are contrasted to a long life and a hopeful future represented by the newborn Timothy.

Wright's final assessment of the film was not carried by Paul Rotha who felt that the message of A Diary for Timothy was 'muddled and uncertain' and that, as with other examples of Jennings' later work, the film was not 'direct and unequivocal'.[5] Rotha's criticism implies a debilitating ambiguity within A Diary for Timothy. In a related way, Lindsay Anderson argued that the film's 'apparently haphazard selection of details' results in an unfruitful ambiguity: the film 'could mean nothing or everything', concludes Anderson.[6] Other critics have followed a similar line, noting ambiguities within the film, which they cast as a failure of creative insight on Jennings' behalf.[7] Such interpretations misread the function of ambiguity within A Diary for Timothy. The film's ambiguity serves as a productive structuring device; recognised as such ambiguity is retrieved from negative, pejorative connotations. In this way, the central, productive, function of ambiguity in A Diary for Timothy is linked to, and informed by, the practice of looking forward.

Looking forward

Looking forward – prognostication – is always a tentative and conditional practice. However, the political and military situation in late 1944 and early 1945, and the possibility of an imminent peace, gave a practical, and in some ways urgent, focus to the activity. As with the preconstruction of *The Silent Village*, the practice of looking forward in *A Diary of Timothy* is expressed in the subjunctive, the central thrust of which is summarised by the question, 'What might be?' Specifically, in the case of *A Diary for Timothy*, the question is implicitly posed as, 'What might befall Britain after the end of the war?' The framing of the point is one of speculation which admits a variety of competing or contradictory, possible or potential answers, thereby begging acknowledgment of the inherent productive presence of ambiguity. In terms of the dogmatism of traditional propaganda – which attempts to eschew ambiguity (not 'What might be?' as an open-ended question admitting a range of responses, but 'This is how it will be') – Jennings' film was deemed by certain official propagandists within the Films Division of the Ministry of Information to be a 'waste of money'.[8] The speculation, openness and ambiguities of *A Diary for Timothy* revise propaganda's typical univocal messages.

One result of the film's complexity has been a dramatic misreading of the film by post-war critics, many of whom have detected a widespread pessimism within the film.[9] In this case the posing of alternatives is interpreted as defeatist and pessimistic. The film's strategic ambiguity – the outcome of open-ended conjecture – is a revelation of Jennings' politics, which bear on this issue. To a jingoist, Timothy's future would be clear and assured: the best experience in the best of all worlds. Ambiguity is a reflection of an eschewal of any such predetermined or guaranteed conclusion and in this way Jennings, though a patriot (and not a jingoist), can be critical of prevailing national policies and directions. As Kevin Jackson, notes: '[h]is patriotism did not blind him to the things about Britain – and specifically about England – which were terrifying or dismaying'.[10] Contrary to this position it has been argued that Jennings' 'view of the British people is blind to the tensions underlying the official picture of "one nation". He has no place in his picture for the strikes which in 1944 brought out a hundred thousand miners in Wales and more in Yorkshire; nothing to say about the regulations penalising "unofficial" strikers with heavy fines or prison sentences'.[11] It is difficult to see how any film at the time sponsored by a government department, let alone one such as *A Diary of Timothy* produced by a Ministry of Information charged with fulfilling the government's propaganda policy, could have explicitly addressed such matters. The criticism proposes a film addressed to specific political concerns. Such a film, while necessary, would be very different from one which poses wide questions about current social (and political) conditions as part of a project of speculation.

Jennings was not, as the criticism just quoted argues, 'blind' to questions of power and rights. Indeed, these issues are directly addressed at the end of the film when the narrator asks of Timothy, 'Are you going to have greed for money and power ousting decency from the world as they had in the past, or are you going to make the world a different place?' In *Towards 2000*, another work of speculation on the future of Britain, the post-war cultural theorist Raymond Williams extrapolates from existing conditions a number of scenarios for the millennium. Among the conditions Williams identifies is that of a possessive individualism, a tendency of market economics to deny communal feeling. The condition is comparable to that identified in *A Diary for Timothy* as the 'greed for money and power ousting decency from the world'. However, like Jennings, Williams was not a pessimist: he also discerned 'resources of hope', a determining presence for change within subordinate cultural forces.[12] In a similar way *A Diary for Timothy* recognises the existence of such resources and implies that they can be drawn upon to transcend current structural limitations to make the future world a different place.

In framing a potential future in these terms Jennings avoids the dual pitfalls which Williams argues attend prognostication: nostalgia or utopianism.[13] The film refuses any sense of 'war nostalgia', a fact that has led many critics to misinterpret Jennings' work.[14] Continually searching in his films for a nostalgic and eulogistic approach to the war, critics can only decry a loss of 'creative powers' when no such signs are evident. Jennings' frequent use of quotations from the canon of traditional English literature is also interpreted as nostalgia. In each case the object of Jennings' practice is the present – to comment on current conditions, not to lament a bygone era. Further, 'war nostalgia' is a particularly inappropriate description of a film such as *A Diary for Timothy* and its questions of the future. The method in *A Diary for Timothy* of posing and ambiguously contrasting questions also denies the certainties and guarantees of utopianism. The suggestion of the world as a 'different place' implicates 'decency' and not a utopian condition of ideal perfection as suggested in other representations from the war era.

Alternate discourses

The attitude to the future in *A Diary for Timothy* can be contrasted to the discourse of 'looking forward' constructed within town planning films of the war era and the immediate post-war period. Planning, as the formulation of policy for developing or reconstructing urban and rural communities, was a concomitant activity of the war. World War II, with its destructive effects on cities such as London, Coventry, Southampton and Plymouth, led, not unexpectedly, to plans for post-war development.[15] The extensive cycle of planning films includes *New Towns for Old* (1942), *When We Build Again* (1942), *A City Reborn* (1945), *New Builders* (1945), *The Plan and the People* (1945) and *Proud City* (1945), each of which is concerned with the future in the form of the rebuilt environments of the post-war era. A pronounced strain of scientific rationality runs through these films as the basis of a system of town planning that disburses resources and thereby abets social improvement. Paralleling and contesting the scientific bases of planning within these films was an acceptance of utopian or visionary schemes. In many cases the dramatic increase in the salience of planning brought about by the war created a situation in which 'even the most idealistic projects no longer seemed unattainable'.[16]

The condition of London in the wake of war was addressed in numerous urban plans, among them the far-ranging development scheme set out by the renowned urban planner Patrick Abercrombie. The scheme was ambitious to the point of being utopian in scope.[17] Abercrombie's plans for the reconstruction of Plymouth contained similar aspirations. Jill Craigie in her film *The Way We Live* (1946) depicts Abercrombie's plans for Plymouth as an expression of public opinion, thereby legitimating the utopianism of Abercrombie's ideas. Craigie, a remarkable documentary filmmaker, was impressed by Abercrombie's designs and admired the celebration of community which suffuses the Plymouth plan. More particularly, *The Way We Live* endorses plans for a new city, which in the terms of the film will herald a bright future. Utopianism embodies a certain dogmatic propositional and assertional stance which is consistent with the aims of propaganda. In this way the core of planning films such as *The Way We Live* is the implicit declaration that the 'future *will* look like this'. In contrast, the evocation of the future presented in *A Diary for Timothy* rallies speculation in place of utopian certainty, and is open to ambivalence and ambiguity in its avoidance of dogmatism. These processes – particularly the structural role of ambiguity – are apparent in the film's deployment of narration and imagery.

Narration

Jennings' return to narration in *A Diary for Timothy* is notable after his eschewal of the practice in his wartime films. The diary form, with its reliance on text and voice, is part of Jennings' broad use of verbal texts

in his work. However, unlike *Words for Battle*, for example, which privi-
leges sounds over verbalisation (to the point where only snatches of
conversation are heard), whole conversations are included in *A Diary
for Timothy*, as in the exchange in a works' canteen. Other instances of
verbal presentations include the voice of BBC news on the radio, and
sections of *Hamlet* delivered onstage. Complementing this variety of
vocalisations, the narration – 'arguably the most elegant written for a
British documentary' – is not the expositional 'Voice of God' commentary of many documentary films.[18] The voice-over avoids omniscience,
and – this being a diary for a child, Timothy – contains homely insights
and clarifications: 'It's the middle of October now ... and the war
certainly won't be over by Christmas, and the weather doesn't suit us ...
And suppose you went up to London. London in November looks like
a nice quiet place, but you'll find things are chancy here too ... In these
days before Christmas the news was bad and the weather was foul'. The
narration was written in part by the liberal novelist E. M. Forster, with
input from Jennings. A commentary by Jennings was available prior
to Forster's involvement with the project, and was used by Jennings
to accompany a screening of a rough cut of the film, which Forster
attended. Redgrave's delivery of the narration emphasises particulari-
ties – rain is ever-present, for example – and the measured and resonant
tones of his voice interact with various sounds on the soundtrack, as
when an air-raid siren warns of a rocket attack and Redgrave calmly and
dryly says, 'I hope you'll never have to hear that sound, Tim'.

Despite the assured narration and the narrative assurances supplied
by the narration, Dai Vaughan, among his praise for the film, finds
fault with the relationship of narration (voice-over) and synchronised
off-screen sounds and voices:

> The film is built up around four characters who are not – we assume –
> personally known to Timothy's family: a farmer, an airman, a coal-miner
> and an engine driver. But there is no consistency in the way the voices
> and image are related in the presentation of these four. The farmer is
> treated with voice-over only, the airman only with synch; the miner is
> given voice-over which, to our surprise, is carried over into synch late in
> the film; and the engine-driver says nothing. It is not that the conven-
> tions of voice-over and voice off-screen are elided, but that they are never
> clearly distinguished in the first place.[19]

Vaughan's critique could be interpreted as a demand for a stronger
narrational presence to integrate the separate components represented
by the four central characters. Such a position is, in effect, disputed
by Kevin Jackson who argues in his criticism that *A Diary for Timothy*
is 'compromised' by a commentary which is 'patronising' and 'though

this stance may be justified by the dramatic logic of an adult addressing a newborn baby, there can be few viewers who do not feel that they, too, are being patted on the head by this know-it-all uncle'.[20] Admittedly, in places the narration exhorts and admonishes in a school-masterly way. However, the dominant tone – in the dual associations of vocal inflection and textual 'voice' – is ruminative, reflective and questioning.[21]

Of the many questions posed by the narrator, arguably the most pointed question of Timothy concerning his future is 'What are you going to do?' In immediate response to this question the film offers a range of occupations as models for the future. The choices are represented in the form of the work of Alan, Bill, Goronwy and Peter. Jennings' refuses to privilege any one occupation, leaving open the potential of each position to serve as a viable way of engaging with the issues that confront Britain in the coming years. In other ways Timothy's childhood itself embodies a host of meanings which implicitly address the question of future paths and activities. The theme of childhood as a way of imagining the future was prominent in British cinema towards the end of World War II. Childhood served as convenient shorthand for the new society that would, as the metaphor would have it, naturally 'grow up' in the wake of the war. The fiction films *In Which We Serve* (1945), *The Way to the Stars* (1942) and *Waterloo Road* (1944), for example, all include a son around whom questions of the future accrue. *Waterloo Road* ends with a baby, Jimmy Colter, in his pram in a bombed and rubble-strewn street as another character asks pointedly: 'I wonder what they'll think of their Mums and Dads? ... Well, Jimmy, me boy, look at you, it's all yours'. In these terms the theme of childhood is a device through which directors evoked the coming of a post-war generation. Jennings' deployment of the metaphor of infancy and childhood is more complex in its exploitation of the ambiguity inherent in the image. Childhood in *A Diary for Timothy* evokes innocence and an absence of complication – conditions which were sorely tested by the war – and simultaneously the representation of childhood bespeaks the inevitability of growth and maturity, which in *A Diary for Timothy* points to the post-war world which will require new approaches to social and political conditions.

Imagery and spectacle

Functioning in tandem with the voice of narration, the film's imagery contributes to the productive ambiguities which inform *A Diary for Timothy*. The condition of innocence implicit within the image of a child is reinforced within one scene of images of natural, undefiled beauty in the form of a field covered in unblemished snow. The startling effect of the scene is achieved in part through a contrast of the bright image and the narration – which introduces the scene with talk of death: 'Death and darkness, death and fog, death across those few miles of water [the battlefields of Europe] ... and death came by telegram to many of us on Christmas Eve. Until, out of the fog, dawned ... loveliness ... Whiteness. Christmas Day [a cut to the snow-covered pasture]'. The scene, which was photographed by Fred Gamage and edited by Alan Orbiston and Jenny Hutt, is arresting. Unlike earlier films such as *Words for Battle* or *Listen to Britain* which commonly juxtapose images from archival sources across scenes, *A Diary for Timothy* more rigorously incorporates images shot specifically for the film, displaying them in formal compositions within the frame, as in this scene – in which, from a close-up of frost on grass, the camera pans to reveal a snowy field, while on the soundtrack a boy sings a Christmas carol. Such a scene is widely described within criticism of Jennings' work as a 'poetic image' or an example of Jennings' visual 'poetry'. While there have been a number of attempts to define the specific characteristics of the poetic image, the term is a loose one referring to features which include framing, the visual beauty of the content, and a 'rhythm' achieved through editing. A more appropriate term than 'poetry' for the effect achieved in such a scene is 'spectacle'. Though typically applied to fiction films such as the musical, wherein spectacular song and dance routines function to halt narrative drive within excessive display, spectacle is a workable term for moments or scenes within documentary or other genres which are to be 'admired not investigated'.[22] In *A Diary for Timothy* the spectacular moment beyond 'investigation' is presented as the enduring beauty of the English countryside. In this scene nature is a point of stasis beyond the social and political changes referred to in the narration. As such the scene partakes of and contributes to the rural myth which Jennings evoked in a number of his earlier films.

However, the film productively renders ambiguous its representation of nature, thus complicating the easy assurances of the rural myth and simple notions of the rural landscape (and, by extension, Britain itself) as outside or beyond change. In particular, a scene in which Alan screens home movies for his family is a device which provides details of the recent past and the rural preparations required for war. Simultaneously the film-within-a-film depicts the ways in which landscape can be altered, by war-like explosions. In place of Jennings' life-long passion for the plough as a symbol of country ways of life, the home movie features the dynamiting of tree stumps as a form of land clearance.[23] Nature and the rural landscape in this scene are not immutable, and the scene thus begs questions concerning the future of what the rural myth insists is the 'essential core' of Britain. The planning films offered one answer to this question, namely, the future of landscape is transformation through modern planning methods and redevelopment schemes. Here again *A Diary for Timothy* presents a useful, constructive ambiguity: is the future of Britain – its landscape and its institutions – to be achieved through a laissez-faire 'natural growth' or via planned intervention – and if the latter, what form should such a directive take? Such issues are embodied within the context of the most pointed question posed in the film. The question, already raised here, is explicitly directed through Timothy at the future of Britain: 'Up to now, we've done the talking, but before long, you'll sit up and take notice. What are you going to do? ... Are you going to have greed for money or power ousting decency from the world as they have in the past? Or are you going to make the world a different place – you and all the other babies?' The approach taken in the film, particularly a willingness to accept ambiguity – an expression of the complexity of Jennings' late style – implies that there will be no easy solutions to these questions in the future.

From *London Can Take It!* to 'Britain Can Make It' and beyond: *The Dim Little Island* and the nation's future

The war in Europe ended soon after Jennings completed *A Diary for Timothy*. The long years of warfare can be measured from Jennings' career, with one of his first films of the war *London Can Take It!* (titled *Britain Can Take It!* for domestic exhibition), produced in 1940. The national conditions depicted in *London Can Take It!* were those of resolve in the face of attack and preparations for further enemy attacks, and possible invasion, with an emphasis on the fortitude and heroism of the capital's citizens. Sandbagged buildings, the presence of military personnel and auxiliary emergency workers in the city's streets all bespeak a people standing by and alert in the presence of war. A year after the end of the war, conditions in Britain had changed demonstrably. The cessation of warfare brought a new set of concerns. Questions of the nation's future implicated the economy and the need to retool industry and modernise the manufacturing sector and to promote consumer spending.

This thrust was carried in the 'Britain Can Make It' exhibition, which opened in September 1946 at the Victoria and Albert Museum. The exhibition, which was organised by the Council for Industrial Design, displayed over 6000 products by 1300 firms and emphasised the latest product designs and labour-saving appliances.[24] Unfortunately for the fascinated and eager crowds that attended the exhibition, the future of a domestic wonderland represented by the products was to be deferred; most of the appliances on display were reserved for export and would not reach the British market for some years.[25] Nevertheless, the purposes of the exhibition were to a degree met: to promote the move by industry from a wartime economy and to place on the social agenda the coming consumerist cornucopia. The emphasis within the exhibition on the future of Britain – its economy, patterns of consumption and social conditions – was plain.

However, the difficulties experienced by the Labour government as a result of strained economic strategies in the following year muted the enthusiasm generated by the 'Britain Can Make It' exhibition. Two years later, in 1949, Jennings' *The Dim Little Island* aimed to lift spirits and reinspire confidence in the future. *The Dim Little Island* has been interpreted as a response to a sense of gloom which, despite the celebrated victory of the Labour Party in 1945, befell the nation in the immediate post-war years.[26] Produced soon after the Labour government's set-backs (*The Dim Little Island* was commissioned in early 1948), the morale boosting of the film can, within this context, be interpreted as a response to specific contemporary political conditions, as opposed to a reply to any lingering despondency over World War II. International political conditions added to contemporary reactions within Britain. In 1948 Orwell was writing *Nineteen Eighty-Four*, a dark vision of a rigidly controlled state that reflected his response to the spread of a harsh Communism, which he first came to doubt and to criticise during the experiences that he acknowledged in *Homage to Catalonia*. Edward Hulton, the proprietor of the *Picture Post*, had praised the Labour victory of 1945: 'I rejoice', he wrote, 'that latter-day Conservatism has been overthrown'. By 1948 his enthusiasm and endorsement of the future opened by the Labour Party's electoral landslide was transformed into fear of Communism.[27] During the war J. B. Priestley had written of and broadcast his hope that a communal spirit would erase social divisions in the post-war years. By 1948 he was not as sanguine concerning the future. As if in answer to the pointed question posed in *A Diary for Timothy* ('Are you going to have greed for money and power ousting decency from the world? Or are you going to make the world a different place?'), Priestley argued in 1948 that political power was being gathered in the hands of a few.[28]

Amidst such contemporary reactions, *The Dim Little Island* sought to reappraise Britain's past, and as with *A Diary for Timothy*, to address the nation's future. Questions concerning the condition of the state of the nation and future challenges were foremost in Jennings' thoughts as he planned the film during the early part of 1948. Jennings spent part of the summer of that year writing a review for the *Times Literary Supplement* of a book titled *The Character of England*. The wide-ranging review is focused on the future of the nation (or, in particular, England). 'There is only one occasion', he wrote, 'when admiration for past deeds may be given full rein, and that is in an epitaph. It is a dangerous tendency for the living'.[29] The script of the film that Jennings worked on during 1948 originated with lines from Kipling's poem 'Chant-Pagan' in which Tommy Atkins, a discharged and disillusioned soldier asks: 'Me that 'ave been what I've been – / Me that 'ave gone where I've gone – / Me that 'ave seen what I've seen – / 'Ow can I ever take on / With awful old England again ... [?]'. In a third treatment of the script, dated 10 June 1948 (which bears the working title 'Awful Old England?') Jennings had already conceived that four 'answers' to the questions posed in Kipling's poem would be provided by four commentators: the cartoonist Osbert Lancaster, John Ormston, an engineer with the Vickers Armstrong company, James Fisher, a naturalist, and the composer Ralph Vaughan Williams. The finished version of the film, released in 1949, follows this general approach, with each of the four commentators presenting their insights into the state of the nation. Within this context, the theme of the film – the same question which motivates *A Diary for Timothy*: 'What will befall Britain?' – is one that centrally occupied Jennings in the post-war years.

The cartoonist Lancaster begins his presentation by sketching his alter-ego, a court jester, the 'licensed fool', whose jibes nevertheless carried the weight of truth. From this perspective he addresses the 'illusion' that 'Great Britain is rather a dim little island ... that now ... the country is going to the dogs'. He refers to Ford Madox Brown's *The Last of England*, painted in the early 1850s during what was a 'time of optimism, of expansion and the Great Exhibition' though which evokes a sombre mood accompanying emigration. To the emigrants, 'England was the land of the twelve-hour day, still suffering the effects of the Hungry Forties'. Lancaster adds, to carry his argument on the relevance of the painting to contemporary conditions: 'Many of these things were indeed realities: the illusion was that they would result in the collapse of Britain'. The other commentators similarly enjoin the audience to take heart at the nation's prospects. John Ormston speaks of engineering feats and his conviction that the Tyneside shipyards will recommence ship production to meet the demands of Britain as a nation of sailors. James Fisher refers to the fate of the country's wildlife and the potential of flora and fauna to offer lessons in living. Vaughan Williams delivers a lecture on the traditions of English music, from Elizabethan lute music to varieties of twentieth-century music. While the potted history is presented as an organised thesis prepared by Vaughan Williams, an undated memorandum relating to the 'Awful Old England?' version of the script reveals that much of the material presented by Vaughan Williams was planned by Jennings. A similar attention to the details of musical scenes to that demonstrated in the Myra Hess piano recital in *Listen to Britain* is illuminated in the memo, and Jennings notes that shots from the Hess sequence could be used in the new film. Under the heading 'Shooting Problems for Music Sequence' Jennings notes suggestions made by Vaughan Williams and the composer Muir Mathieson, and he includes a reminder to himself to check the *Oxford Companion to Music* for relevant illustrations. He adds in another note that, 'For the reference to the Elizabethans' [in the Vaughan Williams segment] and our own "national upheaval" we might find a striking shot from *Fires Were Started*'.[30]

Indeed, a final assessment by each of the four commentators is followed by a dramatic sequence from *Fires Were Started* of buildings ablaze. Vaughan Williams adds, 'so, the fire is ready. Does it require a match to relight it? Some great upheaval of national consciousness and emotion?' The rhetorical questions are followed by another set of such questions put by Lancaster, who, as the music on the soundtrack reaches a crescendo, asks, 'Who can talk of an end when we're scarcely at a beginning?' As in *A Diary for Timothy*, in which the force of the film's narrative is encapsulated in the rhetorical question, 'What will befall Britain?', so too the thematic focus of *The Dim Little Island* is carried in Lancaster's final question. In what is an evocative ending, the film closes with a shot of *The Last of England*. The multiple meanings implicit in the film's closure are encoded within the meanings of the painting, which depicts a couple seated in the stern of a small ship which will take them from their homeland. There is a sense of sadness and apprehension on their faces. The new life ahead is muted; the 'last of England' is the end of a certain way of life for this couple. More particularly the 'painting's title refers not to what the spectator sees but to what the couple are looking – looking *back* – at. In the reverse field of their gaze lies what they will remember as the last sight of their homeland. The promise for them is of a *memory* of England which lies in a future which, being in another place, is also out of frame'.[31] The painting, like Jennings' film, negotiates the ambiguous relationship of past, present and future. In Jennings' film a rich past which, neverthe-less, is not fully sustaining of a present which is marked by disquiet and changed circumstances, begs a better future, which is out of frame. In this way the argumentative drive of the film echoes the method of *A Diary for Timothy* and is summarised in the practice of an open-ended questioning of the future. In the case of *A Diary for Timothy* the relationship of present and future was complicated by the rapidly changing military situation towards the end of the war which militated against the possibility of a conventional closed ending. The outcome is the fitting and justified presence of ambiguity within considerations of the future.

When the director Lindsay Anderson was asked what film he would make if he had total artistic control over the production he expressed a preference for 'a documentary about Britain – the real Britain and what it could be ... a sort of sequel to Jennings' *A Diary for Timothy*'.[32] Anderson astutely defined the aim of *A Diary for Timothy* – and, coincidentally, *The Dim Little Island* – in terms of a description of the reality of Britain and an evocation of the nation's future options and potential – 'what it could be'. In certain ways the sequel to *A Diary for Timothy* referred to by Anderson took the form of the film *Family Portrait*. *Family Portrait*, Jennings' last major work, was commissioned for the 1951 Festival of Britain, a more elaborate version of the 'Britain Can Make It' exhibition of 1946. As with the conjectural method of *A Diary for Timothy*, *Family Portrait* does not necessarily seek to offer definitive answers to the significant question of what Britain could be in the future. In this way *Family Portrait* continues the process of begging questions of the future of the British nation, and posing tentative answers, undertaken in *A Diary for Timothy* and its companion piece *The Dim Little Island*.

Notes

1 Quoted in Sussex, *The Rise and Fall of British Documentary*, p. 158.
2 In Hodgkinson and Sheratsky, *Humphrey Jennings*, p. 73.
3 Reprinted in Jackson (ed.), *The Humphrey Jennings Film Reader*, pp. 96–9.
4 Wright, *The Long View*, p. 202.
5 Rotha, *Documentary Film*, p. 253.
6 Anderson, 'Only Connect', 9.
7 As in, for example, Coultass, *Images for Battle*, p. 190.
8 Quoted in ibid., p. 189.
9 See, for example, Britton, 'Their Finest Hour', 42, and Vaughan, *Portrait of an Invisible Man*, p. 133.
10 Jackson, 'Introduction', to Jackson (ed.), *The Humphrey Jennings Film Reader*, p. xxi.
11 S. Hood, 'A Cool Look at the Legend', in E. Orbanz, *Journey to a Legend and Back: The British Realistic Film* (Berlin: Edition Volker Spiess, 1977), p. 149.
12 R. Williams, *Towards 2000* (Harmondsworth, Middlesex: Penguin, 1985), pp. 243–69.
13 Ibid., pp. 12–14.

14 Britton, 'Their Finest Hour', 41.
15 Within this context Jennings produced a planning film with a different focus: *A Defeated People* (1946) is concerned with post-war plans to redevelop Germany.
16 J. Gold and S. Ward, 'Of Plans and Planners: Documentary Film and the Challenge of the Urban Future, 1935–52', in D. Clarke (ed.), *The Cinematic City* (London: Routledge, 1997), p. 71.
17 P. Mandler, 'New Towns for Old: The Fate of the Town Centre', in B. Conekin, F. Mort and C. Waters (eds), *Moments of Modernity: Reconstructing Britain, 1945–1964* (London: Rivers Oram Press, 1999), p. 221.
18 The comment on the narration is by Brian Winston, *Claiming the Real*, p. 107.
19 Vaughan, *Portrait of an Invisible Man*, p. 135.
20 Jackson, *Humphrey Jennings*, p. 304.
21 Bill Nichols develops the notion of textual 'voice' in 'The Voice of Documentary', in A. Rosenthal (ed.), *New Challenges for Documentary* (Berkeley: University of California Press, 1988), pp. 48–63.
22 Higson, 'Space, Place, Spectacle', pp. 157–77. The role and function of spectacle in documentary is analysed in K. Beattie, *Documentary Display: Re-Viewing Nonfiction Film and Video* (London: Wallflower Press, 2008).
23 Wartime land clearance is the theme of *Spring Offensive* (1940). The film, narrated by A. G. Street, who also narrated *English Harvest* (1939), is set in Suffolk. Jennings uses for the first time a form of dramatised re-enactment to describe the ways in which agricultural workers are contributing to the war economy by reclaiming land and farms which fell into disuse after World War I. Though concerned with contemporary conditions the film's focus on rural life recalls the nostalgia of *The Farm* (1935) and *English Harvest*. However, as in *A Diary for Timothy*, the film looks to the future of peace and asks questions of that future. Street's final words are: 'Remember, we've looked after the land properly only during periods of war … Now the countryside asks you to do something … When peace comes, don't forget the land and its people again'.
24 P. Addison, *Now the War Is Over: A Social History of Britain, 1945–51* (London: British Broadcasting Corporation and Jonathan Cape, 1985), p. 192.
25 Ibid.
26 Kevin Jackson places the film in the context of a response to World War II and a general post-war sense of gloom and malaise. He argues that the film adopted the task of 'bucking-up the battle-weary troops' and was meant to reassure the 'British people that life after the war need be neither as drab or as glum as they may have come to believe'. Jackson, *Humphrey Jennings*, p. 336.
27 Addison, *Now the War Is Over*, p. 203.
28 Quoted in ibid.
29 Quoted in Jackson, *Humphrey Jennings*, p. 335.
30 'Undated Memo on "Awful Old England"', in Jackson (ed.), *The Humphrey Jennings Film Reader*, pp. 116–17.
31 Kuhn, *Family Secrets*, p. 109.
32 Quoted in R. Hughes, 'The Filmmaker and the Audience', in R. Hughes (ed.), *Film: Book 1* (New York: Grove Press, 1959), p. 37.

An ambiguous national iconography: *Family Portrait* 6

A critical shibboleth concerning Jennings' work holds that his best or most accomplished films were produced during the war years. Reflecting this position Lindsay Anderson opened his well-known reappraisal of Jennings' career with the argument that the war 'fertilised [Jennings'] talent and created the conditions in which his best work was produced'.[1] In the same vein another critic has insisted that 'war unmistakably brought out the best in Jennings'.[2] Within the terms of such assessments Jennings' pre-war and post-war films are viewed as impoverished or irrelevant. In this way the position sidelines among other works *Family Portrait*, a film which at the time of its release was praised as a vibrant and creative work. Edgar Anstey, writing in *Film Festival: Third Week*, a publication of the Edinburgh Film Festival, called *Family Portrait* the most important documentary produced since the war.[3] The *Monthly Film Bulletin* praised what its reviewer saw as the film's masterly style and its fine balance of camerawork, editing, voice-over and music.[4] The publication *Today's Camera* declared the film a 'lovely, lingering experience' that would 'stand as a yardstick for contemporary documentary'.[5]

Family Portrait negotiates a theme running through Jennings' work concerned with national identity, which in this case is framed within a particular moment within modernity in Britain. The social theorist Marshall Berman, in his influential work *All That Is Solid Melts into Air*, describes modernity as a 'mode of vital experience – experience of space and time, of the self and others, of life's possibilities and perils'. The experience, he states, results in a sense of 'perpetual disintegration and renewal' and of 'struggle and contradiction, of ambiguity'.[6] The ambiguity at the core of modernity is recast within *Family Portrait* at the intersection of the past and the future. Within this context *Family Portrait* celebrates Britain's past achievements in the fields of industry, science, exploration and the arts and also looks to the nation's future.

The approach is similar to that adopted by Jennings in *The Dim Little Island* which, according to its introductory segment, is a 'short film composed on some thoughts about our past, present and future'. In the relationship of the past and the future in *Family Portrait* Jennings poses, in a similar way to *A Diary for Timothy*, a series of tentative and often rhetorical questions concerning the condition of the nation and the challenges it must confront in the coming years. A refusal to specify answers alludes to the ambiguity at the centre of modernity and reflects the ambiguous meld of characteristics which make up the nation.

Diversity and consensus

Family Portrait was made for the Festival of Britain, a celebration of national achievements which ran from 3 May to 30 September 1951. The film was produced by Wessex Films, a company newly established by Ian Dalrymple after his departure from the Crown Film Unit. Having completed *The Cumberland Story* (1947), a workaday film which mixes dramatic re-enactment and contemporary footage in a history of the new machinery used in coal mines along the north-west coast, Jennings resigned from the Crown Film Unit and moved into the commercial sector of filmmaking when he joined Dalrymple at Wessex. Since he had last worked with Jennings, the editor Stewart McAllister, together with a number of colleagues, had been embroiled in a labour dispute while filming in Africa, with the result that he was attached to the Film Unit of the Central Office of Information. McAllister soon left the Central Office of Information to collaborate with Jennings as editor on the film for Wessex. Another colleague from the past, John Grierson, reappeared in Jennings' working life during the preparations for the film. Grierson was a member of a panel convened in 1949 by Jack Ralph on behalf of the British Film Institute to coordinate all film arrangements for the Festival. Other members of the panel included Michael Balcon, Anthony Asquith, Harry Watt and Arthur Elton. Grierson had earlier soured his relationship with Jennings, as with many subsequent co-workers, through his bullying tactics, and in his new position of power on the panel he used the opportunity it afforded him to criticise Jennings' outline for the proposed film.

The film, which Grierson saw fit to criticise, opens with references to the diversity of nature and landscapes in Britain, and a pointed comment on the 'diversity of the people'. The commentary continues by arguing that such differences produced a host of renowned artists, explorers, scientists and inventors (the commentary and images depict

Drake, Shakespeare, Stephenson, Trevithick, Turner, Milton, Darwin, James Cook, Livingston, Robert Falcon Scott, Faraday and Nelson). The film highlights certain achievements in science and technology, among them radar and aero-turbine engines, and earlier advances such as Stephenson's railway and Trevithick's invention of a steam train, which is illustrated with line drawings similar to those used in Jennings' film *The Story of the Wheel* (1934). Jennings uses Trevithick's boast that his train could outpace a race horse as an opportunity to include two of his favourite images – the horse and the iron horse – which are intercut in shots of a race course and shots of steam and electric trains. The survey of national characteristics and distinctiveness ranges from pre-history to contemporary events, constantly cross-cutting references to scientific discoveries and artistic achievement and linking the past and the present (as in an oblique point concerning Drake, the Spanish Armada and radar). Similarly the many references in the commentary to the diversity of British society are balanced by an equal number of references and allusions to reconciliation and consensus.

Family Portrait was included on a list of films compiled by the British Film Institute for screening at arts festivals, film societies, education institutions and by national and local exhibitors during the five months of the Festival. The film was also screened in the Telekinema (*sic*), a purpose-built theatre on the Festival's London South Bank site devoted to the exhibition of big-screen television broadcasts and documentary films produced for the Festival. As Sarah Easen points out in her detailed and informative history of the place of film within the Festival, *Family Portrait* was one of a dozen films commissioned by the Festival organisers for exhibition on the South Bank site.[7] The official Festival film was *The Magic Box*, a biography by the Boulting brothers of the British cinema pioneer William Friese-Greene. However, *Family Portrait*, subtitled 'A Film on the Theme of the Festival of Britain, 1951', has been referred to in various sources as the 'official' film of the Festival.[8] The claim, though incorrect, points to the way in which *Family Portrait* has been understood to reflect the authorised aims and official policy of the Festival.

Jam and pill: the official policy of the Festival of Britain

The meaning of the Festival of Britain, originally conceived as an event to commemorate the Great Exhibition of 1851, has been subject to a variety of interpretations. The historian Betty Conekin, in a book-length study of the Festival, argues that the 'Festival of Britain was not only an event – or rather, a series of events – designed to demonstrate to the world Britain's proclaimed economic resurgence, it was also an *attempt* at national recovery – an attempt to bolster the low number of tourists, who could stimulate the national economy'.[9] Elsewhere Conekin insists that the Festival 'set the broad parameters of a social democratic agenda for Britain'.[10] James Vernon comments that the Festival was a 'showcase for the art, design and architecture of a Britain determinedly grappling with a "modern" future despite the austerity of the post-war period'.[11] According to David Matless, the broad message of the Festival was of a 'movement into a new world under the guidance of authority above sectional interest'.[12] Geoff Eley claims that the Festival was 'effectively a celebration of the social democratic modernity envisaged by the postwar Labour government'.[13] Michael Frayn argues, in what has become a frequently cited essay, that the Festival reflected a shift in the 'whole tone of public life' which took place during the post-war years.[14]

Many of these meanings are implicit within statements by members of the Festival's planning and organisational committees, which taken together, encode the official policy of the Festival. The Ramsden Committee, set up by the government in 1945 to investigate the possibility of holding an international fair aimed at boosting the post-war export of British products, concluded that a fair 'should be held in London ... to demonstrate to the world the recovery of the United Kingdom from the effect of war in moral, cultural, spiritual and material fields'.[15] In 1947, by which time plans for the exhibition had reduced it from an international to national event, Herbert Morrison, the government minister appointed to oversee planning of the exhibition, described the Festival as a 'great symbol of national regeneration ... new Britain springing from the battered fabric of the old'.[16] At the opening service of dedication Archbishop Fisher stressed the role of the Festival in enhancing national characteristics: 'The chief and governing purpose of the Festival is to declare our belief in the British way of life ... It is good at a time like the present so to strengthen, and in part to recover our hold on all that is best in our national life'.[17]

Against such solemnity there was an emphasis within official quarters on enjoyment and pleasure as objectives for the Festival. The director-general of the Festival, Gerald Barry, talked of the Festival in terms of 'fun, fantasy and colour'. Barry stressed to Ian Cox, the Festival's director of science, that 'we must avoid being too serious and too historical ... People simply will not go to an exhibition to learn a lesson, however perfectly it may be told'.[18] In turn, Morrison wanted to 'see the people happy. I want to hear the people sing'.[19] Max Nicholson, an advisor to Morrison on the project, recalled that Morrison 'wanted it to be a fun thing … He wanted the people to participate in it, he didn't want it to be a "them and us" affair. He wanted the teaching side of it … to be played down, and a great deal of jam spread over the pill'.[20] The pill wasn't entirely sugar-coated. One commentator describes as 'laboriously educational' the red dotted line intended as a guide for patrons to visit in strict order the Festival's twenty-seven pavilions.[21] An emphasis on the educational was also in evidence in the Festival's rigorous concentration on the arts and sciences as elements of the general theme of the 'Land and the People'.[22]

The Festival theme was translated into a physical presence within the Lion and Unicorn Pavilion, which, according to the official guide to the exhibition, was designed to symbolise two of the main qualities of the national character: realism and strength [the Lion], and fantasy, independence and imagination [the Unicorn].[23] Reflecting the fantastic, the pavilion's celebration of 'British Character' tended towards an expression of the frivolous or the absurd. Dylan Thomas noted the emphasis on the fantastic and the eccentric within the pavilion's exhibits when he commented that, 'What everyone I know, and have observed, seems to like most, about the exhibition are the irreverent touches, such as the linked terracotta man and woman fly-defying gravity and elegantly hurrying up a w.c. wall'.[24]

A family affair: national identity

In a somewhat less whimsical way the Festival's focus on assumed national characteristics is a central theme of *Family Portrait*, which Jennings, in keeping with the emphasis within the Festival on 'fun', is able to represent in ways that are visually pleasurable. *Family Portrait* is a visually lyrical celebration of the nation's past, present and future, which includes views that can be admired and enjoyed for their expressive and, in places, spectacular sights. Any sense within such an approach of an effect similar to a travelogue is reduced within the intimacy in which content is presented. *Family Portrait* is arguably Jennings' most personal work, a point noted by a number of observers who have called the film a 'personal essay', and personal 'in the sense that it is his summing-up of his notions about England'.[25] The point comes across in Grierson's slightly condescending remark, made in a slim volume published in tribute to Jennings soon after his death, that '*Family Portrait* is not so much a film as a meditation'.[26] Echoing the official slogan of the Festival – 'autobiography of a nation' – Jennings' film applies autobiographical elements, in the sense of his feelings about Britain, within his idiosyncratic autobiography of the national family.

A personal, intimate quality is reinforced within the narration, spoken by Michael Goodliffe, which is presented in the first person plural mode of address. The familiar is further emphasised within the film's title and the various references within the film to the 'family' of Britain. The elements are stressed in the film's opening narrative: 'Perhaps because we in Britain live on a group of small islands, we like to think of ourselves as a family – and of course with the unspoken affection and outspoken words that families have. And so the Festival of Britain is a kind of family reunion. So let us take a look at ourselves; to let the young and the old, the past and the future, meet and discuss. To pat ourselves on the back, to give thanks that we still are a family. To voice our hopes and fears, our faith for our children'. The allusions to family are appropriately contained within a family snapshot album, images of which open and close the film, with its photographs of seaside holidays, a baby's christening, children with Santa Claus, and a family against the backdrop of war-damaged houses. Through its multiple references to personal, familial ties the film mobilises an image of the nation as, in effect, one big (dominantly happy) family which is united in and through common characteristics which transcend sectional divisions and social difference. Linking the nation and family activates powerful commonsensical meanings which accrue to the concept of the family as a 'natural' social unit. In these terms the ideological construct of the nation is 'naturalised' within meanings expressive of belonging, identity and shared or common interests and sentiments.

As *Family Portrait* demonstrates, the end of the war did not spell a waning of emphasis on national identity. The Festival was a prime venue for renewed attention to the topic, and the connections between national identity and the metaphor of family were also replayed in the feature film *The Happy Family* (1951), a fictional narrative set on the site of what was to become the Festival of Britain. The story concerns members of the Lord family, who have barricaded themselves into their home in an attempt to resist government orders which would clear the neighbourhood for the exhibition. The fittingly named Mr Filch, the 'government chap that's trying to pinch the house', in the words of a younger Lord, cannot understand the family's refusal to move: 'You'll be refusing to help your country, you must oblige', he insists. As the family becomes increasingly resistant and revolutionary in the presence of government pressure the patriarch Mr Lord proposes a toast at a family gathering: 'Let's drink to us – to living quietly and being left alone, and not being led about like sheep; to our Englishman's castle, and to all the millions of little castles belonging to little people all over the country. That's nicer than revolution, eh? Let's drink to the family'. As the forces of change and the state approach, the lord of his castle retreats to references to seemingly immutable and essential national characteristics.

The conservatism of *The Happy Family* is in contrast to the image of the 'national family' constructed a decade earlier by George Orwell in his essay 'The Lion and the Unicorn'. Orwell asserts within the essay that England 'resembles a family, a rather stuffy Victorian family ... [with] its private language and its common memories'.[27] Orwell recognises that the family is divided by class, region, religion and politics, though he proposes a democratic socialism as the balm for social divisions and a viable future for the imagined community (the essay is subtitled 'Socialism and the English Genius'). Caught between the conservatism of *The Happy Family* and Orwell's progressive patriotism and socialism – and touched with elements of both – is Jennings' *Family Portrait*. Jennings' film is, like *The Happy Family*, a celebration of essentialisms within the nation; however, as with Orwell's reflections, *Family Portrait* recognises contradictions and ambiguities which cut across, though do not subvert, the apparently unique characteristics of the 'family'. The narration refers to the inhabitants of Britain as a 'very mixed family' and acknowledges a 'diversity of the people' and 'rifts in the family' within the national space. One way in which the diversity is exemplified is within the contrast between leading figures in British history and 'ordinary' citizens. References in *Family Portrait* to a pantheon of 'great Britons' (Shakespeare, Newton, Darwin, Watt, Turner and so on) are posed against images of the British people not as heroes, 'but [as] individual people with souls of their own', a line from the commentary which is delivered over shots of a man drinking in a pub. Elsewhere contradictions and distinctions between occupations and economies are evoked when the narrator poses the question: 'How to reconcile the farm and the factory?'

Orwell felt that the national differences and the 'characteristic [social] fragments' he outlined in 'The Lion and the Unicorn' were not understandable without recourse to a unifying principle. For Orwell a crucial question was, 'How can one make a *pattern* out of this *muddle*?'[28] The question – couched in the same terms of 'muddle' and 'pattern' – is also central to *Family Portrait*. The reference in the narration to the 'mixture of muddle and orderliness' of everyday life in Britain alludes to the condition of contemporary reality and modernity as one of change and flux. The cultural theorists David Morley and Kevin Robins depict the effect of modernity in similar terms and argue that modernity also offers a strategy to negotiate muddle and flux: 'The project of modernity is [to quote Marshall Berman] "to make oneself somehow at home in the maelstrom" that is daily life'.[29] *Family Portrait* literalises a 'home in the maelstrom' in the practice of the national characteristic referred to in the film as 'sitting quiet at home'. In addition to private domesticity, the solid ground within the muddle is based on 'tradition' and 'pageantry', all of which, according to the narration, form 'part of the pattern of life'. Such features also include what the narrator of *Family Portrait* refers to as 'the very things that make the family, the pattern, possible: tolerance, courage, faith [and] the will to be disciplined and free'. Other central components of this pattern referred to widely in the film are 'poetry' – artistic imagination and creativity – and 'prose' – scientific and industrial innovation. In one sense the two conditions are complementary; in another sense they are ambiguous, or at least ambivalent and unreconciled tendencies, which are nevertheless held in balance within the nation's history and character. Used in these ways the terms recast classical distinctions between Reason and Imagination, concepts which inform Jennings' collagist study of the coming of the machine, *Pandæmonium*, and which anticipate C. P. Snow's reference in the late 1950s to the 'two cultures' of science and the arts.[30]

The road ahead

In Jennings' terms 'poetry' and 'prose' form part of a tradition of practical skill and theoretical understanding which informs the development and current expression of British social experience. The distinction between science and the arts encoded in the film's use of the terms poetry and prose reflected the assertion by members of the executive committee of the Festival of Britain 'that Britain was uniquely placed in the constellation of post-war powers to mark out a new course for the integration of science and the arts'. The members further pointed out that a 'festival planning document from 1948 had stated that perhaps "the greatest single contribution which Britain could make would be to bring Science and the Humanities into step"'.[31] Contesting such aims the historian Paul Addison bluntly criticises the representation of poetry and prose in *Family Portrait*: 'The cosy presentation of British society as a family divided, not by class, but by a rift between the imaginative and the practical sides of the national character is sentimental guff'.[32]

While Addison's focus on class is a fitting reminder of the relevance and importance of the experience to analyses of post-war film, a recognition of historical content complicates his conclusion. In particular, the reality of the Cold War of the early 1950s underlines the cogency of the emphasis in *Family Portrait* on the seemingly misplaced notions of 'poetry' and 'prose'. The rise of the Cold War was attended by a widespread anxiety over the excesses of science, especially in the form of the development of atomic weapons. The critical and commercial success of the Boulting brothers *Seven Days to Noon* (1950), in which a nuclear scientist steals an atomic bomb and threatens to detonate it unless Britain cease further production of such weapons, was not the only reflection at the time of widespread Cold War fears. Within this context the rational expression of science – 'prose' – was capable of slipping into something more sinister and devastating. Given such potential, the film's emphasis on science alluded to, if not foregrounded, political conditions and potential outcomes every bit as pressing as class distinctions. Jennings' script for *Family Portrait* aims to balance the capabilities of science against humanist rationality as a way of plotting a future for society. In this way references to poetry and prose form part of the practice within the film of 'looking forward', which is developed within an argument concerning the condition of the nation in coming years.

The consideration of the future evident within the film has, however, been overlooked within a dominant critical interpretation of what is perceived to be Jennings' nostalgic longing for the glories of a bygone era. The focus of this critical assessment is a brief shot at the end of the film depicting the procession of the mace, a symbol of authority, into the House of Commons, a site of constitutional democracy.[33] Accompanying the image the narrator inquires what can Britain contribute to a world from which it has gained so much: 'Perhaps the very things that make the family, a pattern, possible – tolerance, courage, faith'. In his influential criticism of this scene, Lindsay Anderson recycles the argument that Jennings in some way 'needed' the war to stimulate his creative sensibilities. For Anderson, *Family Portrait* demonstrates Jennings' 'traditional spirit', which 'was unable to adjust itself to the changed circumstances of Britain after the war'.[34] Traditionalism, notes Anderson, 'does not always have to be equated with Conservatism. But somehow by the end of the war, Jennings' traditionalism had lost any touch of the radical'. According to Anderson, signs of the waning of Jennings' radical sprit were found in *Family Portrait*: '[Jennings] found himself invoking the great names of the past (Darwin, Newton, Faraday and Watt) in an attempt to exorcise the demons of the present ... The symbol at the end of the film is the mace of Authority, and its last image is a preposterous procession of ancient and bewigged dignitaries. The Past is no longer an inspiration: it is a refuge'.[35]

Anderson correctly notes that *Family Portrait* invokes the names of significant personages from the past – as he did frequently in other of his films. *Words for Battle*, for example, is based on references to notable poets, writers and statements of the past and present. Significantly, Anderson does not find in *Words for Battle* an attempt to deny the present. Aspects of Jennings' filmmaking – such as the invocation of 'great names of the past' – did not demonstrably change between his wartime work and the post-war *Family Portrait*. Writing in 1954, Anderson's detection of what he felt to be a reactionary nostalgia in *Family Portrait* is more a reflection of the then prevailing critical line to Jennings' work – which held that the war was essential to his film-making skill – than evidence of the presence of a nostalgia in the film or a sign of a marked departure from the 'poeticism' of his wartime work. The infectiousness of the dominant critical interpretation leads Anderson to misread the shots from Parliament: literally and contextually within the film the footage is used to represent 'democracy' which, though it draws on the past, is in *Family Portrait* projected into the future in the form of a liberalism that invests democracy with features such as discipline and faith. Rather than an obsession with the past, as Anderson argues, the film is constructed around conceptions of the future – a future not immune to danger, particularly the dangers associated with science, such as the development of the atomic bomb. In these terms the film is not obsessed with 'the Past' but, instead, looks to the future, while implicitly criticising conceptions that would cast the *future* as refuge.

A more sustained reference to the past is presented in the film's allusions to empire. The British empire, once a mainstay of nationhood and British identity, was, by the time of *Family Portrait*, assailed by anti-imperialism, a process which expanded in the post-war period of political and national realignments. Quoting the historian Gareth Stedman Jones and the sociologist Bill Williamson, Betty Conekin notes that 'by 1951 the retreat from Empire had begun, and therefore by 1949, with Labour in power, the Empire was no longer an appropriate or comfortable foundational structure around which to build British national identity ... [An outcome of this situation was] the gradual realisation that Great Britain was not the world power it once had been'.[36] What Conekin calls a retreat from empire was reflected in the Festival of Britain, which 'represented Britain and British "contributions to civilisation" with little mention of Empire'.[37] *Family Portrait* was among the few exhibitions within the Festival that did mention empire. As he explains components of the 'pattern' of British life, the film's narrator points out that Britons have gone 'to the violent ends of the earth ...

Cape Town, Cairo and Canada ... We have been to the poles and every time the return has brought us back food and food for machines'. The narrator adds that this imperial exploration (the narrative is not one of imperial exploitation) also 'brought us experience and responsibility'. According to Conekin, who has analysed the Festival at length, '[t]his is one of the most direct references to Empire in the Festival of Britain, replete with the version of British imperialism represented as paternalistic and conscientious'.[38]

Among his criticisms of *Family Portrait* Lindsay Anderson draws attention to the film's articulation of a 'fantasy of Empire', evident in the voice-over which, he argues, facilely supports the notion of imperial beneficence in comments such as, 'The crack of the village bat is heard on the Australian plains'.[39] Here, as elsewhere, the film ignores the specifics of the legacies of British colonialism and imperialism. However, the experience of empire is evoked, to be relegated to the past; a process which is reinforced through the use of the past tense in referring to empire. The concept of empire is not perpetuated into the present or future, rather the imperialist fantasy is (to realign Anderson's observation of the film) encoded in nostalgia for the glories of the past. In these ways the relationship in the film of past and present is reinforced in a tension between the past of empire and a future of emergent geopolitical alliances. *Family Portrait* depicts Britain at a particular moment, caught between the past of imperial relations (and war) and a future that will demand a restructuring of global power. In the process the condition of the nation, the focus of the film, is rendered ambiguous through the simultaneous expression of the sureties of the past and the invocation of an uncertain future entailing new political alignments. An intimation of emerging conditions is present in the narrator's acknowledgment that 'We are too small, too crowded to stand alone'. The social historian Robert Hewison argues that the solution to this predicament offered in the film follows conventional British post-war foreign policy, in the form of closer ties with Europe.[40] The narration does briefly mention that 'We have become ... inside the family of Europe' but, significantly, it goes on to add, 'and the pattern overseas'.

This latter reference introduces the topic of Britain's post-war negotiation of a relationship with the US. Against an image of a scientist conducting an experiment the narrator again refers to a crucial concern, the relationship of 'prose' and 'poetry': 'We have just had the knack of putting prose and poetry together'. This achievement is matched later in the commentary by an important recognition that 'we also belong to a community across the Atlantic'. The statements, and their relationship, are dense with meaning. The meeting of prose and poetry is achieved within scientific experimentation – the process which, in the contemporary context of the 1950s, alludes to concerns about nuclear weapons and their place in a Cold War participated in by the United States. Britain's relationship to the US in the midst of global political realignments resulting from the Cold War is reinforced directly through reference in the commentary to Britain's place within a 'community' coordinated by the US.

It has been argued that the representation of social conditions in *A Diary for Timothy* offers an indication of 'why Britain went Labour' at the first post-war national election of 1945.[41] *Family Portrait*, with its intimations of a future of internationalism, the global realignment of political power, and rapid change associated with modernity – themes consonant with the focus within the Festival of Britain's forward-looking representations – is one of the clearest examples of why the nation went Conservative in the elections of October 1951. Faced with a new global and domestic situation such as the one alluded to in the film, and the accompanying anxiety generated by the experiences, voters returned to an inward-looking 'little England' Conservatism as a refuge from the future. As if fulfilling Raymond Williams' dictum that 'There is no useful way of thinking about the future which is not based in [the] values of close continuity of life', *Family Portrait* analyses what the film proposes as essential, continuous components of national identity in relation to suggestions concerning Britain's future.[42] Within these terms the film demonstrates the ways in which Jennings in his first and last major work of the post-war era continued to engage the complexities of national experience in ruminative, open-ended and tentative (as opposed to bombastic) ways.

Such a position contests the argument posed at the opening of this chapter, which maintained that Jennings required the war to produce significant representations of British life. The argument implicates in an unacknowledged way an 'end of history' position, one which implies that post-war history was bankrupt or devoid of the type of experiences that would have further provoked or inspired Jennings' 'genius' in the same way as World War II. Rather than the question, 'Did Jennings need the war to produce significant films?' (which frames his filmmaking in a backward-looking, nostalgic way – the very terms which were levelled by certain critics at Jennings' films), the pertinent question raised by his untimely death is, 'How would Jennings have responded to coming post-war experiences?' In these terms it is interesting to speculate on how Jennings' films would, for example, have responded to the rise in the late 1950s of a political New Left and its impact on British society or, alternatively, to the presence in the early 1960s of a British cinematic

New Wave. Such questions lead, inevitably, to the issue of the ways in which Jennings' work influenced the future of documentary film-making.

Notes

1 Anderson, 'Only Connect', 5.
2 P. Strick, 'Fires Were Started', *Films and Filming*, 7: 8 (May 1961), 16. The notion that Jennings 'needed' the war in order to produce his 'best' work is a not particularly subtle version of another widespread critical position – the infamous claim that documentary representation thrives in times of crisis.
3 Quoted in S. Easen, 'Film and the Festival of Britain', in MacKillop and Sinyard (eds), *British Cinema of the 1950s*, p. 57.
4 Ibid.
5 Quoted in Easen, 'Film and the Festival of Britain', p. 57.
6 M. Berman, *All That Is Solid Melts into Air: The Experience of Modernity* (London: Verso, 1982), p. 15.
7 Easen, 'Film and the Festival of Britain', p. 56.
8 See, for example, B. Conekin, '*The Autobiography of a Nation': The 1952 Festival of Britain* (Manchester: Manchester University Press, 2003), p. 91.
9 Ibid., p. 26.
10 B. Conekin, '"Here Is the Modern World Itself": The Festival of Britain's Representations of the Future', in Conekin, Mort and Waters (eds), *Moments of Modernity*, p. 228.
11 J. Vernon, 'Conference Report', *Social History*, 22: 2 (May 1997), 214.
12 Matless, *Landscape and Englishness*, p. 268.
13 G. Eley, 'Finding the People's War: Film, British Collective Memory, and World War II', *American Historical Review*, 106: 3 (June 2001), 834.
14 M. Frayn, 'Festival', in M. Sissons and P. French (eds), *Age of Austerity* (London: Hodder and Stoughton, 1963), p. 323.
15 Quoted in Conekin, '*The Autobiography of a Nation*', p. 28.
16 Quoted in R. Hewison, *Culture and Consensus: England, Art and Politics since 1940* (London: Methuen, 1995), p. 58.
17 Quoted in ibid., p. 61.
18 Quoted in A. Briggs, 'Exhibiting the Nation', *History Today*, 50: 1 (January 2000), 21.
19 Quoted in Hewison, *Culture and Consensus*, p. 61.
20 Quoted in Addison, *Now the War Is Over*, p. 207.
21 Ibid., p. 209.
22 I. Cox, *The South Bank Exhibition: A Guide to the Story it Tells* (London: HMSO, 1951), p. 8.
23 Ibid., p. 67.
24 Quoted in Matless, *Landscape and Englishness*, p. 272.
25 Jackson, *Humphrey Jennings*, p. 351; Lovell and Hillier, *Studies in Documentary*, p. 115.
26 J. Grierson, 'Humphrey Jennings', in *Humphrey Jennings: A Tribute*, prepared by D. Powell, B. Wright, and R. Manvell (n.p.: The Humphrey Jennings Memorial Fund Committee, n. d.).
27 Orwell, 'The Lion and the Unicorn', pp. 149–50.
28 Ibid., p. 139.

29 D. Morley and K. Robins, 'No Place Like Heimat: Images of Home(land) in European Culture', *New Formations*, 12 (winter 1990), 2.

30 C. P Snow, *The Two Cultures* (Cambridge: Cambridge University Press, 1998). The argument was originally made in an address in 1959.

31 Conekin, '"Here Is the Modern World Itself"', p. 228.

32 Addison, *Now the War Is Over*, p. 207.

33 Shots of a mace occur in four separate places throughout the film. The final shot of a mace entering the House of Commons is the one that has most troubled the film's critics.

34 L. Anderson, 'Postscript' (to a reprint of his essay 'Only Connect: Some Aspects of the Work of Humphrey Jennings', originally published in 1954), in M.-L. Jennings (ed.), *Humphrey Jennings: Film-Maker, Painter, Poet* (London: BFI in association with Riverside Studios, 1982), p. 59.

35 Ibid.

36 Conekin, '*The Autobiography of a Nation*', p. 28.

37 Ibid., p. 32.

38 Ibid., p. 93.

39 Anderson, 'Postscript', p. 59.

40 Hewison, *Culture and Consensus*, p. 58.

41 E. Rhode, *Tower of Babel: Speculations on the Cinema* (London: Weidenfeld and Nicolson, 1966), p. 80.

42 Williams, *Towards 2000*, p. 6.

Legacies

Summarising the legacy of what he called Jennings' 'precious handful of films', Lindsay Anderson wrote in 1981 that while the films 'may not seem directly dedicated to our dilemmas ... they can still stir and inspire us with their imaginative and moral impulse'.[1] More appropriately, to rephrase Anderson's observation, Jennings' films continue to 'stir and inspire' precisely because they continue in various ways to raise issues relevant to the present: among them, forms of representation capable of effectively expressing everyday experience and national identity. Within acknowledgments of the importance of Jennings' films to the history of documentary representation, certain assessments of his filmmaking have unintentionally denied legacies by arguing that his work is too idiosyncratic for emulation.[2] This may well be the case when referring to Jennings' use of collage and ambiguity, formal characteristics which are not commonly copied or duplicated in documentary filmmaking. Further, beyond idiosyncratic elements, not all of Jennings' films have been influential. *Sequence* magazine in the 1950s criticised *The Cumberland Story* (1947), for example, as unimpressive, an estimation that has been widely upheld within critical circles.[3] However, the significant selected work analysed in this book, though difficult to emulate, has made lasting impressions in various quarters. The legacies of Jennings' films are examined here in relation to the history and memory of the British home front during World War II; a number of trends and specific works from the field of film and television; and ongoing questions of national identity and patriotism.

History, memory and World War II

Jennings' work constitutes a broad framework for re-examinations of the history and memory of World War II. In particular his images –

more so than many other contemporary depictions – came to signify the impact of the war on the home front. In this way Jennings' particular forms of documentary representation of a crucial moment in the nation's experience have been imprinted within the nation's history and collective memory. The memory work associated with Jennings' films is exemplified in the use of Jennings' images in numerous cinematic and televisual histories of the war. Just as McAllister and Jennings frequently recycled newsreel or other images in a number of films, so too footage from Jennings' films constitutes a rich archive of shots of the wartime home front which has been mined and applied in various contexts. This process was inaugurated during the latter years of the war. For example, Frank Capra used shots from *London Can Take It!*, *Words for Battle* and *Listen to Britain* at salient moments in his *Why We Fight* wartime series of films. Television has extended this effect. J. B. Priestley, for instance, used shots from *London Can Take It!* and *Listen to Britain* in *1940: A Reminiscence*, screened by the BBC in 1965.[4] The historian Angus Calder mentions a television series he was associated with dealing with the Second World War which, among its footage of the Blitz, included a 'wonderful shot (of a fireman filthy after a night attacking a conflagration)' from *Fires Were Started.*[5] Jennings' images are striking and memorable, and not coincidentally were shot in black-and-white. The recycling of his imagery, and its forceful impact on collective memory, is one of the reasons why, as Calder points out, the 'Blitz is a black-and-white story'.[6]

In these terms Jennings' is valued not only as a filmmaker, but as a historian – or, more precisely, the filmmaker as historian. The position is summarised in a comment by Ian Dalrymple when he wrote that 'no work recalls the atmosphere and feeling of the times more poignantly than Humphrey's [wartime] films'.[7] The filmmaker and producer Richard Attenborough reinforced the point when he stated that 'if you want to know what Britain was like in the 1940s, what we put up with and what our motivations were, go and see one of [Jennings' wartime] films'.[8] Jeffrey Richards defines the essence of Jennings as 'historian' in his perceptive assessment: 'For those generations born since the Second World War, the experience of life in Britain on the home front is now encapsulated in a series of black–and-white documentary images, endlessly recycled in film and television accounts of the conflict. Many of the most striking images are drawn from the films of Humphrey Jennings, who has been called Britain's greatest documentarist. His vision has become our vision'.[9] In another way Jennings' vision of the nation, and the forms and styles he used to represent his vision, have been reflected and perpetuated in a range of film and television productions not restricted to depictions of World War II.

Film and television productions

Kevin Jackson, in the epilogue to his biography of Jennings, stressed that 'Jennings is a living presence in contemporary cinema – one of the Old Masters' who inspires and informs new audiences.'[10] In one way, Jennings' presence is felt in the fact that his films continue to be screened in a variety of venues, notably international film festivals. In recent years Jennings' films have been exhibited at, among other festivals and meetings, the Imperial War Museum (in September 2000 and May 2006) and the Huesca Film Festival in June 2005, and in 2007 *Words for Battle* was exhibited in the Classics Section of the Cannes Film Festival. Other screenings in 2007 of Jennings' films included the Documentary Film Institute at San Francisco State University in March, his birthplace of Walberswick in September, the Hull International Short Film Festival in October, and Anthology Film Archives in New York in November. In the exhibition at the Documentary Film Institute in San Francisco, *Listen to Britain*, *Fires Were Started* and *A Diary for Timothy* were screened in a programme themed around the US invasion of Iraq. As if in answer to a question raised by the film critic David Thomson in an appreciation of Jennings' work ('Why should anyone re-view wartime propaganda films, from a war fifty years old now?'), Jennings' films continue to be screened because they provide insights into contemporary social and political conditions.[11]

Jackson's assessment of Jennings as a 'living presence' in cinema bespeaks wide-ranging impacts and effects, and indeed Jennings' films are not only shown to new audiences, they are also regarded with respect by workers within the film and television industries and inspire, 'whether directly or in more oblique ways, the shape and tone of content of the films that today's practitioners are making'.[12] In this way Jennings' films have influenced various documentary and fiction-based productions for the cinema and television. The efflorescence of documentary filmmaking in Britain during the later part of the 1950s known as Free Cinema was, as many of its practitioners have commented, indebted to Jennings' work. Karel Reisz, whose films, together with those of Lindsay Anderson, were central to Free Cinema, stated that Jennings' films bequeathed the 'notion that you could make films out of observation rather than [a] pre-thought reconstruction of ideas'.[13] Certain scenes in Free Cinema films apply this notion in forms of montage reminiscent of Jennings' work. In his book *The Technique of Film Editing*, first published in 1953, Reisz explicates the formal components of the documentary film of ideas' through reference to an excerpt from *Diary for Timothy*. Reisz notes that Jennings structured his films through associative juxtaposition and commentary in a way which, according to Reisz, heeded Eisenstein's admonition to avoid 'fanciful montage structures arousing the fearsome eventuality of meaninglessness'.[14]

Lindsay Anderson acknowledged his debt to Jennings a number of times during his long and varied career in both documentary film-making and fiction-film production. Writing in 1954, before the emergence of Free Cinema, Anderson praised Jennings' wartime films as works which 'will speak for us to posterity'.[15] In 1964 Anderson noted that the editorial style and the use of sound in his documentaries *Wakefield Express* (1952) and *Every Day Except Christmas* (1957) owed much to Jennings' films.[16] (Indeed, in terms of content – working-class leisure – Anderson's *O, Dreamland* (1953) is comparable to *Spare Time*.) In 1981 Anderson continued to praise Jennings' films for their ability to 'still stir and inspire us with their imaginative and moral impulse'.[17]

In an entirely different way the montage of sound and image in *Listen to Britain* arguably provides a model for Jean-Luc Godard's experiments with image and sound relations in *British Sounds* (1970). In the first sequence of the film the camera tracks along an assembly line that produces MG spots cars. Against this long take the sound track plays three different sonic elements: a male voice reading passages from *Communist Manifesto*, a girl's voice announcing significant dates in the history of the English working class, and factory noises. As with *Listen to Britain*, *British Sounds* presents noise and sounds in tension with each other and with other images, and within this relationship image and sound are productively rendered ambiguous, leaving 'material on which the spectator must work', as one assessment notes.[18]

Jennings' films have also been influential among producers of documentary for television. Dennis Mitchell, described as 'perhaps the most important and influential documentarist working in television' during the late 1950s and early 1960s, produced among his many programmes the documentary *Morning in the Streets* (BBC, 1959).[19] The programme was shot on location, primarily in Liverpool and Salford, and focuses on the working-class areas of these and other northern industrial cities to reveal the resilience and good humour of many of the people who live in these areas. In its subject and locations the programme echoes Jennings' *Spare Time*, and as film historian John Corner points out, stylistically Mitchell's films also resemble Jennings' filmmaking. As

Corner notes, 'In *Morning in the Streets* the informational function is ... carried by recoded speech, used for the most part as voice-over. But this is now accompanied by a more stylistically expansive use of the camera, connecting the film back to rhetorical elements in the "classic" work of the 1930s and particularly to the Humphrey Jennings of *Spare Time*'.[20]

Robert Vas, who made films on a wide variety of subjects during his career at the BBC, speaking in 1980, cited Jennings as the key influence on his work. His debt to Jennings is highlighted in his production of the programme *The Heart of Britain* (BBC, 1970), a study of Jennings' films and reflections by numerous colleagues and commentators.[21] In another television documentary on Jennings' work, Kevin Macdonald's *Humphrey Jennings: The Man Who Listened to Britain* (BBC, 2001), various directors described the ways in which Jennings has affected their filmmaking. Elsewhere the director Michael Grigsby has recounted how Jennings' films excited him, forcing him to re-examine experience in innovative ways in his various television documentaries.[22] Grigsby's *Living on the Edge* (ITV, 1987) applies an associative method of montage, in which sound and image are combined into a narrative and argument without need for commentary, in a manner that resembles methods deployed by Jennings in films such as *Listen to Britain*.

The influence of Jennings' work has extended beyond the realm of documentary production into fiction filmmaking across the past sixty years. While it would be overstating a case to argue that Jennings' films directly influenced Italian neorealism, Martin Scorsese is not the only commentator to point out resemblances between the genre and Jennings' films.[23] Karel Reisz also noted the way in which the reconstructive method of *Fires Were Started* preceded similar forms in Roberto Rossellini and other neorealist directors of the late 1950s.[24] In his analysis of movements in British and Italian cinema the film historian Roy Armes argues that though certain wartime documentaries could have provided a basis for a British neorealist movement there was, instead, with the end of the war, a turn away from the critical concerns of films such as *Rome, Open City* (1945).[25] However, while differing in stylistics to Italian neorealism, the British New Wave of the late 1950s and early 1960s did to an extent work with similar themes while it simultaneously retrieved and reworked the realistic tradition of British documentary filmmaking. In these terms it was Jennings, and not Rossellini, who can be directly linked with paving a way for films such as *Room at the Top* (Jack Clayton, 1959), *Saturday Night and Sunday Morning* (Karel Reisz, 1960), and *The Loneliness of the Long Distance Runner* (Tony Richardson, 1963). The focus in New Wave films on the quotidian within northern industrial cities reworks Jennings' attention in *Spare Time, Heart of Britain* and *The Cumberland Story* to regional diversity and northern ways of life. Similarly the 'kitchen sink' realism of New Wave films exploits the form of realism and a partial emphasis on melodramatic effect associated with the reconstructive mode of a film such as *Fires Were Started*. Jennings' acceptance of the coincidental, serendipitous moment in filmmaking (Ian Dalrymple remembers once when Jennings went to film a cargo ship 'for a symbolic purpose he discovered, to his joy and amazement, that her name was BRITISH GENIUS'[26]) was also felt in the working methods of New Wave film-makers. As Sue Harper and Vincent Porter astutely note in an assessment of Jennings' influence: '[t]he New Wave cinematographers ... liked to combine a sense of contingency – the random and aleatory quality of the "real" world – with an explicitly poetic conception'.[27]

The attention evident in *Fires Were Started* to character and location and the theme of everyday fortitude in the face of the Blitz are features of John Boorman's *Hope and Glory* (1987). Boorman's film, like *Fires Were Started*, ignores the war as a battle experience and concentrates on the nature of the home front in the East End during, and in response to, periods of aerial bombardment. As with *Fires Were Started*, Boorman's film evokes the period in terms of extraordinary sights and defers to an image of the nation as both fractured by social differences yet unifiable in common feelings of good will. In a different way, Terence Davies' *The Long Day Closes* (1992), a portrait of a boy growing up in Liverpool in 1956, echoes Jennings' sonic innovations. Many of the scenes in Davies' film are accompanied by a rich tapestry of music and popular songs. Davies uses a 'coming of age' narrative as a metonym for a history of the nation's experience and applies music as a way of creating what he calls 'a pattern of timeless moments'.[28] In so doing Davies recycles the word so important to Jennings' *Family Portrait*, 'pattern', in reference to a film that, in its use of sound and music in the service of national themes, is indebted to *Listen to Britain*.[29] Davies has acknowledged that his documentary film *Of Time and the City* (2008) was in certain ways inspired by Jennings' work. Davies has said that whereas 'Jennings was trying to capture the very nature of being British and being at war', his own intentions in *Of Time and the City* were a more modest attempt to represent his home town of Liverpool during the years 1945 to 1973.[30] Nevertheless, *Of Time and the City*, with its echoes of *Spare Time*, can, like *The Long Day Closes*, be directly linked through its heavy reliance on music to *Listen to Britain*. 'I love *Listen to Britain* because it's greater than a documentary', Davies has explained, 'it's a complete poem: 19 minutes and you feel you've seen a feature'.[31]

In his assessment of Jennings' career, David Thomson makes the intriguing suggestion that Jennings' thought has much in common with ideas in David Hare's play *Plenty* (filmed by Fred Schepisi in 1985). Susan Traherne, the heroine of Hare's play, follows a trajectory that leads from the camaraderie of the wartime home front to disillusionment with the quality of life in Harold Macmillan's Britain of the early 1960s. For Thomson, 'the mystery in [Jennings'] best films is the same as the moral hesitation and private rapture Hare seeks to explore'.[32] Hare has emphasised that 'ambiguity is central' to *Plenty*. 'The audience is asked to make up its own mind about each of the actions. In the act of judging the audience learns something about its own values'.[33] As Thomson adds, reinforcing the role of a productive ambiguity in Jennings' films, '[s]urely Jennings would have appreciated that openness'.[34]

Beyond the resonances of Jennings' work within specific films and other cultural productions, his legacy can also be gauged in terms of the forms he helped establish and popularise, among them the reconstructive mode of the story-documentary. Caryl Doncaster's claim, published in 1956, that the 'dramatised story documentary is one of the few art forms pioneered by television' overlooked the development of the form during World War II in the work of Harry Watt, Pat Jackson and, in particular, Humphrey Jennings.[35] Writing in his memoir published in 1987, Harry Watt did a service to the historical record when he modestly pointed out the influence on British cinema of the mix of documentary and fiction techniques in the story-documentary form which he helped develop in association with colleagues working in wartime cinema, among them Jennings.[36] Paul Rotha, not always a strong supporter in print of Jennings' work, wrote in 1970 that through the work of directors such as Humphrey Jennings documentary techniques 'achieved the widest public recognition' through their integration with the approach to fiction exemplified in feature-length films. 'The achievement was substantial and lasting', he noted at the time.[37] The wartime marriage of 'documentary' and 'fictional' elements was, as Doncaster points out, applied in television productions of the late 1950s, and subsequently in a relatively widespread use in television and cinema of 'dramatised documentary', a form that employs documentary realism as a structural basis upon which dramatisations are used to reconstruct events and to add dramatic tension as a basis of entertainment appeal.[38]

Comparing and contrasting Jennings' films and those of Eisenstein, Karel Reisz argued in 1953 that 'if the intellectual essay film is to develop in the future, it will have to do so along the lines used by Jennings rather than those envisaged by Eisenstein'.[39] The comment is borne out in the impact of Jennings' work on the essay film, a loose term used to describe expressive, experimental work which, like the written essay, questions, tests and reflects on ideas. In these terms what Peter Wollen identifies as a neoromantic strain in British cultural production runs from Jennings to the essay films of Derek Jarman, notably his film *The Last of England* (1987).[40] Jarman's imagery in this film, with its recurring views of a blitzed and fire-ravaged London, recalls memorable scenes of London in Jennings' wartime films, though Jarman's themes of the 'sickness' and moral bankruptcy of late twentieth-century England are not ones Jennings would have necessarily endorsed. The avant-gardist film essays of Patrick Keiller also analyse many of the themes and topics raised in Jennings' films. Keiller acknowledges an intellectual debt to Jennings and discusses the legacies of Jennings' filmmaking to contemporary filmmakers in the television portrait *Humphrey Jennings: The Man Who Listened to Britain*. Keiller's film *London* (1994), a work that mixes fact and fiction in a hybrid form distinct from the meeting of these elements in Jennings' reconstructions, directly refers to Jennings in the context of the film's analysis of national identity. Indeed, both Jennings and Keiller, albeit in differing ways, examine the condition of the English nation, questioning and rephrasing notions of national belonging within innovative forms, which rework traditional approaches to documentary representation.

Questions of national identity and patriotism

Not surprisingly, the issues of national identity and patriotism which inform Jennings' films were to the fore of popular thought during an era when the concept of independent nations was sorely tested by global warfare. George Orwell was one of the more astute contemporary commentators on these topics. The ideas contained in Orwell's wartime writings – which Jennings commented on more than once in his letters to his wife Cicely[41] – are in certain respects comparable to the ideas and positions espoused by Jennings in his films. In turn, the views of Jennings and Orwell on national character and patriotism represent a significant marker of the ways in which these concepts and practices were addressed by sections of British society during the war.

   Orwell analysed these topics in, among other writings, his long essay 'The Lion and the Unicorn'. The first part of the essay, 'England Your England', written in 1940 and published in 1941, begins with an outline of the immediate political situation. Overhead, as he writes, German bombers are being flown by 'kind-hearted law-abiding men' whose motivation for 'committing murder' is the force of patriotism.[42] However,

Orwell goes on to argue in the essay that patriotism is neither inherently good nor bad (such attributes depend on the content of 'patriotic' ideas), that it is not equitable to fascism or conservatism, and that it is a social necessity, one of the features of 'English character'. For Orwell patriotism 'takes different forms in different classes, but it runs like a connecting thread through nearly all of them'.[43] Orwell applied a sense of history to his analysis of patriotism in England, which he argued had roots within radical political and social thought that was willing to confront and incorporate cosmopolitan trends. Jennings' films bespeak similar strains of a 'patriotism' understood as an endorsement of certain values. Typically Jennings, like Orwell, invoked these values through reference to features of what he saw as the English national character. The references in certain of his films to selected poets and statesmen, as in *Words for Battle*, and to engineers and scientists, as in *Locomotives*, *Family Portrait* and his unfinished compendium *Pandæmonium*, demonstrate in a way that is remarkably consonant with Orwell, the radical and innovative bases of the variety of thought referred to as patriotic. Jennings' cosmopolitanism – as evident in, for instance, his negotiation of Continental theories such as Surrealism – informed his patriotism.

Questions of patriotism and national identity, which are never far away in national politics, were prominently inflected in particular ways in various cultural spheres during the Thatcher era. The title of a collection of essays on films of the era – *Fires Were Started: British Cinema and Thatcherism*[44] – reflects the impact of Jennings' films and thought as a standard against which to measure the vagaries of contemporary 'patriotic' thought. In another way the lingering effects of the experience of Thatcherism have led to re-examinations of national identity and patriotism within a wider cultural context beyond cinema. One outcome of this move has been the analysis provided by the popular singer Billy Bragg in his recent book *The Progressive Patriot* in which he has sought to reclaim patriotism from the many abuses of practice conducted in its name during the Thatcher years.[45] Bragg, like Orwell in 'The Lion and the Unicorn', plots the antecedents of contemporary patriotism through a tradition of political radicalism, and ranges widely over British history to argue his central theme that patriotism does not have to be the sole preserve of advocates of various forms of political conservatism or flag-waving football hooligans. Bragg's conclusion – that patriotism can be a meaningful and progressive impulse capable of producing a sense of belonging – owes a debt to Orwell's writings and similar strands of thought in films by Jennings, which Bragg quotes in his book. The broad range of effects, impacts, impressions and influences connoted by the term legacies demonstrates in various ways the relevance of Jennings' work to contemporary filmmaking and social and political experience. It is now almost sixty years since Jennings made his last film, but he 'still matters. He still asks awkward questions'.[46]

Notes

1 Anderson, 'Postscript', p. 59.
2 See 'Mike Leigh on Humphrey Jennings', at www.channel4.com/culture/microsites/J/jennings/leigh.html (accessed 31/03/06).
3 Quoted in R. Durnat, *A Mirror for England: British Movies from Austerity to Affluence* (London: Faber and Faber, 1970), p. 121.
4 Calder, *The Myth of the Blitz*, p. 229.
5 Ibid.
6 Ibid., p. 229.
7 Quoted in R. Manvell, *Films and the Second World War* (London: J. M. Dent, 1974), p. 159.
8 Quoted at www.boltonmuseums.org.uk/HTML/spender/history_humphrey_jennings (accessed 18/03/07).
9 J. Richards, 'Humphrey Jennings: The Poet as Propagandist', in M. Connolly and D. Welch (eds), *War and the Media: Reportage and Propaganda, 1900–2003* (London: I. B. Tauris, 2005), p. 127.
10 Jackson, *Humphrey Jennings*, p. 385.
11 D. Thomson, 'A Sight for Sore Eyes', *Film Comment*, 29: 2 (March–April 1993), 54.
12 Jackson, *Humphrey Jennings*, p. 385.
13 Quoted in 'Free Cinema', a transcript of a discussion chaired by Kevin MacDonald at the National Film Theatre in 2001, at www.bfi.org.uk/features/interviews/free-cinema.html (accessed 17/04/07).
14 Reisz and Millar, *The Technique of Film Editing*, p. 162.
15 Anderson, 'Only Connect', 12.
16 P. Cowie, 'An Interview with Lindsay Anderson', *Film Quarterly*, 17: 4 (summer 1964), 14.
17 Anderson, 'Postscript', p. 59.
18 C. McCabe, with M. Eaton and L. Mulvey, *Godard: Images, Sounds, Politics* (London: BFI Publishing and Macmillan, 1980), p. 22.
19 J. Corner, 'Documentary Voices', in J. Corner (ed.), *Popular Television in Britain: Studies in Cultural History* (London: BFI Publishing, 1991), p. 49.
20 Ibid., p. 52.
21 R. Vas, '*My Homeland* and *Nine Days in '26*', in A. Rosenthal (ed.), *The Documentary Conscience: A Casebook in Film Making* (Berkeley: The University of California Press, 1980), pp. 261–75.
22 In an interview with Julian Petley on 25 June 25 2004 at www.bfi.org.uk/features/interviews/grigsby.html (accessed 17/04/07).
23 Scorsese quoted in P. Horne, 'Moving at the Speed of Emotion', www.bfi.org.uk/sightandsound/feature/65 (accessed 17/94/07).
24 Quoted at www.bfi.org.uk/features/interviews/freecinema.html (accessed 17/04/07).
25 R. Armes, *A Critical History of the British Cinema* (New York: Oxford University Press, 1978), p. 186.
26 I. Dalrymple, 'Personal Tribute', in *Humphrey Jennings: A Tribute*, prepared by D.

142 HUMPHREY JENNINGS

Powell, B. Wright and R. Manvell (n.p.: The Humphrey Jennings Memorial Fund Committee, n.d.].

27 S. Harper and V. Porter, *British Cinema of the 1950s: The Decline of Deference* (Oxford: Oxford University Press, 2003), p. 210.

28 D. Thomson, 'Sound and Fury: Terence Davies', *Sight and Sound*, 17: 4 (April 2007), 36.

29 The relationship of the films of Jennings and Davies leads critic David Thomson to imagine possibilities for other versions of Davies' film. Thomson's revelry on Davies' use of music includes a production, '*The Umbrellas of Liverpool*, Britain's first all-signing romance, by Terence Davies', as introduced by Humphrey Jennings.

30 Quoted in S. Anthony, 'Terence Davies' Thoughtful Eccentric Hymn to Liverpool', *The Guardian* (13 October 2008), at www.guardian.co.uk/film/2008/oct/13/ terence-davies-time-and-the-city (accessed 20/10/08).

31 Ibid.

32 Thomson, 'A Sight for Sore Eyes', 59.

33 Ibid.

34 Ibid.

35 C. Doncaster, 'The Story-Documentary', in P. Rotha (ed.), *Television in the Making* (London: The Focal Press, 1956), p. 44.

36 Watt, *Don't Look at the Camera*, p. 186.

37 Rotha, *Documentary Film*, p. 251.

38 On dramatised documentary see K. Beattie, *Documentary Screens: Non-fiction Film and Television* (Houndsmills, Basingstoke, Hampshire: Palgrave Macmillan, 2004), chapter 8.

39 Reisz and Millar, *The Technique of Film Editing*, p. 163.

40 P. Wollen, 'The Last New Wave: Modernism in the British Films of the Thatcher Era', in L. Friedman (ed.), *Fires Were Started: British Cinema and Thatcherism* (Minneapolis: University of Minnesota Press, 1993), p. 46.

41 See, for example, a letter dated 10 May 1941, reprinted in Jackson (ed.), *The Humphrey Jennings Film Reader*, p. 29.

42 Orwell, 'The Lion and the Unicorn', p. 138.

43 Ibid., p. 145.

44 L. Friedman (ed.), *Fires Were Started: British Cinema and Thatcherism* (Minneapolis: University of Minnesota Press, 1993).

45 B. Bragg, *The Progressive Patriot: A Search for Belonging* (London: Bantam Press, 2006).

46 Thomson, 'A Sight for Sore Eyes', 59.

Afterword

A certain effect of Jennings' mode of documentary filmmaking is evident in *Spare Time*. The film has minimal voice-over commentary spoken in quiet tones, a soundtrack in which sounds are often used contrapuntally to the images, and a narrative composed of individual vignettes which gives the appearance of a series of snapshots in which lives and experiences are captured at discrete, well-timed moments. As such, *Spare Time* stands apart from the realism of numerous films of the British documentary film movement. Not coincidentally, perhaps, traditionalists within the Griersonian documentary movement disliked *Spare Time*.[1] The example says a great deal about Jennings' filmmaking and its relationship to the tradition of British documentary.

The British documentary film movement under Grierson's steward-ship emphasised a rhetoric of social persuasion grounded heavily in an expository mode in which images were aligned with, though frequently subservient to, a stentorian voice-over. Grierson argued that documen-tary was, from its inception, an 'anti-aesthetic' medium overtly intended as a tool of social 'betterment' and a purveyor of the ideological aim of advancing a particular form of social reformism.[2] In promoting partic-ular styles and aims for documentary film Grierson knowingly sought to separate documentary from the aesthetics and potential of nonfiction film undertaken by a sizeable segment of the international avant-garde.[3] As the example of *Spare Time* suggests, Jennings' films stand apart from the Griersonian agenda. Reinforcing this point Geoffrey Nowell-Smith notes that '[a]t no time did [Jennings] share the governing principles of the [British documentary] movement. Politically and ideologically he was not a meliorist or even a reformist. He was disparaging of realism, and of the practice that went with it'.[4]

In these and other ways Jennings' films inform the modernist experiment in the arts conducted during the early and mid-twentieth century.[5] This contribution is traceable through reference to Jennings' understanding of Surrealism and its use of collage, a practice he centrally employed within an associative montage that exploited the productive ambiguities available within disjunctive, collagist juxtapositions. The contextualising focus on ambiguity associated with the films of Humphrey Jennings analysed here does not suggest that Jennings' work is reducible to a single concept. The meaning of ambiguity denies such a reduction. Ambiguity is plenitude, paradox, contradiction, and is open-ended. As such, it evokes differing experiences and refers to differing points of view and multiple meanings. This is the modernist terrain of Jennings' filmmaking. Recently various commentators have called for a 'post-Griersonian documentary' and have interrogated the possibility of a documentary form that exceeds the traditional strictures of documentary representation.[6] Jennings' foundational effect and lasting achievement is a similar contribution to revised understandings of the techniques, approaches and the very conception of 'documentary'. As such, it must be remembered, Jennings' films exceed the boundaries of an accepted documentary filmmaking practice mapped out by Grierson and the forms and styles maintained within the documentary canon. This is the core of his legacy, and a viable feature of the future of an innovative documentary practice.

Notes

1 Julian Petley, at www.screenonline.org.uk/people/id/453623/index.html (accessed 08/08/08).
2 Grierson, 'The Documentary Idea: (1942)', p. 105.
3 See chapter 1 of Beattie, *Documentary Display*.
4 Nowell-Smith, 'Humphrey Jennings', p. 322.
5 Ibid.
6 See, for example, Winston, *Claiming the Real*, p. 258, and J. Corner, 'Documentary in a Post-Documentary Culture? A Note on Forms and their Functions', at www.info.lut.ac.uk/research/changing.media/John%20Corner%20paper.htm (accessed 08/04/05).

Filmography

Locomotives 1934, 9 mins, b/w

Production: GPO Film Unit
Director: Humphrey Jennings
Musical Direction: John Foulds
Music: excerpts from Schubert's *Rosamunde*, arranged by John Foulds
Note on credits: 'From models in the Science Museum'.

Pett and Pott: A Fairy Story of the Suburbs 1934, 33 mins, b/w

Production: GPO Film Unit
Producer: John Grierson
Director/Script/ Writer/ Editor: Alberto Cavalcanti
Associate Directors: Basil Wright, Stuart Legg
Photography: John Taylor
Sets: Humphrey Jennings
Sound Recording: John Cox
Music: Walter Leigh

Post Haste 1934, 10 mins, b/w

Production: GPO Film Unit
Producer: John Grierson
Editor: Humphrey Jennings

The Story of the Wheel 1934, 12 mins, b/w

Production: GPO Film Unit
Editor: Humphrey Jennings
Note on credits: 'Photographed from models and drawings from the British Museum, London Museum, and Science Museum'.

The Birth of the Robot 1936, 7 mins, Gasparcolor

Production: Shell-Mex Oil Company
Producer/Director: Len Lye
Script: C. H. David
Photography: Alex Strasser
Colour Décor and Production: Humphrey Jennings
Models: John Banting, Alan Fanner
Sound Recording: Jack Ellit
Music: excerpts from Gustav Holst's *The Planets*

Farewell Topsails 1937, 9 mins, Dufaycolor

Production: Adrian Klein/Dufay Chromex Ltd
Director: Humphrey Jennings
Photography: J. D. Davidson

Design for Spring (alternative title: Making Fashions) 1938, 18 mins, Dufaycolor

Production: ABFD, Dufay Chromex Ltd
Producer: Adrian Klein, in collaboration with Norman Hartnell
Director: Humphrey Jennings
Photography: Jonah Jones

The Farm 1938, 9 mins, Dufaycolor

Production: Dufay Chromex Ltd
Producer: Adrian Klein
Director: Humphrey Jennings
Photography: J. D. Davidson
Unit Manager: R. L. M. Davidson

Penny Journey: The Story of a Post Card from Manchester to Graffham 1938, 8 mins, b/w

Production: GPO Film Unit
Director: Humphrey Jennings
Photography: H. E. Fowle, W. B. Pollard

Speaking from America 1938, 10 mins, b/w

Production: GPO Film Unit
Producer: Alberto Cavalcanti

Director: Humphrey Jennings
Photography: W. B. Pollard, Fred Gamage
Diagrams: J. Chambers
Commentary spoken by: Robin Duff
Sound: Ken Cameron

English Harvest 1939, 9 mins, Dufaycolor

Production: Dufay Chromex Ltd
Producer: Adrian Klein
Director: Humphrey Jennings
Assistant Director: Cecil Blacker
Photography: J. D. Davidson
Commentary spoken by: A. G. Street
Music: excerpts from Beethoven's Sixth Symphony

The First Days (alternative title: *A City Prepares*) 1939, 23 mins, b/w

Production: GPO Film Unit
Producer: Alberto Cavalcanti
Directors: Humphrey Jennings, Harry Watt, Pat Jackson
Editor: R. Q. McNaughton
Commentary spoken by: Robert Sinclair

S.S. Ionian (alternative title: *Her Last Trip*. A 9 minute version was released as *Cargoes*) 1939, 20 mins, b/w

Production: GPO Film Unit
Director: Humphrey Jennings
Sound: Ken Cameron

Spare Time 1939, 18 mins, b/w

Production: GPO Film Unit
Producer: Alberto Cavalcanti
Director/Script: Humphrey Jennings
Assistant Director: D. V. Knight
Photography: H. E. Fowle
Commentary spoken by: Laurie Lee
Sound: Yorke Scarlett
Music: Steel, Peach and Tozer Phoenix Works Band; Manchester Victorian Carnival Band; Handel Male Voice Choir

London Can Take It! (alternative title of a shorter version for domestic distribution: **Britain Can Take It!**) 1940, 9 mins, b/w

Production: GPO Film Unit
Directors: Humphrey Jennings and Harry Watt
Photography: Jonah Jones and H. E. Fowle
Editors: Stewart McAllister, Jack Lee
Commentary spoken by: Quentin Reynolds
Sound: Ken Cameron
Music: *A London Symphony* by Vaughan Williams

Spring Offensive (alternative title: **An Unrecorded Victory**) 1940, 20 mins, b/w

Production: GPO Film Unit
Producer: Alberto Cavalcanti
Director: Humphrey Jennings
Photography: H. E. Fowle, Eric Cross, Jonah Jones
Script: Hugh Gray
Designer: Edward Carrick
Editor: Geoff Foot
Artistic Director: Edward Carrick
Commentary written and spoken by: A. G. Street
Sound: Ken Cameron
Musical Direction: Muir Mathieson
Music: excerpts from the music of Liszt, arranged by Brian Easdale

Welfare of the Workers 1940, 10 mins, b/w

Production: GPO Film Unit
Producer: Harry Watt
Assistant Producer: J. B. Holmes
Director: Humphrey Jennings
Photography: Jonah Jones
Editor: Jack Lee, Joe Mendoza
Commentary spoken by: Ritchie Calder
Sound: Ken Cameron

Heart of Britain (alternative title of a longer 'American and Empire version': **This Is England**, with a commentary spoken by Ed Murrow) 1941, 9 mins, b/w

Production: Crown Film Unit

Producer: Ian Dalrymple
Director: Humphrey Jennings
Photography: H. E. Fowle
Editor: Stewart McAllister
Commentary spoken by: J. B. Holmes
Sound: Ken Cameron
Music: the Huddersfield Choir singing the 'Hallelujah Chorus' from
   Messiah by Handel, and excerpts from Elgar's *Introduction and Allegro*
   and Beethoven's Fifth Symphony, played by the Hallé Orchestra

Words for Battle 1941, 8 mins, b/w

Production: Crown Film Unit
Producer: Ian Dalrymple
Director/Script: Humphrey Jennings
Editor: Stewart McAllister
Commentary spoken by: Laurence Olivier
Sound: Ken Cameron
Music: excerpts from the music of Beethoven and Handel, played by the
   London Philharmonic Orchestra

Listen to Britain 1942, 18 mins, b/w

Production: Crown Film Unit
Producer: Ian Dalrymple
Director/Script/Editor: Humphrey Jennings and Stewart McAllister
Assistant Director: Joe Mendoza
Production Manager: Dora Wright
Foreword spoken by: Leonard Brockington
Photography: H. E. Fowle
Sound: Ken Cameron

'Fires Were Started – ' (alternative title of a longer version: *I Was a Fireman*) 1943, 63 mins, b/w

Production: Crown Film Unit, with the cooperation of the Ministry of
   Home Security and the National Fire Service
Production: Ian Dalrymple
Production Manager: Dora Wright
Production Assistant: Francis Cockburn
Director/Script: Humphrey Jennings
Unit Manager: Nora Dawson

Photography: C. Pennington-Richards
Editor: Stewart McAllister
Assistant Editor: Jenny Stein
Story Collaboration: Maurice Richardson
Set Construction: Edward Carrick
Sound: Jock May
Recordist: Ken Cameron
Musical Director: Muir Mathieson
Music: William Alwyn
Cast: Commanding Officer George Gravett (*Sub-Officer Dykes*); Leading Fireman Philip Wilson-Dickson (*Section Officer Walters*); Leading Fireman Fred Griffiths (*Johnny Daniels*); Leading Fireman Loris Rey (*J. Rumbold, 'Colonel'*); Fireman Johnny Houghton (*Sidney 'Jacko' Jackson*); Fireman T.P. Smith (*B.A. Brown*); Fireman John Barker (*Joe Vallance*); Fireman William Sansom (*Mike Barrett*); Assistant Group Officer Green (*Mrs Townsend*); Firewoman Betty Martin (*Betty*); Firewoman Eileen White (*Eileen*)

The Silent Village 1943, 36 mins, b/w

Production: Crown Film Unit
Producer: Humphrey Jennings
Director/Script: Humphrey Jennings
Assistant Director: Diana Pine
Photography: H. E. Fowle
Editor: Stewart McAllister
Sound: Jock May, Ken Cameron
Music: title and incidental music composed by Beckitt Williams, Welsh songs sung by Morriston United Male Choir, hymns sung by the Cwmgiedd Chapel Congregation

The 80 Days 1944, 14 mins, b/w

Production: Crown Film Unit
Producer: Humphrey Jennings
Director: Humphrey Jennings
Photography: Cyril Arapoff, Teddy Catford
Editor: Stewart McAllister
Commentary spoken by: Ed Murrow
Sound: Ken Cameron

The True Story of Lili Marlene 1944, 30 mins, b/w

Production: Crown Film Unit
Producer: J. B. Holmes
Director/Script: Humphrey Jennings
Assistant Director: Graham Wallace
Photography: H. E. Fowle
Sets: Edward Carrick
Editor: Sid Stone
Sound: Ken Cameron
Music: Denis Blood

V1 (re-edited version of The 80 Days for US distribution) 1944, 10 mins, b/w

Production: Crown Film Unit
Producer: Humphrey Jennings
Director/Script: Fletcher Markle
Assistant Directors: Nora Dawson, Jack Kranz
Photography: Cyril Arapoff
Commentary spoken by: Fletcher Markle
Sound: Ken Cameron

A Diary for Timothy 1945 (released 1946), 39 mins, b/w

Production: Crown Film Unit
Producer: Basil Wright
Director/Script: Humphrey Jennings
Production Unit: Dusty Buck, Diana Pine, Richard Warren
Photography: Fred Gamage
Supervising Editor: Alan Osbiston
Cutter: Jenny Hutt
Commentary written by: E. M. Forster
Commentary spoken by: Michael Redgrave
Sound: Ken Cameron, Jock May
Music: Richard Addinsell (and an extract from Chopin's *Polonaise Militaire*) played by the London Symphony Orchestra, conducted by Muir Mathieson
Note on credits: 'Produced with the help and co-operation of people all over Great Britain among them Dame Myra Hess and John Gielgud'.

A Defeated People 1946, 19 mins, b/w

Production: Crown Film Unit
Producer: Basil Wright
Director/Script: Humphrey Jennings
Photography: Fred Gamage and Army Film Unit cameramen
Commentary spoken by: William Hartnell
Sound: Ken Cameron
Music: Guy Warrack, played by the London Symphony Orchestra

The Cumberland Story 1947, 39 mins, b/w

Production: Crown Film Unit
Producer: Alexander Shaw
Director/Script: Humphrey Jennings
Photography: H. E. Fowle
Camera Operator: Noel Rowland
Editor: Jocelyn Jackson
Production Manager: Dusty Buck
Unit Manager: Richard Warren
Art Direction: Scott MacGregor, John Cooper
Research: Diana Pine
Sound: Jock May
Music: Arthur Benjamin, played by the Philharmonic Orchestra

The Dim Little Island 1949, 11 mins, b/w

Production: Wessex Films, Grand National
Producer/Director: Humphrey Jennings
Assistant Director: Harley Usill
Photography: Martin Curtis
Editor: Bill Megarry
Commentary spoken by: Osbert Lancaster, John Ormston, James Fisher,
    Ralph Vaughan Williams
Music: Ralph Vaughan Williams

Family Portrait 1950, 26 mins, b/w

Production: Wessex Films
Producer: Ian Dalrymple
Director/Script: Humphrey Jennings
Unit Manager: R. L. M. Davidson
Assistant Director: Harley Usill

Photography: Martin Curtis
Editor: Stewart McAllister
Commentary spoken by: Michael Goodliffe
Sound: Ken Cameron
Music: composed and arranged by John Greenwood, directed and
conducted by Muir Mathieson

The Good Life 1951, 30 mins, colour

(A segment of the six-part film *The Changing Face of Europe,* 116 mins)
Production: Wessex Films
Director: Graham Wallace
Initial research toward direction undertaken by Humphrey Jennings
Photography: Fred Gamage

References

Adamowicz, E. *Surrealist Collage in Text and Image: Dissecting the Exquisite Corpse* (Cambridge: Cambridge University Press, 1998).

Addison, P. *Now the War Is Over: A Social History of Britain, 1945–51* (London: British Broadcasting Corporation and Jonathan Cape, 1985).

Aitken, I. *Alberto Cavalcanti: Realism, Surrealism and National Cinema* (Trowbridge, Wiltshire: Flicks Books, 2000).

Aitken, I. *Film and Reform: John Grierson and the British Documentary Movement* (London: Routledge, 1990).

Aldgate, A. and J. Richards, *Britain Can Take It: The British Cinema in the Second World War* (Oxford: Basil Blackwell, 1986).

Anderson, B. *Imagined Communities: Reflections on the Origin and Spread of Nationalism* (London: Verso, 1991).

Anderson, L. 'Only Connect: Some Aspects of the Work of Humphrey Jennings', *Film Quarterly*, 15: 2 (winter 1961–62), 5–11.

Anderson, L. 'Postscript', in M.-L. Jennings (ed.), *Humphrey Jennings: Film-Maker, Painter, Poet* (London: BFI in association with Riverside Studios, 1982), pp. 58–9.

Anthony, S. 'Terence Davies' Thoughtful Eccentric Hymn to Liverpool', *The Guardian* (13 October 2008), at www.guardian.co.uk/film/2008/oct/13/terence-davies-time-and-the-city (accessed 20/10/08).

Armes, R. *A Critical History of the British Cinema* (New York: Oxford University Press, 1978).

The Arts Enquiry. *The Factual Film: A Survey Sponsored by the Darlington Hall Trustees* (London: Oxford University Press, 1947).

Auden, W.H. 'Squares and Oblongs', in C. Abbott (ed.), *Poets at Work* (New York: Harcourt, 1948), pp. 163–81.

Balfour, M. *Propaganda in War, 1939–1945: Organisations, Policies and Publics in Britain and Germany* (London: Routledge and Kegan Paul, 1971).

Barr, C. 'The National Health: Pat Jackson's *White Corridors*', in I. MacK-illop and N. Sinyard (eds), *British Cinema of the 1950s: A Celebration* (Manchester: Manchester University Press, 2005), pp. 64–73.

Barsam, R. *Non-Fiction Film: A Critical History* (Bloomington: Indiana University Press, 1992).

Barthes, R. *Mythologies* (New York: Hill and Wang, 1972).

Bazin, A. *What Is Cinema?* volume 2 (Berkeley: University of California Press, 1971).

Beattie, K. *Documentary Display: Re-Viewing Nonfiction Film and Video* (London: Wallflower Press, 2008).

Beattie, K. *Documentary Screens: Non-fiction Film and Television* (Houndsmills, Basingstoke, Hampshire: Palgrave Macmillan, 2004).

Beddington, J. Memorandum to Ian Dalrymple, 26 November 1942. The National Archives, INF 1/212.

Benjamin, W. 'The Work of Art in the Age of Mechanical Reproduction' (1936), in *Illuminations: Essays and Reflections* (New York: Schocken, 1969), pp. 217–52.

Berman, M. *All That is Solid Melts into Air: The Experience of Modernity* (London: Verso, 1982).

Berry, D. *Wales and Cinema: The First Hundred Years* (Cardiff: University of Wales Press, 1994).

The Blitz: The Photography of George Rodger, introduced by T. Hopkinson (Harmondsworth, Middlesex: Penguin, 1994).

Bragg, B. *The Progressive Patriot: A Search for Belonging* (London: Bantam Press, 2006).

Briggs, A. 'Exhibiting the Nation', *History Today* 50: 1 (January 2000), 16–25.

'Britain Can Take It', production file, The National Archives, INF 6/328.

Britton, A. 'Their Finest Hour: Humphrey Jennings and the British Imperial Myth of World War II', *CineAction!* 18 (fall 1989), 37–44.

Bromhead, A.C. Letter to Jack Beddington, 27 November 1942. The National Archives, INF 1/212.

Brown, S. 'Dufaycolor: The Spectacle of Reality and British National Cinema', a report to the Centre for British Film and Television Studies (London: Birkbeck College, University of London) at www.bftv.ac.uk/projects/dufaycolor.htm (accessed 18/03/07).

Bryant, M. *Auden and Documentary in the 1930s* (Charlottesville, Virginia: University Press of Virginia, 1971).

Calder, A. *The Myth of the Blitz* (London: Jonathan Cape, 1991).

Cavalcanti, A. 'Sound in Films', in E. Weis and J. Belton (eds), *Film Sound: Theory and Practice* (New York: Columbia University Press, 1985), pp. 98–111.

Cecil Beaton: War Photographs, 1939–45, introduction by G. Buckland (London: Imperial War Museum and Jane's Publishing Co., 1981).

Chapman, J. 'British Cinema and "the People's War"', in N, Hayes and J. Hill (eds), *'Millions Like Us?' British Culture in the Second World War* (Liverpool: Liverpool University Press, 1999), pp. 33–61.

Chapman, J. *The British at War: Cinema, State and Propaganda, 1939–1945* (London: I. B. Tauris, 1998).

Chapman, J. 'Cinema, Propaganda and National Identity: Film and the Second World War', in J. Ashby and A. Higson (eds), *British Cinema, Past and Present* (London: Routledge, 2000), pp. 193–206.

Chapman, J. 'Our Finest Hour: The Second World War in British Feature Film since 1945', *Journal of Popular British Cinema*, 1 (1998), 63–75.

Chapman, J. *Past and Present: National Identity and the British Historical Film* (London: I. B. Tauris, 2005).

Chapman, J., M. Glancy and S. Harper (eds), *The New Film History: Sources, Methods, Approaches* (Houndsmills, Basingstoke, Hampshire: Palgrave, 2000).

Chion, M. *The Voice in Cinema*, trans. C. Gorman (New York: Columbia University Press, 1999).

Colls, R. and P. Dodd, 'Representing the Nation: British Documentary Film, 1930–45', *Screen*, 26: 1 (January–February 1985), 21–33.

Conekin, B. *'The Autobiography of a Nation': The 1952 Festival of Britain* (Manchester: Manchester University Press, 2003).

Conekin, B. '"Here is the Modern World Itself": The Festival of Britain's Representations of the Future', in B. Conekin, F. Mort and C. Waters (eds), *Moments of Modernity: Reconstructing Britain, 1945–1965* (London: Rivers Oram Press, 1999), pp. 228–81.

Corner, J. 'Documentary in a Post-Documentary Culture? A Note on Forms and their Functions', at www.info.lut.ac.uk/research/changing.media/John%20Corner%paper.htm (accessed 08/04/05).

Corner, J. 'Documentary Voices', in J. Corner (ed.), *Popular Television in Britain: Studies in Cultural History* (London: BFI Publishing, 1991), pp. 42–59.

Coultass, C. 'British Feature Films and the Second World War', *Journal of Contemporary History*, 19: 1 (January 1994), 7–22.

Coultass, C. *Images for Battle: British Film and the Second World War, 1939–1945* (Newark: University of Delaware Press, 1989).

Cowie. P. 'An Interview with Lindsay Anderson', *Film Quarterly* 17: 4 (summer 1964), 12–14.

Cox, I. *The South Bank Exhibition: A Guide to the Story it Tells* (London: HMSO, 1951).

Cunningham, V. *British Writers of the Thirties* (Oxford: Oxford University

Press, 1989).

Dalrymple, I. 'The Crown Film Unit, 1940–43', in N. Pronay and D. W. Spring (eds), *Propaganda, Politics and Film, 1918–45* (London: Macmillan, 1982), pp. 209–20.

Dalrymple, I. 'Personal Tribute', in *Humphrey Jennings: A Tribute*, prepared by D. Powell, B. Wright and R. Manvell (n.p.: The Humphrey Jennings Memorial Fund Committee, n.d.], n.p.

Delany, P. *Bill Brandt: A Life* (Stanford, California: Stanford University Press, 2004).

Dickinson, M. and S. Street, *Cinema and State: The Film Industry and the Government, 1927–84* (London: BFI Publishing, 1985).

Documentary News Letter, 4 (1942), 200 (review of '*Fires Were Started* –').

Dodd. K. and P. Dodd, 'Engendering the Nation: British Documentary Film, 1930–1939', in A. Higson (ed.), *Dissolving Views: Key Writings on British Cinema* (London: Cassell, 1996), pp. 38–50.

Dodd, P. 'Lowryscapes: Recent Writings about "the North"', *Critical Quarterly*, 32: 2 (1990), 17–28.

Doncaster, C. 'The Story-Documentary', in P. Rotha (ed.), *Television in the Making* (London: The Focal Press, 1956), pp. 44–7.

Drazin, C. *The Finest Years: British Cinema of the 1940s* (London: Andre Deutsch, 1998).

Durnat, R. *A Mirror for England: British Movies from Austerity to Affluence* (London: Faber and Faber, 1970).

Easen, S. 'Film and the Festival of Britain', in I. MacKillop and N. Sinyard (eds), *British Cinema of the 1950s: A Celebration* (Manchester: Manchester University Press, 2003), pp. 51–65.

Edwards, S. 'Disastrous Documents', *Ten-8*, 15 (1984), 12–23.

Eisenberg, E. *Strategic Ambiguities: Essays on Communication, Organization, and Identity* (Thousand Oaks, California: Sage, 2007).

Eley, G. 'Finding the People's War: Film, British Collective Memory, and World War II', *American Historical Review*, 106: 3 (June 2001), 818–38.

Empson, W. *Seven Types of Ambiguity* (Harmondsworth, Middlesex: Penguin Books in association with Chatto and Windus, 1961 [1930]).

Empson, W. *Some Versions of Pastoral: A Study of the Pastoral Form in Literature* (Harmondsworth, Middlesex: Penguin, 1966 [1935]).

Fox, J. *Film Propaganda in Britain and Nazi Germany: World War II Cinema* (Oxford: Berg, 2007).

Frayn, M. 'Festival', in M. Sissons and P. French (eds), *Age of Austerity* (London: Hodder and Stoughton, 1963), pp. 319–38.

Friedman, L. (ed.), *Fires Were Started: British Cinema and Thatcherism* (Minneapolis: University of Minnesota Press, 1993).

Frizzell, D. *Humphrey Spender's Humanist Landscapes: Photo-Documents,*

1932–1942 (New Haven, Connecticut: Yale Center for British Art, 1997).

Gamboni, D. *Potential Images: Ambiguity and Indeterminacy in Modern Art* (London: Reaktion Books, 2003).

Geraghty, C. 'Disguises and Betrayals: Negotiating Nationality and Femininity in Three Wartime Films', in C. Gledhill and G. Swanson (eds), *Nationalising Femininity: Culture, Sexuality and British Cinema in the Second World War* (Manchester: Manchester University Press, 1996), pp. 230–7.

Gold, J. and S. Ward, 'Of Plans and Planners: Documentary Film and the Challenge of the Urban Future, 1935–52', in D. Clarke (ed.), *The Cinematic City* (London: Routledge, 1997), pp. 229–58.

Greene, G. *The Confidential Agent* (Harmondsworth, Middlesex: Penguin, 1992 [1939]).

Grierson, J. 'The Documentary Idea: (1942)', in I. Aitken (ed.), *The Documentary Film Movement: An Anthology* (Edinburgh: Edinburgh University Press, 1998), pp. 103–14.

Grierson, J. *Eyes of Democracy*, edited with an introduction by Ian Lockerbie (Stirling: The John Grierson Archive, 1978).

Grierson, J. 'First Principles of Documentary (1932)', in I. Aitken (ed.), *The Documentary Film Movement: An Anthology* (Edinburgh: Edinburgh University Press, 1998), pp. 81–92.

Grierson, J. 'Humphrey Jennings', in *Humphrey Jennings: A Tribute*, prepared by D. Powell, B. Wright and R. Manvell (n.p.: The Humphrey Jennings Memorial Fund Committee, n. d.), n.p.

Guynn, W. *A Cinema of Nonfiction* (Rutherford, New Jersey: Fairleigh Dickinson University Press, 1990).

Hall, S. 'The Social Eye of *Picture Post*', Working Papers in Cultural Studies, no. 2 (Birmingham: The University of Birmingham, 1972).

Harding, A. 'The Closure of the Crown Film Unit in 1952: Artistic Decline or Political Machinations?', *Contemporary British History*, 18: 4 (winter 2004), 22–51.

Harper, S. 'The Years of Total War: Propaganda and Entertainment', in C. Gledhill and G. Swanson (eds), *Nationalising Femininity: Culture, Sexuality and British Cinema in the Second World War* (Manchester: Manchester University Press, Manchester, 1996), pp. 193–211.

Harper, S. and V. Porter, *British Cinema of the 1950s: The Decline of Deference* (Oxford: Oxford University Press, 2003).

Harrisson, T. 'Films and the Home Front: The Evaluation of their Effectiveness by "Mass-Observation"', in N. Pronay and D. W. Spring (eds), *Propaganda, Politics and Film, 1918–45* (London: Macmillan, 1982), pp. 234–45.

Heath, S. *Questions of Cinema* (Bloomington: Indiana University Press, 1981).

Heimann, J. *The Most Offending Soul Alive: Tom Harrisson and His Remarkable Career* (London: Aurum Press, 2002).

Henderson, B. 'Toward a Non-Bourgeois Camera Style', *Film Quarterly*, 24: 2 (winter 1970–1971), 2–14.

Hewison, R. *Culture and Consensus: England, Art and Politics since 1940* (London: Methuen, 1995).

Highmore, B. *Everyday Life and Cultural Theory: An Introduction* (London: Routledge, 2002).

Higson, A. '"Britain's Outstanding Contribution to the Film": The Documentary-Realist Tradition', in C. Barr (ed.), *All Our Yesterdays: 90 Years of British Cinema* (London: BFI Publishing, 1986), pp. 81–8.

Higson, A. 'Five Films', in G. Hurd (ed.), *National Fictions: World War Two in British Films and Television* (London: BFI Publishing, 1984), pp. 22–6.

Higson, A. 'Space, Place, Spectacle: Landscape and Townscape in "Kitchen Sink" Films', in A. Higson (ed.), *Dissolving Views: Key Writings on British Cinema* (London: Cassell, 1996), pp. 133–56.

Higson, A. *Waving the Flag: Constructing a National Cinema in Britain* (Oxford: Clarendon Press, 1995).

Hodgkinson, A. and R. Sheratsky, *Humphrey Jennings: More than a Maker of Films* (Hanover: University Press of New England, 1982).

Hood, S. 'A Cool Look at the Legend', in E. Orbanz, *Journey to a Legend and Back: The British Realistic Film* (Berlin: Edition Volker Spiess, 1977), pp. 141–50.

Horne, P. 'Moving at the Speed of Emotion', www.bfi.org.uk/sightandsound/feature/65 (accessed 17/04/07).

Hughes, R. 'The Filmmaker and the Audience', in R. Hughes (ed.), *Film: Book 1* (New York: Grove Press, 1959), pp. 36–8.

Hutchings, P. '"When the Going Gets Tough …": Representations of the North-East in Films and Television', in T. E. Faulkner (ed.), *Northumbrian Panorama: Studies in the History and Culture of North East England* (London: Octavian Press, 1996), pp. 273–90.

Inwood, S. *A History of London* (London: Macmillan, 1998).

Jackson, K. *Humphrey Jennings* (London: Picador, 2004).

Jackson, K. (ed.), *The Humphrey Jennings Film Reader* (Manchester: Carcanet Press, 1993).

Jackson, P. *A Retake Please! Night Mail to Western Approaches* (Liverpool: Royal Navy Museum Publications and Liverpool University Press, 1999).

Jennings, H. 'Colour Won't Stand Dignity', in D. Macpherson (ed.), *British Cinema: Traditions of Independence* (London: BFI Publishing, 1980), pp. 182–83.

Jennings, H. *Pandæmonium: 1660–1886: The Coming of the Machine as Seen by Contemporary Observers*, M.-L. Jennings and C. Madge (eds) (New York: The Free Press, 1985).

Jennings, H. Untitled treatments of 'Backbone of Britain', The National Archives, INF 5/77.

Jennings, H. Working papers and treatments of *'Fires Were Started –'*, item 6, box 1, the Humphrey Jennings Collection, BFI Special Collections, the British Film Institute.

Jennings, H. and Jack Holmes, 'The Documentary Film', item 16, box 2, the Humphrey Jennings Collection, BFI Special Collections, the British Film Institute.

Jennings, H. and C. Madge (eds), with contributions by T. O. Beachcroft, J. Blackburn, W. Empson, S. Legg and K. Raine, *May the Twelfth: Mass-Observation Day-Surveys 1937 by Over Two Hundred Observers* (London: Faber and Faber, 1987 [1937]).

Jennings, M.-L. 'Chronology and Documents' compiled by Mary-Lou Jennings, in M.-L. Jennings (ed.), *Humphrey Jennings: Film- Maker, Painter, Poet* (London: BFI in association with Riverside Studios, 1982).

Jennings, M.-L. (ed.), *Humphrey Jennings: Film-Maker, Painter, Poet* (London: BFI in association with Riverside Studios, 1982).

Joseph, N. *The Silent Village: A Story of Wales and Lidice Based on the Crown Film Production* (London: The Pilot Press Ltd., 1943).

Kuhn, A. 'British Documentary in the 1930s and "Independence": Recontextualising a Film Movement', in D. Macpherson (ed.), *Traditions of Independence: British Cinema in the Thirties* (London: BFI Publishing, 1980), pp. 24–33.

Kuhn, A. *Family Secrets: Acts of Memory and Imagination* (London: Verso, 1995).

Kushner, T. *We Europeans? Mass-Observation, 'Race' and British Identity in the Twentieth Century* (Aldershot, Hampshire: Ashgate, 2004).

Lambert, G. 'Interview: Alberto Cavalcanti and Gavin Lambert', *Screen*, 143: 2 (1972), 33–53.

Lant, A. *Blackout: Reinventing Woman for Wartime British Cinema* (Princeton, New Jersey: Princeton University Press, 1991).

Leach, J. 'The Poetics of Propaganda: Humphrey Jennings and *Listen to Britain*', in B. K. Grant and J. Sloniowski (eds), *Documenting the Documentary: Close Readings of Documentary Film and Video* (Detroit: Wayne State University Press, 1998), pp. 154–70.

Lovell, T. 'Landscape and Stories in 1960s British Realism', in A. Higson (ed.), *Dissolving Views: Key Writings on British Cinema* (London: Cassell, 1996), pp. 157–77.

Lovell, A. and J. Hillier, *Studies in Documentary* (London: Secker and Warburg, 1972).

MacClancy, J. 'Brief Encounter: The Meeting, in Mass-Observation, of British Surrealism and Popular Anthropology', *Journal of the Royal Anthropological Institute*, 1 (n.s): 3 (1995), 495–512.

Macpherson, D. and J. Evans, 'Introduction', to 'Nation, Mandate, Memory', in J. Evans (ed.), *The Camerawork Essays: Context and Meaning in Photography* (London: Rivers Oram Press, 1997), pp. 145–52.

Madge, C. 'A Note on Images', in M.-L. Jennings (ed.), *Humphrey Jennings: Film-Maker, Painter, Poet* (London: BFI in association with Riverside Studios, 1982), pp. 47–9.

Mandler, P. 'New Towns for Old: The Fate of the Town Centre', in B. Conekin F. Mort and C. Waters (eds), *Moments of Modernity: Reconstructing Britain, 1945–1964* (London: Rivers Oram Press, 1999), pp. 208–32.

Manvell, R. *Films and the Second World War* (London: J. M. Dent, 1974).

Matless, D. *Landscape and Englishness* (London: Reaktion Books, 1998).

McCabe, C. with M. Eaton and L. Mulvey, *Godard: Images, Sounds, Politics* (London: BFI Publishing and Macmillan, 1980).

McLaine, I. *Ministry of Morale: Home Front Morale and the Ministry of Information in World War II* (London: George Allen and Unwin, 1979).

Mellor, D. 'London-Berlin-London: A Cultural History: The Reception and Influence of the New German Photography in Britain, 1927–1933', in D. Mellor (ed.), *Germany: The New Photography, 1927–1933* (London: Arts Council of Great Britain, 1978), pp. 113–31.

Mellor, D. 'Mass Observation: The Intellectual Climate', in J. Evans (ed.), *The Camerawork Essays: Context and Meaning in Photography* (London: Rivers Oram Press, 1997), pp. 132–44.

Merralls, J. 'Humphrey Jennings: A Biographical Sketch', *Film Quarterly*, 15: 2 (winter 1961–62), 29–34.

'Mike Leigh on Humphrey Jennings', at www.channel4.com/culture/microsites/J/jennings/leigh.html (accessed 31/03/06).

Millar, D. 'Fires Were Started', *Sight and Sound*, 38: 2 (spring 1969), 100–4.

Ministry of Information, *Front Line, 1940–41: The Official Story of the Civil Defence in Britain* (London: HMSO, 1942).

Monegal, E. 'Alberto Cavalcanti', in R. Barsam (ed.), *Nonfiction Film Theory and Criticism* (New York: Dutton, 1976), pp. 239–49.

Morley, D. and K. Robins, 'No Place Like Heimat: Images of Home(land) in European Culture', *New Formations*, 12 (winter 1990), 1–23.

Morton, H.V. *In Search of England* (Harmondsworth, Middlesex: Penguin, 1960 [1927]).

Murphy, R. *Realism and Tinsel: Cinema and Society in Britain, 1939–1949* (London: Routledge, 1992).

Nichols, B. 'Documentary Film and the Modernist Avant-Garde', *Critical Inquiry*, 27: 4 (summer 2001), 580–610.

Nichols, B. *Representing Reality: Issues and Concepts in Documentary* (Bloomington: Indiana University Press, 1991).

Nichols, B. 'The Voice of Documentary', in A. Rosenthal (ed.), *New Challenges for Documentary* (Berkeley: University of California Press, 1988), pp. 48–63.

Nowell-Smith, G. 'Humphrey Jennings: Surrealist Observer', in C. Barr (ed.), *All Our Yesterdays: 90 Years of British Cinema* (London: BFI Publishing, 1986), pp. 321–33.

Orwell, G. 'The Lion and the Unicorn', in *George Orwell: Essays* (London: Penguin Books in association with Martin Secker and Warburg, 2000), pp. 138–87.

Orwell, G. *The Road to Wigan Pier* (London: Penguin, 2001 [1937]).

Plantinga, C. 'The Scene of Empathy and the Human Face on Film', in C. Plantinga and G. Smith (eds), *Film, Cognition, and Emotion* (Baltimore: Johns Hopkins University Press, 1999), pp. 239–55.

Priestley, J. B. *English Journey: Being a Rambling but Truthful Account of What One Man Saw and Heard and Felt and Thought during a Journey through England during the Autumn of the Year 1933* (Harmondsworth, Middlesex: Penguin, 1984 [1934]).

Pudovkin, V. I. 'Asynchronism as a Principle of Sound Film', in E. Weis and J. Belton (eds), *Film Sound: Theory and Practice* (New York: Columbia University Press, 1985), pp. 86–91.

Raine, K. *Defending Ancient Springs* (West Stockbridge, Massachusetts: The Lindisfarne Press, 1985 [1967]).

Reeves, N. *The Power of Film Propaganda: Myth or Reality?* (London: Cassell, 1999).

Reisz, K. and G. Millar, *The Technique of Film Editing* (London: Focal Press, 1973 [1953]).

Remy, M. *Surrealism in Britain* (Aldershot, Hampshire: Ashgate, 1999).

Reynolds, Q. *By Quentin Reynolds* (London: William Heinemann Ltd., 1964).

Reynolds, Q. (commentary), *Britain Can Take It: The Book of the Film* (London: John Murray, 1941).

Rhode, E. *A History of the Cinema: From its Origins to 1970* (Harmondsworth, Middlesex: Penguin, 1978).

Rhode, E. *Tower of Babel: Speculations on the Cinema* (London: Weidenfeld and Nicolson, 1966).

Richards, J. *The Age of the Dream Palace: Cinema and Society in Britain, 1930–1939* (London: Routledge and Kegan Paul, 1984).

Richards, J. *Films and British National Identity: From Dickens to Dad's Army* (Manchester: Manchester University Press, 1997).

Richards, J. 'Humphrey Jennings: The Poet as Propagandist', in M. Connolly and D. Welch (eds), *War and the Media: Reportage and Propaganda, 1900–2003* (London: I.B. Tauris, 2005), pp. 127–38.

Richards, J. and D. Sheridan (eds), *Mass-Observation at the Movies* (London: Routledge and Kegan Paul, 1987).

Roberts, G. 'Soluble Fish: How Surrealism Saved Documentary from John Grierson', in G. Harper and R. Stone (eds), *The Unsilvered Screen: Surrealism on Film* (London: Wallflower Press, 2007), pp. 90–101.

Robins, K. and F. Webster, *Times of the Technoculture: From the Information Society to Virtual Life* (London: Routledge, 1999).

Roscoe, J. 'Real Entertainment: New Factual Hybrid Television', *Media International Australia*, 100 (August 2001), 9–20.

Rose, S. 'Engendering the Slum: Photography in East London in the 1930s', *Gender, Place and Culture*, 4: 3 (1997), 277–300.

Rose, S. *Which People's War: National Identity and Citizenship in Britain, 1939–1945* (Oxford: Oxford University Press, 2003).

Rotha, P. *Documentary Diary: An Informal History of the British Documentary Film, 1928–1939* (New York: Hill and Wang, 1972).

Rotha, P. *Documentary Film: The Use of the Film Medium to Interpret Creatively and in Social Terms the Life of the People as it Exists in Reality* (New York: Hastings House, 1970 [1935]).

Russell, C. *Experimental Ethnography: The Work of the Film in the Age of Video* (Durham, North Carolina: Duke University Press, 1999).

Sansom, W. 'The Making of *Fires Were Started*', *Film Quarterly*, 15: 2 (winter 1961–62), 27–8.

Shearman, J. 'Wartime Wedding', *Documentary News Letter*, 6: 54 (November–December 1946), 53.

Smith, A. 'Humphrey Jennings' *Heart of Britain* (1941): A Reassessment', *Historical Journal of Film, Radio and Television*, 23: 2 (2003), 133–51.

Smith, M. *Britain and 1940: History, Myth and Popular Memory* (London: Routledge, 2000).

Smith, M. 'Narrative and ideology in *Listen to Britain*', in J. Hawthorn (ed.), *Narrative: From Malory to Motion Pictures* (London: Edward Arnold, 1985), pp. 145–57.

Snow, C.P. *The Two Cultures* (Cambridge: Cambridge University Press, 1998).

Sorenssen, B. 'The Documentary Aesthetics of Humphrey Jennings', in J. Corner (ed.), *Documentary and the Mass Media* (London: Edward Arnold, 1986), pp. 47–64.

Spender, H. *'Lensman' Photographs, 1932–52* (London: Chatto and Windus, 1987).

Spender, H. *Worktown People: Photographs from Northern England, 1937–38*, ed. J. Mulford (Bristol: Falling Wall Press, 1982).

Stenton, M. 'British Propaganda and Raison d'Etat, 1935–40', *European Studies Review*, 10 (1980), 47–74.

Strick, P. 'Fires Were Started', *Films and Filming*, 7: 8 (May 1961), 14–16, 35.

Sussex, E. *The Rise and Fall of British Documentary: The Story of the Film Movement Founded by John Grierson* (Berkeley: University of California Press, 1975).

Swann, P. *The British Documentary Movement, 1926–1946* (Cambridge: Cambridge University Press, 1989).

T. S. 'At the World', *New York Times* (2 October 1943), at http://movies2.nytimes.com/mem/movies/review.html?_r=1&title1=silent%20village (accessed 15/04/07).

Taylor, J. *A Dream of England: Landscape, Photography and the Tourists' Imagination* (Manchester: Manchester University Press, 1994).

Taylor, J. *War Photography: Realism in the British Press* (London: Routledge, 1991).

Taylor, P. *British Propaganda in the Twentieth Century: Selling Democracy* (Edinburgh: Edinburgh University Press, 1999).

Thomson, D. 'A Sight for Sore Eyes', *Film Comment*, 29: 2 (March–April 1993), 54–9.

Thomson, D. 'Sound and Fury: Terence Davies', *Sight and Sound*, 17: 4 (April 2007), 36–9.

Thorpe, F. and N. Pronay, with C. Coultass, *British Official Films in the Second World War* (Oxford: Clio Press, 1980).

Trilling, L. *Sincerity and Authenticity* (London: Oxford University Press, 1972).

Vas, R. '*My Homeland* and *Nine Days in '26*', in A. Rosenthal (ed.), *The Documentary Conscience: A Casebook in Film Making* (Berkeley: The University of California Press, 1980), pp. 261–75.

Vaughan, D. *Portrait of an Invisible Man: The Working Life of Stewart McAllister, Film Editor* (London: BFI Publishing, 1983).

Vernon, J. 'Conference Report', *Social History*, 22: 2 (May 1997), 208–15.

Watt, H. *Don't Look at the Camera* (London: Paul Elek, 1974).

Wiener, M. *English Culture and the Decline of the Independent Spirit, 1850–1980* (Cambridge: Cambridge University Press, 1981).

Williams, R. 'Culture is Ordinary' [1958], in *Resources of Hope: Culture, Democracy, Socialism* (London: Verso, 1989), 3–18.

Williams, R. *Towards 2000* (Harmondsworth, Middlesex: Penguin, 1985).

Winston, B. *Claiming the Real: The Griersonian Documentary and its Legitimations* (London: BFI Publishing, 1995).

Winston, B. *'Fires Were Started – '* (London: BFI Publishing, 1999).

Winston, B. '"Honest, Straightforward Re-enactment": The Staging of Reality', in K. Bakker (ed.), *Joris Ivens and the Documentary Context* (Amsterdam: Amsterdam University Press, 1999), pp. 160–70.

Wollen, P. 'The Last New Wave: Modernism in the British Films of the Thatcher Era', in L. Friedman (ed.), *Fires Were Started: British Cinema and Thatcherism* (Minneapolis: University of Minnesota Press, 1993), pp. 35–51.

Wright, B. 'First Period, 1934–1940' in *Humphrey Jennings: A Tribute*, prepared by D. Powell, B. Wright and R. Manvell (n.p.: The Humphrey Jennings Memorial Fund Committee, n.d.), n.p.

Wright, B. *The Long View* (London: Secker and Warburg, 1974), pp. 178–9.

Wright, B. and B. V. Brown, 'Manifesto: Dialogue on Sound', *Film Art*, 3 (spring 1934), reprinted in D. Macpherson (ed.), *Traditions of Independence: British Cinema in the Thirties* (London: BFI Publishing, 1980).

Index

Note: 'n' after a page number indicates the number of a note on that page.

DH

791.
430
230
92
BEA